# OXFORD ENGLISH MONOGRAPHS

*General Editors*

# The Joycean Labyrinth

Repetition, Time, and
Tradition in *Ulysses*

UDAYA KUMAR

CLARENDON PRESS · OXFORD
1991

Oxford University Press, Walton Street, Oxford OX2 6DP
Oxford New York Toronto
Delhi Bombay Calcutta Madras Karachi
Petaling Jaya Singapore Hong Kong Tokyo
Nairobi Dar es Salaam Cape Town
Melbourne Auckland
and associated companies in
Berlin Ibadan

Oxford is a trade mark of Oxford University Press

Published in the United States
by Oxford University Press, New York

British Library Cataloguing in Publication Data
(data available)

Library of Congress Cataloging in Publication Data
Kumar, Udaya.
The Joycean Labyrinth: repetition, time, and tradition in Ulysses/Udaya Kumar.
(Oxford English monographs)
Includes bibliographical references and index.
1. Joyce, James, 1882–1941. Ulysses. I. Title. II. Series.
PR6019.09U6735  1991  91–11767
823'.912—dc20
ISBN 0–19–811221–1

Typeset by Cambrian Typesetters
High Street, Frimley, Surrey
Printed and bound in
Great Britain by Bookcraft Ltd.
Midsomer Norton, Bath

*For my parents*

# Acknowledgements

THIS book began as a thesis submitted for D.Phil. at the University of Oxford in 1988. Several parts have been considerably revised and expanded since then. I should like to thank Mr Christopher Butler who supervised my thesis work. His comments and observations inform several arguments in the book. Dr John Kelly and Professor Derek Attridge, while examining the thesis, provided valuable suggestions. Andrew and Howard read through a draft of the thesis and assisted in clarifying several aspects of the argument. Arvind and Eivor went through the later revisions, and helped much in improving the text. Thanks are due to them all.

Thanks are also due to the Inlaks Foundation and to St John's College, Oxford for funding my research at Oxford.

A special note of thanks must be recorded for the support and affection of a large number of friends and colleagues in India, England, and Switzerland. Without their help, this book would not have been possible. Finally, I must thank Leonor, who shared all my worries and pleasures and toil in working on this book for the past three years.

U. K.

*Geneva*

# Contents

# Abbreviations

THE following abbreviations have been used in referring to Joyce's works:

U                               *Ulysses*, A Critical and Synoptic Edition, ed.
                                Hans Walter Gabler, 3 vols. (New York:
                                Garland Press, 1984).

FW                              *Finnegans Wake* (London: Faber & Faber, Ltd.,
                                1960). All references are followed by page and
                                line numbers.

References to other texts of Joyce are followed by page numbers.

P                               *A Portrait of the Artist as a Young Man*
                                (London: Jonathan Cape, 1968).

SH                              *Stephen Hero*, ed. Theodore Spencer (1944),
                                revd. J. J. Slocum and H. Cahoon (London:
                                Jonathan Cape, 1956).

Exiles                          *Exiles: A Play in Three Acts* (London: Jonathan
                                Cape, 1952).

Critical Writings               *The Critical Writings of James Joyce*, ed.
                                Richard Ellmann and Elsworth Mason
                                (London: Faber & Faber, Ltd., 1959).

Letters                         *The Letters of James Joyce*, 3 vols., ed. Stuart
                                Gilbert (vol. i) and Richard Ellmann (vols. ii–
                                iii) (New York: Viking, 1966).

JJQ                             *James Joyce Quarterly*

# *Note on the Citations of* Ulysses

ALL references to *Ulysses* are indicated in the text within brackets, followed by the episode and line numbers. For example, (*U*, 3. 406–9) indicates a reference to lines 406–9 of 'Proteus'. However, the displayed quotations from *Ulysses* do not follow the individual line divisions of the Critical and Synoptic Edition. They have been presented as continuous prose.

# 1

# Introduction

THERE is an inescapable contemporaneity to Joyce's texts, even half a century after his death. However, this contemporaneity is itself the symptom of a history—that of our ways of reading. More profoundly, it is also a symptom of the continuous modifications and redefinitions that have taken place in our understanding of the task of interpretation itself. The enigmas and puzzles that Joyce put in his texts have continued to ensure his immortality, but our notions of enigmas and puzzles in literary texts have also undergone changes. The context of a reading of Joyce involves these several levels of history. Inevitably, this book is itself a contemporary reading of Joyce. However, it also seeks to situate itself, recognizing that the ground occupied by a contemporary reading of Joyce is complex and rather ill-defined.

The transformations in our understanding of literary texts, primarily due to a series of events in contemporary philosophy, literary theory, and other disciplines, have immensely contributed to a rereading of Joyce's work. What has come to be called post-structuralist theory has been the primary strand in this rereading. It has taken the form of a psychoanalytical, or deconstructionist, or feminist reassessment of Joyce's work.

One of the major contributions of post-structuralist theory to a rereading of Joyce has been in relieving a reading of the formal elements in the work from over-schematic interpretations of a conservative kind. By this, I mean that most of these new readings did not seek to justify the formal complexity of *Ulysses* and *Finnegans Wake* as the realization of an organic form. A characteristic example of the more traditional interpretation in this respect is Richard Ellmann's *Ulysses on the Liffey*.[1] Ellmann, even though he regards Joyce's own schema as not fully realized in the actual composition of the novel, proposes another schema, even more unifying and rigorous. According to this, the organizational principles underlying *Ulysses* can be seen as forming a consistent

[1] Richard Ellmann, *Ulysses on the Liffey* (London: Faber & Faber, Ltd., 1972).

pattern of ascending dialectic. The formal diversity of the novel is resolved at a deeper level in favour of a more complex totality. It is precisely this totalizing impulse that post-structuralist readings of Joyce put into question.

Much of the post-structuralist work on Joyce relies primarily on the argument that Joyce's work reveals an incessant textual play and the postponement of a meaning based on identity. The early ventures in Joyce criticism to employ this argument—e.g. the work of Stephen Heath and Colin MacCabe—developed this in relation to a number of notions elaborated in contemporary philosophy, primarily the work of Derrida and Lacan.[2] Joyce was seen as the writer of *différance*, of the liberation of the signifier. In recent years, his attributes have multiplied. Among other things, he is also seen as a woman writer, a post-modernist, and a masochist in his textual practice.

In abandoning the totalizing interpretations of the earlier critics—be they ethical, philological, philosophical—these readings had implicitly reclaimed another kind of identity for Joyce's work. It came to signify the subversion of code, the radicalism of language and of politics. These readings relied on two distinct strategies. They make a distinction between Joyce's self-under-standing as a writer—the innumerable texts that surround Joyce's own work, in the form of letters, conversations, notebooks, Joyce's library—and his textual practice. This operation in itself is not simplistic and is perhaps presupposed in much of the literary criticism of our times to various degrees. However, in some critics, this led to a rejection of certain patterns of thought closely related to the context of Joyce's writing—e.g. theology—as a reactionary critical strategy in itself. Hélène Cixous, for example, criticizes a strategy of reading that trusts 'the known facts about Joyce's work, particularly his intensive use of symbols, and his obsessive and often explicit concern to control word-order, thus prejudging the work as a "full" text, governed by "the hypostasis of the signified".' To this, she opposes 'a reading that accepts "discourage-ment" . . . by seeing in that trap which confiscates signification the sign of the willed imposture which crosses the *whole* of Joyce's

---

[2] Stephen Heath, 'Ambiviolences', in Derek Attridge and Daniel Ferrer (eds.), *Post-Structuralist Joyce: Essays from the French* (Cambridge: CUP, 1984), 31–68; Colin MacCabe, *James Joyce and the Revolution of the Word* (London: Macmillan, 1979).

work, making that betrayal the very breath (the breathlessness) of the subject.'[3] Perhaps there is more to Joyce's conscious textual strategies than what this opposition allows. Accordingly, there have been attempts to reinterpret Joyce's extra-textual texts in a radically new way, disengaging them from the context of their inscription and reading them in the light of his textual practice. MacCabe's book presents this impulse in a rather extreme form, trying to read a political radicalism commensurate with the radicalism of Joyce's textual practice, into his letters and essays.[4] Have these critics misrecognized Joyce not only in their attribution of an apparently radical, post-structuralist, identity to him? Or, even more profoundly, have they underestimated Joyce's radicalism in attributing to him the identity they conferred on his textual practice?

I think the answer to both these questions is in the affirmative. The versions of post-structuralist criticism that I mentioned above often involve an understanding of Joyce's textual practice as aiming towards a liberation from symbolic orders that is usually described only in negative terms. Even where more positive characterizations seem to have been given, they rely at a deeper level on notions such as 'the Imaginary', which is further defined in its relation to the symbolic order. The influence of deconstruction has been, in the main, to make Joyce a deconstructor. The theorist identifies in Joyce his own image, a proto-theorist whose texts anticipate theory itself. This is where I feel that the identity often attributed to Joyce is mistaken—in making Joyce the subversive textual practitioner, these critics reduce his practice to a new essence, based on a set of new philosophemes that were not clearly intended to form a system. Perhaps Joyce was not outside the terrains of familiar discourse, nor even on the margins, but at a certain crossroads 'where roads parallel merge and roads contrary also'.[5] Perhaps the identity of Joyce's textual practice reveals a complexity and a process of reflection on previous representations that is only inadequately indicated in terms such as 'rupture', 'break', or 'liberation'. And, possibly, this complex scenario shows a more

---

[3] See Hélène Cixous, 'Joyce: the (r)use of writing', in Attridge and Ferrer (eds.), *Post-Structuralist Joyce*, 21.

[4] See MacCabe, *James Joyce*; see, for contrasting evidence, Domenic Manganiello, *Joyce's Politics* (London: Routledge & Kegan Paul, Ltd., 1980).

[5] *Letters*, i. 148.

radical engagement and a more profound critique than the 'revolution of the word' or 'the Imaginary' would permit us.

This book attempts to propose a reading of *Ulysses* against the background of the questions raised above. It shares a number of concerns with post-structuralist theory, but also argues for a rethinking of the use of theory in relation to the text. It treats *Ulysses* as a complex transitional text, where widely heterogeneous and even contradictory impulses are at work. However, it is not enough to recognize this complexity; it is necessary to describe its relations and modes, and to trace its effects. An attempt at this has been made by following a strand of problems through the text. It is this strand that has determined the structure of this book—beginning with an examination of repetition and ending with a consideration of the notion of tradition in Joyce. I shall try to make the topos of this itinerary clearer in this introduction.

It has been said that Joyce oversystematized *Ulysses*. The proliferation of principles and patterns of organization is what clearly marks out *Ulysses*, especially its second half, from Joyce's earlier works and aligns it more closely with *Finnegans Wake*. However, *Ulysses* is the book of the day, and clearer identities are at least tentatively discernible while its nocturnal successor went ahead to evolve a greater flexibility in the use of patterns, a fluidity in their association. Among the patterns that permeate *Ulysses*, one finds not only the Homeric analogues and several other schematic elements, but also a perverse naturalism in the attempt to reproduce the geographical details of Dublin as well as the precision of the public, chronometric time of 16 June 1904. This naturalistic impulse might, at first sight, seem to ground the text in an external world to which representation can measure up or correspond. However, there is in this naturalism a propensity to accumulate detail so prolixly that it cannot be contained in any reasonable notion of relevance. This naturalistic impulse, rather than grounding the text in an external world, makes this relation a principle that violates the economy of naturalistic representation. Like the obsessive Borgesian cartographers who ultimately draw the perfect map which corresponds to their country on a scale of one to one, the representation breaks down by overreaching itself. The Joycean naturalism, with its expansiveness, includes everything until representation cannot bind it together, until it fails.

The other schematic patterns, too, work in much the same way in so far as they also function fragmentarily and asymmetrically in various parts of the text and create problems for unification. However, these principles did not seek to found *Ulysses* on the grounds of an external world but on that of arbitrary principles, and of arts, techniques, and images culled from a repertoire which we can probably call the tradition of representation. There is a devalorization of natural as opposed to arbitrary ones, involved in this development of representation beyond its limits. Just as the Borgesian map stands at the crossroads of the two impulses of cartography that it seeks to satisfy—namely projection and correspondence—so *Ulysses* creates an internal fragmentation through an oversystematization based on principles that derive from opposing impulses—the naturalistic and the schematic.

The schematism of *Ulysses* thus seems to generate a variety of effects on different parts of the text in an asymmetric and partial way. The elements and patterns that organize certain parts of the text do not have much validity in other parts. The acts of synthesis and unification that we attempt tend to be valid only locally and are not generalizable to the entire text. To demonstrate Joyce's innovation in *Ulysses* or to describe adequately his textual practice, it is important to show how these patterns function in the text and what specific effects they generate. In other words, it is important to take account of the totalizing impulses that operate in *Ulysses*, as well as to show how they frustrate the production of a totality in terms of structure within the text.

In a text such as *Ulysses*, consequently, the distinction between narrative structures and textual organization seems to blur. Narrative structures are operative in *Ulysses* primarily through their partial, local, and contingent relations to other structures at the surface level of the text. The textual surface shows an interplay of patterns that cannot be reduced to narrative deep structure. A reading of *Ulysses* in terms of such deep structures alone will give only a distorted and highly abstract picture of the novel.

In spite of all these deep structures or schematic elements, the kind of attention that *Ulysses* demands constantly is similar to that of modern poetry. It is a demand for attention to the verbal surface of the novel, to the event of language, and to the modalities of the text. Joyce's compositional strategies, often compared to that of mosaic artists, warrant this close attention. One of the strategies that Joyce uses in the text to demand this close attention is repetition. There is a frequent repetition of verbal elements in *Ulysses* as well as in *Finnegans Wake*. In the latter text, freed from mimetic obligations, repetition provides a fluid organizational pattern. In *Ulysses*, repetition often problematizes the narrative logic implied in the naturalistic impulse at work in the novel. It questions identities and demands forms of attention incommensurable with the linear progress of naturalistic narrative.

It could be argued that the repetition of verbal elements is part of an old epic tradition, thus forming another element in the organization of *Ulysses*. It has also been suggested that the Wagnerian leitmotif has been a source for this strategy in Joyce.[6] However, Joyce puts repetition to a radically different use in the text, highlighting a dislocation of contexts rather than reaffirming a familiar identity in meaning. The kind of repetition that Bloom thinks about in *Ulysses*, based on prayer and advertising, belongs to the latter function—it intensifies and reaffirms the identity of an act or of a proposition. Joyce's use of verbal repetition in *Ulysses* disrupts such identities to a large extent. This is not to deny the presence of the other strategy of repetition in *Ulysses*. As in most mimetic novels, repetition also confers identities and stabilizes the referents. However, the disruptive use of repetition puts several of these identities into question. The present book begins by examining some of the modes of repetition in *Ulysses*. Repetition forms a convenient point of departure for this study for two reasons. First, its operations cannot adequately be described in terms of a unifying logic. Secondly, repetition opens up a way of thinking about the totalizing impulse in *Ulysses* that does not produce any totality in terms of a structure. To make this latter point clearer, a brief digression about some philosophical aspects of repetition that inform the novel needs to be made.

In recent years, increased attention has been given to repetition in contemporary philosophy as well as in literary theory. However, the philosophical meditation on repetition goes back presumably to the beginnings of philosophy itself. In the West, the Stoic notion of natural law and the Platonic theory of forms could be seen as attempts to deal with repetition, to subordinate it to a law or an

---

[6] See Stuart Gilbert, *James Joyce's 'Ulysses': A Study* (Harmondsworth: Penguin, 1963), 213–14; Anthony Burgess, *Joysprick: An Introduction to the Language of James Joyce* (London: André Deutsch, 1973), 83.

identity.[7] In relation to Joyce's own interests, the philosophy of Vico shows the prevalence of cycles that are 'similar without being identical' in human history.[8] In German idealism, notably in the speculative logic of Hegel, identity and difference seem to be united and opposed to each other in patterns of repetition. In Nietzsche and Kierkegaard, repetition assumes a liberating role. In Nietzsche, it is related to a supreme act of affirmation that wills the eternal return. In Kierkegaard, repetition is assigned the task of freedom itself.

There has been a centrality given to repetition in post-structuralist thinking, notably in the work of Derrida and Deleuze. In the texts of Derrida, repetition is seen as preceding the establishment of identities. Iterability becomes a condition of writing, an idea implicit in the notion of *différance*: iterability involves the repetition of the same as the different, inducing differentiation and the deferring of an identical meaning. The primacy of repetition to notions of identity renders the search for an undifferentiated origin problematic.[9]

Deleuze's work concerns us more here since repetition and difference form the central concerns in his work, from his early monographs on Proust and Nietzsche to his recent work on cinema. The major elaboration of his examination of repetition is to be found in *Différence et répétition*. In Deleuze's work, too, repetition is assigned primordiality in relation to identity. Repetition is seen there as the mode of articulation of difference, of the uniquely particular. Furthermore, Deleuze makes a distinction between naked and clothed repetition: the former signifies repetition of the same as the same, while the latter denotes repetition with variation, i.e. with difference. While naked repetition accomplishes the reproduction of an original identity, so that each occurrence of the

---

[7] See, for a discussion of the notion of repetition in the history of philosophy, Gilles Deleuze, *Différence et répétition* (Paris: Presses Universitaires de France, 1968), 43–95. The passages cited from this text are in my translation from the French.

[8] *James Joyce Archive*, ed. Michael Groden (New York: Garland, 1977–80), iii. 391.

[9] A preoccupation with the question of repetition can be seen in many of Derrida's writings. See e.g. Jacques Derrida, *Speech and Phenomena and Other Essays on Husserl's Theory of Signs*, tr. David B. Allison (Evanston, Ill.: Northwestern University Press, 1973); *Writing and Difference*, tr. Alan Bass (Chicago: University of Chicago Press, 1978); *Of Grammatology*, tr. G. C. Spivak (Baltimore: Johns Hopkins University Press, 1976).

repeated element is only a copy of the original, the other form of repetition makes it impossible to think of such an original model. Plato's theory of forms can be seen as an example of the model presupposed by naked repetition. The original form is the model behind the copies. Clothed repetition annuls the distinction between the original and the copy. Each act of repetition is an affirmation of singularity—repetition is the mode that articulates difference without the mediation of identity or analogy. Deleuze argues:

Consider two propositions: only similar things differ; only differences resemble each other. The first formula poses resemblance as the condition of difference; undoubtedly, it also requires the possibility of an identical concept for two things on the condition of their resemblance and also implies an analogy in the relation of each thing to its concept. Finally, it entails the reduction of difference to an opposition determined by these three moments.[10]

Against this model, Deleuze opposes the other formula according to which resemblance, identity, analogy, opposition, etc. are specific effects of difference: 'According to this formula, it is necessary that difference immediately relates the different terms to one another.'[11] Deleuze proposes the notion of *différenciant*, or of the differentiation of difference to elaborate this relationship. What would interest us particularly are the conditions of a system of organization that allows difference to be articulated in this way.

The first feature of such a system, according to Deleuze, is serial organization:

It is necessary that a system constitutes itself on the basis of two or more series, each series being defined by the differences between the terms that compose it. If we suppose that the series enter into communication under the action of some force, it appears that this communication relates differences to other differences, or constitutes within the system differences of differences—these differences at the second degree play the role of *différenciant*, i.e. they relate the differences at the first degree to one another.[12]

For Deleuze, sometimes there is an element at play that provides an apparent identity or similarity in order to establish communication between these diverse series. He describes this pseudo-identity as a

---

[10] Deleuze, *Différence et répétition*, 153.        [11] Ibid. 154.
[12] Ibid.

'dark precursor' (*précurseur sombre*), which determines in advance
the path of the lightning that flares up between different intensities.
It is defined as 'difference in itself, in the second degree, which puts
in relation heterogeneous or disparate series'.[13]

The pseudo-identity functions to produce a system of relations
which does not give rise to a totality. It puts series of differences or
of repetitions into communication to articulate their difference. All
this points towards a new schematism of synthesis. As distinct from
the Kantian model of a synthesis by the imagination and its
subsumption under the concept, here the organizing, or the
apparently totalizing principle, does not induce a totality, it only
creates the direct relations of series of differences. For Deleuze, such
dark precursors are provided in Joyce's work by the epiphany in
general and by the esoteric or the portmanteau word in *Finnegans
Wake*.[14] Another example that Deleuze cites for the operation of
the dark precursor is the work of Raymond Roussel and the role
played by quasi-homonyms in it. Roussel himself has demonstrated
the construction of his novels as based on the verbal similarity of
two dissimilar words, the story being a device for connecting them.
The homonym does not induce an identity between two words. It
only elaborates their difference so that the story can fill the space of
this difference.

The reason for this digression has been to show how the
meditation on repetition in contemporary philosophy can give rise
to an account of textual organizations that cannot ultimately be
contained under a principle of totalizing identity, and which, none
the less, use grids of organization unceasingly till more and more
series of differences and interrelations come into play. Earlier in this
introduction, I considered some of the complexities generated by
these patterns for totalizing interpretations of Joyce. The question
is not only to formulate an account of the disruptive effects of the
text but also to show how the organizing principles participate in it
or contribute to it. The generality of the arguments related to
'writing' or 'liberation of the signifier' or 'the Imaginary' often fails
to provide this.

On the one hand, the proliferation of such organizing principles
belongs to a number of writings in early modernism. On the other
hand, they anticipate without entirely belonging to it many

---

[13] Ibid. 157.          [14] Ibid. 159–60.

experiments in fiction as well as other arts, that have come to be called 'post-modern'. The specificity of these labels and of the often complex and ambiguous relations that obtain between them and the texts often depend on the particularity of the configuration of textual elements—for example, the specific ways in which external principles of organization are chosen and how they function within the text. A generalized argument concerning the production of meaning often fails to make these distinctions clearly. The result of this is usually a suppression or a misrecognition of the historicity of a text. This historicity is operative within the text in determining and elaborating procedures which exceeded the self-understanding of the author or his contemporaries. However, this self-understanding functions at the border of the text, sometimes invisibly and insensibly, like Deleuze's dark precursor. Joyce's aesthetic theory and his schema play analogous roles in relation to *Ulysses*. They need to be understood in the light of the text. But this is essential not only for understanding them, but for understanding *Ulysses* as well.

This book sets out to study some aspects of this organization and some of their effects. I begin by examining the various kinds of repetition at work in *Ulysses* and the way they generate several intersecting series. These series indeed come into incommensurable relations with a number of identities that some of the conservative readings of Joyce take for granted. For example, sometimes it works across characters, making it difficult to understand the notion of a character-subjectivity and its memory as the founding principles of repetition. Sometimes, it does not work to convey any identical sense in meaning for the fragment concerned. Here too, repetition questions an identity, whether it be in the form of an *arkhe* or of a *telos* or of a law.

However, to speak about repetition purely in terms of its negative function will make it vulnerable to precisely the kind of criticism that I raised against the rather simplistic versions of post-structuralist readings of Joyce. Repetition creates effects which need to be described in their own terms rather than in relation to their opposites or of some identity that is disrupted or violated. An attempt is made below to develop an argument that would describe some of these effects and to show how totalizing impulses operate in the text in conjunction with impulses that are contrary to this. There are three major areas where I explore these procedures in relation to *Ulysses*. The first of them concerns the question of time. Modern narrative theory has examined aspects of temporal synthesis that are presupposed by narration. Lukács's *Theory of the Novel*, as Jay Bernstein convincingly argues, relies on the Kantian schema of perception for describing the narrative act.[15] Paul Ricœur's *Time and Narrative*, once again, takes as its conceptual terrain the Kantian schema.[16] The procedures of repetition and of the serial organization with its frustration of totalizing syntheses have their implications for the experience of time in *Ulysses* as well. I examine in some detail how the schematism of *Ulysses* functions, in producing localities of temporal experience that do not fit into an overall temporal schema. This creates an experience of differential temporality, where the only originary experience of time is the experience of a process of differentiation.

This is perhaps where Joyce's endeavour finds itself paralleling that of Bergson, albeit in a very different way. In Bergson's texts, *durée* is seen as a qualitative multiplicity, a pure heterogeneity that constantly differs from itself.[17] *Durée* is the originary experience of time in so far as it is this differentiation that is eventually arrested by representation, by the spatializing and quantifying impulse in reason. *Durée* is pure temporality in that it creates a proliferation of differences that constitutes an experience that is prior to as well as that exceeds representations.[18]

Joyce seems to give a specifically linguistic turn to these meditations on time. In his works, the temporality of the text insistently comes to the surface, presenting the innumerable patterns of partial syntheses that do not fit into one another and which only create more differences, differences of a second degree. At the origin, we have only processes of differentiation at work, machineries that produce an increasing number of levels, and modes in which these differences operate.

From this perspective, the episode of *Ulysses* that thematizes its archaeology is 'Oxen of the Sun'. It is an episode of gestation and

[15] Jay Bernstein, *Philosophy of the Novel: Lukács, Marxism and the Dialectic of Form* (Brighton: Harvester Press, 1984).

[16] Paul Ricœur, *Time and Narrative*, tr. Katherine McLaughlin and David Pellauer, 3 vols. (Chicago: University of Chicago Press, 1984–8).

[17] Henri Bergson, *Time and Free Will: An Essay on the Immediate Data of Consciousness*, tr. F. L. Pogson (London: George Allen & Unwin, Ltd., 1910).

[18] See Gilles Deleuze, *Bergsonism*, tr. Hugh Tomlinson (New York: Zone Books, 1988).

birth, a birth and a gestation enacted at several apparently homologous levels—the embryo, the earth, language—the pre-human, the human, and the post-human. However, in each of these cases, gestation is not seen as evolution, in the sense of a gradual growth of a seed to its goal. It is seen as differentiation, a series of differences or sets of differences supplanting one another. Even the embryonic chart Joyce works with is no more than a set of differences—it is only a dark precursor. This is equally true of the other levels as well, all the more so in the case of language where one particular set of stylistic characteristics is supplanted by another set. The voice that mimes these styles does not provide an identity but only a relation of differences. The text of the episode itself fills in between all these various series, setting up an interminable process of interpretation which cannot subsume the text under a totalizing meaning. The meditation on origins shows only processes of differentiation. Gestation itself is seen as a re-enactment of life, beginning and ending in forms of chaos.

This also shows a structure of recollection, a recollection that is also an abandonment of identity and of style, that often arises in Joyce's work. This can be described through a discussion of the specific ways in which Joyce and Proust appropriate and transform the tradition of *Bildungsroman* into novels of self-discovery as well as of self-reflexive writing. The *Portrait* and *À la recherche du temps perdu* abandon a reduction of the past experience to what it comes to mean in the present. They recognize, structurally speaking, the interplay of the past and the present, or of a genesis that was experienced by the hero and of a structure that the hero only finds at the end. Both novels apparently rely on structures of circularity in that the novels rehearse their own pre-history—the hero of the last pages goes on to write the first pages of the novel. However, neither Proust nor Joyce reduces genesis to the structure it engenders—the experienced past cannot be contained by the knowing present. In Proust, this leads to a reliance on memory and on art where the immediate intensity of the experience and its later, more detached, appropriation as knowledge are reconciled. Both memory and art, in various ways, show us essences which preserve, without uniting, intensity as well as distance. However, the identity of the narrator's voice is kept intact, since it embodies the insight that there are several different strands of time at work in its constitution.

Joyce's device for tuning the *Bildungsroman* in relation to these dual demands of time was different. It is the identity of the narrator's voice that is ruptured to several territories of discourse, where intensity is experienced and meaning contemplated. Thus the novel is really not the story of an articulation, but of articulations, and characteristically the metaphor of language recurs towards the conclusion of the various sections of the *Portrait*, whether it be in the form of the sensory music of water falling into a still pool, or of the new language given to Stephen in a kiss in the brothel, or of the Communion. Articulation is seen as engagement in a discourse, in a universe of meaning that eventually comes to be supplanted by another world. The role of memory in this Joycean schema is quite different from that in Proust's novel. In Proust, memory unites intensity and the revelation of an essence. It confers on the language of the present an amplitude that the present would lack, were it to be deprived of memory. In the future anterior of Proust's prose, memory lets language oscillate between an anterior which was the lived present and a future which is the present of writing. In Joyce's *Portrait*, on the other hand, memory evokes and presents discursive traces of a world that has been disarticulated. There is no single past, but a series of pasts, various ways of articulating a world and a self. In Proust, the narrator and the character are united by memory in the same narrative voice. In Joyce, they function in an amorphous system where the narrator is coloured by the character's consciousness. The narrator of each section of the *Portrait* is itself a product of the memory which recalls the past as it was embodied in style. The remembered image is an image of language, an image which carries with it the discursive world where it arose.

In *Ulysses* too the faculty of memory which sometimes provides a source for interior monologues creates articulations which are discontinuous. It often recalls a discursive fragment that is contextually associated with the present. It circulates fragments from other parts of the text that constitute the character's past, and induces tensions and dislocations within the text. This is where Jacques Aubert's beautiful analysis of 'Proteus' in terms of the simulacrum becomes pertinent.[19] Memory in the simulacrum of the text is a textual memory that repeats fragments in new articulations.

---

[19] Jacques Aubert, *Introduction à l'esthétique de James Joyce* (Paris: Didier, 1973).

The collision of chains of articulation creates the suspension of the notion of identity that is in command or in control.

In the third chapter of the book, an attempt is made to examine some aspects of the complex temporal structure of *Ulysses* and the necessary partiality of the syntheses and connections that can be made. I examine two major positions elaborated in Joyce criticism— one in relation to 'time-mind' and Bergson's notion of *durée*, and the other in relation to the notion of 'spatial form'. Joyce's schema and other organizational principles do not give any unified temporal structure to the novel either.

This is indeed true of the sign as well. One of the aspects of repetition is to deeply implicate the meaning of the sign in the various series in which it participates. Therefore, instead of a simple articulation between the signifier and the signified, the series of repetitions of the sign, the context in which it is used, seem to enter its constitution. This interiorization of contextual displacement reveals an inner temporality within the sign—the sign itself is neither closed nor total. It is subject to a constant retotalization, where elements or contexts from its prehistory come to determine its meaning. This temporalizing of the sign is indeed analogous to the function of memory that I described above. It brings with it traces of its previous articulations. The sign becomes a palimpsest or, more precisely, a constant rehearsal of its own history.

There are other significant complications of the sign, primarily a result of the different regularities of discourse in which it is articulated in various parts of the text. Since Joyce often works with a group of semantemes for inducing a specific pattern in the text, the number of interpretative connections or series in which the sign partakes abounds.

Finally, the last two chapters are concerned with a certain dimension of Joyce's art which it is necessary to understand in the context of our discussion of the internal temporality of the sign. This dimension concerns Joyce's use of allusions in *Ulysses*. There are two ways in which this phenomenon has been discussed from the perspective of literary theory. One of them is to subsume this under a notion of intertextuality. However, a distinction would need to be made between a generalized notion of intertextuality that has been proposed as a feature of textuality in general and the specific and more explicit mode of allusions that Joyce uses. The second way is closer to the idea of the library that Foucault discerns as being operative in Flaubert's *La Tentation de saint Antoine*, one of Joyce's models for 'Circe'.[20] It presupposes a notion of the tradition of Western representation and liberates allusion from ideas of authority and authorization, traditionally attached to allusions. A variation of the second way in which literary theory has responded to Joyce's relation to the tradition of representation has been articulated in some of Derrida's writings on Joyce. Here Joyce's strategies are related to the questions of history and of recollection.[21] Again Derrida's own texts are arguably not unified in the elaboration of this argument. I shall discuss some of these texts in the fourth chapter.

I argue below that it is profoundly useful to consider allusion as a form of repetition in relation to the history of representation. This has consequences for two questions. On the one hand, the idea of artistic creation and that of aesthetic apprehension become inalienably tied up with notions of repetition. This necessitates a rereading of Joyce's early aesthetic theories. This indirectly involves the relationship that obtains between singularity and repetition. The young Joyce's notions of essence, of *claritas*, etc. would need to be interpreted in this light. On the other hand, the idea of tradition itself undergoes a questioning. The use of allusions, instead of grounding the text on tradition, constructs various series that do not necessarily lead to a totality. Like the disruptive repetition I mentioned above, allusion too, in the hands of Joyce, is a way of implicating the original in a process of differentiation and of constant reinterpretation. The original meaning no longer determines the meaning of discourse. Like the first inscription on a palimpsest, it already presupposes its own overwritings, where the original and the repeated become difficult to distinguish.

According to this use, tradition is essentially a performance of elements which disrupt their identities and engage in new series. This is quite different in its basic impulse from another notion of tradition prevalent in early modernism, and which finds a lucid

[20] Michel Foucault, 'Fantasia of the Library', in id., *Language, Counter-Memory, Practice*, ed. D. F. Bouchard, tr. D. F. Bouchard and Sherry Simon (Oxford: Basil Blackwell, 1977), 87–109.

[21] See Jacques Derrida, *Edmund Husserl's 'Origin of Geometry': An Introduction*, tr. J. P. Leavy (Brighton: Harvester Press, 1978), 103 ff.; id., 'Des tours de Babel', tr. Joseph F. Graham, in Joseph F. Graham (ed.), *Difference in Translation* (Ithaca, NY: Cornell University Press, 1985), 165–207; id., 'Two Words for Joyce', in Attridge and Ferrer (eds.), *Post-Structuralist Joyce*, 147–58.

theoretical articulation in T. S. Eliot's 'Tradition and the Individual Talent'.[22] Instead of a continuum of monuments, Joyce's method presupposes fantasms, imitations, and distortions of representations from the past. Joyce's text interiorizes them, not to form a totality that subsumes them, but to form a proliferation of new series. This results in a presentation of differences, an internal resonance in the system that arises from the communication of various series with one another. In the constitution of the monument, it is precisely this difference that is annulled. Joyce's method affirms this difference—in fact, tradition is nothing but the articulation of this difference.

These are indeed the major concerns of this book. However, it needs to be clarified that the attempt has not been to describe *a* single structure, or *a* single system that legislates over *Ulysses*. On the contrary, the attempt here has been to show how contrary impulses incite interpretations that need to found meaning on structures and how these interpretations come to be frustrated. This frustration is essential to the Joycean enterprise. It creates zones of meaning which do not fit together, discursive territories where different regularities hold.

[22] T. S. Eliot, 'Tradition and the Individual Talent' (1919), in id., *Selected Essays* (3rd edn.) (London: Faber & Faber, Ltd., 1951), 13–22.

# 2

# Repetition:
# Its Modes and Levels

In the Introduction, while discussing the theoretical implications of repetition, I cited Deleuze's distinction between two kinds of repetition. The first, which he calls 'naked' repetition, involves the unvarying repetition of the same. The first occurrence of the element functions as an original model here, and the subsequent occurrences can be seen as copies of this model. The second kind, 'clothed' repetition, introduces difference at each of its occurrences. The relation between 'model' and 'copy' does not obtain in this case. While 'naked' repetition functions to reaffirm and stabilize an identity given at the beginning, 'clothed' repetition questions such stability.

This distinction can serve as an introduction to Joyce's use of repetition in *Ulysses*. The repetition of verbal elements is indeed one of the noticeable peculiarities of *Ulysses*. William Schutte's compilation of recurrent elements runs into more than three hundred pages.[1] However, all the elements that Schutte lists are not interpretatively significant acts of repetition. For example, the names of characters, while repeated, do not invite attention to their new occurrence as an act of repetition.[2] There are several such elements in narrative discourse that are often repeated with unvaried meaning, such as places, objects, events. They function as acts of naked repetition, where repetition only confirms and reiterates the sense of the original use. It aids the reader's retentive memory and stabilizes the identity of the element. This kind of repetition is not the object of discussion in this chapter.

However, there is another kind of repetition in *Ulysses*. In 'Nestor', Deasy tells Stephen:

—The ways of the Creator are not our ways . . . All human history moves towards one great goal, the manifestation of God. (*U*, 2. 380–1)

---

[1] William M. Schutte, *Index of Recurrent Elements in James Joyce's 'Ulysses'* (Carbondale, Ill.: Southern Illinois University Press, 1982).

[2] Ibid. p. vi.

In 'Proteus', as Stephen observes the dog on the beach, we come across this passage:

His speckled body ambled ahead of them and loped off at a calf's gallop. The carcass lay on his path. He stopped, sniffed, stalked round it, brother, nosing closer, went round it, sniffling rapidly like a dog all over the dead dog's bedraggled fell. Dogskull, dogsniff, eyes on the ground, moves to one great goal. Ah, poor dogsbody! Here lies poor dogsbody's body. (*U*, 3. 347–52)

Here, the use of 'moves to one great goal' in the second passage calls our attention to the earlier use of the phrase. In other words, the memory of the earlier use of the word makes it possible to establish an interpretatively relevant connection between the two passages. There are several ways of interpreting this connection. It can be related to Stephen's memory or to a general textual strategy. The second instance of the use of the phrase does not stabilize or confirm the first one. It calls attention to both uses of the phrase, to the difference between them. This act of self-focusing repetition opens up a gap that interpretation needs to bridge. The apparent identity of the phrase conceals a deeper difference: a difference in the context and associations in which the phrase is placed. It is this second kind of repetition, destabilizing identities and creating differences, that I shall examine in this chapter.

The monologues of Stephen and Bloom show an abundance of instances of this latter kind of repetition. Phrases and words from earlier parts of the text are repeated, sometimes transformed or distorted, to fit an entirely new context. In some cases, the ostensible meaning of the phrase becomes less important than the earlier *context* of its use. For example, the recurrence of 'smell of burn' in Bloom's monologues several times in the novel does not often seem to refer to the smell of burn as such. It can be understood adequately only if we go back to the context in which it was originally used, i.e. the smell of burn of kidney in the morning, making Bloom rush to the kitchen from the bedroom where he had earlier delivered Boylan's letter to Molly.

Not all the instances of repetition in *Ulysses* can be understood or accounted for in terms of the psychological recollection of characters. An extreme example of this is the occurrence of the same passage in the monologues of both Stephen and Bloom:

Do and do. Thing done. In a rosery of Fetter lane of Gerard, herbalist, he walks, greyedauburn. An azured harebell like her veins. Lids of Juno's eyes, violets. He walks. One life is all. One body. Do. But do. (*U*, 9. 651–3).

In Gerard's rosery of Fetter lane he walks, greyedauburn. One life is all. One body. Do. But do. (*U*, 11. 907–8).

Here, repetition seems to function as a strategy that goes beyond character-subjectivity and its memory. Naturalizing interpretations of Joyce find it difficult to interpret such strategies.[3] However, an examination of them can throw light on the ways in which Joyce seems to explore recollection in terms of language.

Some parts of *Ulysses* show a use of repetition that goes even further away from being subordinated to characters and their memory. In 'Sirens', the overture presents a series of disjointed fragments which are later repeated in the text, where they form part of intelligible sentences. Some of the fragments are already instances of repetition from earlier episodes. For example, 'Blue Bloom is on the' (*U*, 11. 6) recalls '*Leopoldo or the Bloom is on the Rye*' (*U*, 10. 524), and the 'Bronze by Gold' motif (*U*, 11. 1) had occurred in 'Wandering Rocks' (*U*, 10. 962). Here the justification of repetition seems to be at the level of narrative organization, in the use of *fuga per canonem* as the technic of the episode. In 'Oxen of the Sun', phrases from earlier parts of the text are repeated. Joyce explained to Budgen that this was an organizational principle for the episode: 'this progression is also linked back subtly at each part with some foregoing episode of the day.'[4] Examples include 'the ghost of his own father' (*U*, 1. 556–7, 14. 1033–4), 'old Nobodaddy' (*U*, 9. 787, 14. 419), and 'wheatkidneys' (*U*, 3. 119, 14. 155). In 'Circe', there is a systematic repetition of earlier events of the day in the form of fantasy. Some of them can be understood in terms of character-subjectivities, but others show a different kind of determination.[5] The figure of Shakespeare appears to both Stephen and Bloom (*U*, 15. 3820–3), and the daughters of Erin

---

[3] Robert Adams discusses this passage and remarks that it is unclear as to when it appeared for the first time in the compositional history of *Ulysses*. Michael Groden, on the other hand, refutes Adams's position and points out that Joyce added this passage to the earliest extant draft of 'Sirens'. Groden's claim appears to be validated by Buffalo MS, V A 5, fo. 27ᵛ. See Michael Groden, '*Ulysses' in Progress* (Princeton, NJ: Princeton University Press, 1977), 42 n.; *James Joyce Archive*, ed. Michael Groden, xiii (New York: Garland Press, 1977), 46. [4] *Letters*, i. 140.

[5] John Paul Riquelme, *Teller and Tale in Joyce's Fiction: Oscillating Perspectives* (Baltimore: Johns Hopkins University Press, 1983), 242–4.

seem to operate at a metatextual level, recapitulating the episodic divisions of the text (*U*, 15. 1940–52).

So far I have considered instances of repetition from within the text. How about allusions, where verbal fragments from outside the text are chosen for circulation within *Ulysses*? Joyce uses an amazingly large number of allusions from a variety of sources. In most cases, allusion functions in a way similar to that of destabilizing repetition. There is often a difference between the original context of the verbal fragment and its use in *Ulysses*. This again invites interpretative connections. What internal repetition does in relation to earlier parts of the text seems to be paralleled by what allusion does in relation to other texts. To complicate matters further, a number of allusions are repeated within *Ulysses*. This involves a double repetition where strategies of repetition of verbal fragments and those of allusion function together. The series that a repeated allusion generates connects the present use to previous uses of the fragment within and outside the text. Questions of identity and origin become even more problematic here.

I shall examine below three major modes that destabilizing or self-focusing repetition takes in *Ulysses*. The first mode concerns the repetition of verbal fragments within *Ulysses*. In the second group, I consider the case of repeated allusions in order to study the effects of the intensification of repetition in them. Finally, I examine the repetition of events and situations, or repetition that occupies the level of signified content.

It should be remembered, however, that the distinction between these three modes is not a hard and fast one. Repetition of allusions, empirically speaking, forms a subset of the repetition of verbal fragments. None the less, the doubling of repetition in their case makes it useful to examine them separately. Similarly, it is not always easy to make the distinction between repetition at the level of signified content and that at the level of the verbal surface. The interior monologue, dense with recollections, straddles this distinction. Here much of the recollection is actually realized in the form of verbal repetition. The specific effects created by the act of recollection are to a large extent determined by the play of identity and difference that I indicated above in relation to verbal repetition. I treat such cases as repetition of verbal elements. This appears to be a useful way to explore Joyce's use of memory and the role of language in this. However, there are a number of instances where events or situations seem to recall one another without being accompanied by verbal repetition. This can take the form of the recollection of the same event by different characters, or of the repetition of a certain configuration of elements in a variety of situations. These are far less numerous than verbal repetition in *Ulysses*. I consider only these instances as repetition at the level of signified content.

## Memory and the Metempsychosis of the Word

In 'Calypso' we have the beginning of a series of verbal repetition. The elements of this series are clustered around Molly's mispronunciation of the word 'metempsychosis', a word that semantically signifies a play of identity and difference. In 'Calypso' we do not directly hear Molly's utterance:

—Met him what? he asked.
—Here, she said. What does that mean?
  He leaned downward and read near her polished thumbnail.
—Metempsychosis?
—Yes. Who's he when he's at home?
—Metempsychosis, he said, frowning. It's Greek: from the Greek. That means the transmigration of souls.
—O, rocks! she said. Tell us in plain words. (*U*, 4. 336–43)

We find Bloom's monologues returning to this incident several times during the day. This return takes the form of verbal repetition, each time induced by a new context. In 'Lestrygonians', intrigued by the word 'parallax', Bloom thinks:

Par it's Greek: parallel, parallax. Met him pike hoses she called it till I told her about the transmigration. O rocks! (*U*, 8. 111–13)

Here we see Molly's mispronunciation for the first time. The opacity of the word 'parallax' is what induces the recollection, and 'Greek' forms the associational link. However, when 'met him pike hoses' is recalled, it presents itself with other traces of its earlier context. 'O rocks!' appears as a disjunctive fragment without being appropriated by the surrounding passage. It is connected to the new context only through the recollection of its earlier occurrence. Later, in the same episode, Bloom recalls 'met him pike hoses' but it is not immediately in relation to Molly nor to the incident in the morning. 'Karma they call the transmigration of sins you did in a past life the reincarnation met him pike hoses' (*U*, 8. 1147–8). '[T]ransmigration' recalls 'Metempsychosis' from the original context, but the latter is replaced by 'met him pike hoses'. The literal meaning (or lack of it) of the phrase is abandoned in favour of the memory of the earlier context. Bloom's memory invokes a part of the text that the reader is familiar with—it invokes a set of discursive elements that were presented together earlier in the text. In other words, the memory of characters functions here in close proximity to our memory of the text, or of discursive connections.

In 'Sirens', as Bloom's thoughts anticipate Boylan's visit to Molly, we come across this passage:

> Mrs Marion. Met him pike hoses. Smell of burn. Of Paul de Kock. Nice name he. (*U*, 11. 500–1)

Here 'Met him pike hoses' does not have any relation to 'metempsychosis', 'transmigration', or 'Greek'. It forms part of a chain of discursive fragments, recirculated from 'Calypso'. 'Mrs Marion' comes from Boylan's letter in the morning: 'Mrs Marion Bloom. His quickened heart slowed at once. Bold hand. Mrs Marion' (*U*, 4. 244–5). 'Smell of burn' recalls the smell of burn of kidney (*U*, 4. 380–1). 'Of Paul de Kock' and 'Nice name he' come from Molly's conversation, again in the same context: 'Yes. Get another of Paul de Kock's. Nice name he has' (*U*, 4. 358). Memory here works through repetition of verbal fragments whose only connection to one another lies in their previous history within the text. Furthermore, it is interesting to note that this whole chain of associations is evoked through verbal similarity. It is the fragment 'Mrs Marion Bloom' from Simon Dedalus's words a few lines earlier in the text (*U*, 11. 496) that triggers off the chain of recollection. This chain is reunited with the conversation once again, immediately after 'Nice name he': 'What's this her name was? A buxom lassy. Marion ...?' (*U*, 11. 502).

It is difficult to determine whether the passage (*U*, 11. 500–1) belongs to Bloom's monologue or to the narrator. The nature of repetition makes such determination impossible. On the one hand, the passage invokes a set of elements that clearly come from Bloom's world. On the other, it is the discourse of the other characters, Simon Dedalus and Father Cowley, that begins and completes the chain. The individual recollection of Bloom, a series connected through contextual associations, thus forms part of a larger chain that relies on verbal similarities as well.

In 'Sirens', after Bloom's recollection of the 'Spinoza incident', we find another reference to 'metempsychosis':

Nature woman half a look. God made the country man the tune. Met him pike hoses. Philosophy. O rocks! (*U*, 11. 1061–2)

At the surface level, 'Met him pike hoses' and 'philosophy' seem to be connected to Spinoza, but on closer examination the number of vague associations multiplies. 'God made the country man the tune' is an allusion to 'God made the country and man made the town', a line from William Cowper. Here, two levels of being are suggested: divine and human. In Bloom's mind, meditations on this question relate to theosophical lore in a rather imprecise way. Metempsychosis could be one way of connecting them. Earlier in the novel, Stephen had elaborated this idea: 'God becomes man becomes fish becomes barnacle goose becomes featherbed mountain' (*U*, 3. 477–9). A complex textual memory seems to mediate between the phrase and its context.

Later, in 'Sirens', we come across another passage that continues this series of verbal repetition:

Up the quay went Lionelleopold, naughty Henry with letter for Mady, with sweets of sin with frillies for Raoul with met him pike hoses went Poldy on. (*U*, 11. 1187–9)

This passage occurs in the narrator's discourse. However, narration also seems to behave in a way similar to Bloom's monologues, recycling discursive fragments which are not related to one another except through their prior history. '[M]et him pike hoses' does not evoke the meaning of metempsychosis here. It refers the reader back to the earlier contexts of its use. It brings under its surface the various discursive domains where the fragment was embedded before.

The later repetition of the phrase in the text displays some of the tendencies that we have already seen. In 'Nausicaa' it returns to its original spelling and meaning:

Thinks I'm a tree, so blind. Have birds no smell? Metempsychosis. They believed you could be changed into a tree from grief. (*U*, 13. 1117–19)

The original meaning of metempsychosis appears here, as it was explained in 'Calypso':

—Metempsychosis, he said, is what the ancient Greeks called it. They used to believe you could be changed into an animal or a tree, for instance. (*U,* 4. 375–6)

The word is used here in its original literal meaning, as if it were a case of stabilizing repetition. However, 'changed into a tree' further recalls the original context of the use of the word, calling attention to its status as a repeated element. Moreover, since the word has already been repeated several times in the text in a self-focusing way, it is difficult to ignore the repetition. Towards the end of the episode, the phrase recurs in a collection of disjointed fragments (*U,* 13. 1279–81) which are united only through textual memory. In 'Oxen of the Sun', 'metempsychosis' forms part of Bloom's sober meditations on the levity of medical students (*U,* 14. 896–902) and later the word is used in the sense of transformation (*U,* 14. 1100).

In 'Circe' it reappears with the ghost of Paddy Dignam:

PADDY DIGNAM
Bloom, I am Paddy Dignam's spirit. List, list, O list!
BLOOM
The voice is the voice of Esau.
SECOND WATCH
(*blesses himself*) How is that possible?
FIRST WATCH
It is not in the penny catechism.
PADDY DIGNAM
By metempsychosis. Spooks.
A VOICE
O rocks. (*U,* 15. 1217–28)

Here the repetition of 'metempsychosis' is again accompanied by 'O rocks' uttered by an anonymous voice. This is in keeping with strategies of 'Circe': the entire episode can be seen as an elaborate repetition machine where elements presented earlier in the text are transformed and repeated as fantasy. Later in the episode, among the '*shaking statues of several naked goddesses*', we find '*Venus Metempsychosis*' (*U,* 15. 1706), a repetition that combines two different series of associations: Bloom's thoughts about the statues of naked goddesses and the series of verbal repetitions of 'metempsychosis'.

In 'Eumaeus' the phrase is absorbed by the language of textual commentaries, perhaps occasioned by *Ruby: Pride of the Ring:*

I looked for the lamp which she told me came into his mind but merely as a passing fancy of his because he then recollected the morning littered bed etcetera and the book about Ruby with met him pike hoses (*sic*) in it which must have fell down sufficiently appropriately beside the domestic chamberpot with apologies to Lindley Murray. (*U*, 16. 1470–5)

In 'Ithaca' the word occurs again in a comment on Molly's mispronunciation (*U*, 17. 686), and in 'Penelope' we find Molly trying to remember the word: 'and that word something with hose in it' (*U*, 18. 565).

These occurrences of 'metempsychosis' and its variants constitute a series of self-focusing repetition. Each instance of recurrence invites attention to the act of repetition and refers back to the earlier contexts of its use. In most instances, the literal meaning of the word becomes secondary in relation to the series of discursive contexts it highlights. The different ways in which the same verbal element is used in different discourses seem to be the primary object of attention here. In contrast to naked repetition, where the use of names or other verbal elements with unvaried meaning aids the reader's retentive memory, here the reader's memory is used in the service of a textual strategy. Instead of reaffirming an identity which unites all acts of repetition, here repetition creates a series of differences and dislocations.

These dislocations can be seen in the various ways in which the repeated verbal element is connected to its new discursive surroundings. Sometimes this is done through verbal similarity, as in the case of 'A jumping rose on satiny breast of satin, rose of Castile' (*U*, 11. 8). Here 'rose' evokes *The Rose of Castile*, the name of the opera in Lenehan's riddle (*U*, 7. 591). Verbal similarity provides a tenuous connection between fragments of two diverse discourses. More often, we find contextual associations connecting the repeated verbal element to its new context. This is especially the case in the monologues. In the example from 'Sirens' (*U*, 11. 500–1) that I discussed above, it is the earlier context where the fragments were used in the text that ensures the connection between 'metempsychosis' and its surroundings. These connections rely on the reader's textual memory: the operation of such a memory is invited by the apparent disjunction between elements in the passage. Sometimes, the repetition of a verbal element is occasioned by an association at the level of meaning. In most instances of this kind, there is a slight semantic dislocation that makes a reference to the earlier context necessary. In 'God made the country man the tune. Met him pike hoses. Philosophy. O rocks!' (*U*, 11. 1061–2), a vague invocation of the original meaning is involved. However, this is too imprecise for the fragment to function independently—it functions more like an allusion to the earlier use of the word.

In all these cases, there is a slight disparity between the recurring verbal element and its surroundings. This disparity invites interpretative connections to be made between the earlier and the new occurrences of the element. As I have tried to show, the various occurrences are not united in terms of a single meaning. Rather, it is a difference that is highlighted, and a series rather than a totality that emerges.

There are some instances where an even greater disjunction occurs between the earlier and the new contexts of use of verbal fragments. The repetition of 'In a rosery of Fetter lane of Gerard, herbalist, he walks, greyedauburn' (*U*, 9, 651–2, 11. 907–8) is an example of this. The occurrence of the fragment of the monologues of both Bloom and Stephen complicates the problem of interpretation here. The reference to the earlier context does not resolve, but rather exacerbates, the problem. This makes it necessary to think of the strategy of repetition in *Ulysses* as essentially operating at the level of the text rather than at the level of character-subjectivities. The recollection of characters seems to be one specific mode of verbal repetition rather than vice versa. The use of repetition in the overture of 'Sirens' and in the 'Oxen of the Sun' points in the same direction. It is not enough to attribute this strategy to the narrator or to the 'author as arranger'. Such an attribution only begs the question in relation to the relevance and function of this strategy. It is necessary to describe the effects of repetition and to see how these relate to other aspects of Joyce's textual strategies. In the later chapters of this book, I shall try to examine the implications of repetition for the experience of time, the notion of the sign, and attitudes to tradition.

## Allusions: The Echo of an Echo

The repetition of allusions forms a special case of verbal repetition. Allusions are already instances of repetition in relation to earlier texts. In other words, they constitute a specific mode of inter-textuality. Allusions are different from quotations and commentary. In *Ulysses*, by and large, allusions function as instances of implied or indirect reference. Often they leave the source of the allusion for the reader to discover. This is to a large extent due to the associative connections in which allusions are implicated by the interior monologue. However, a certain degree of suggestion and revelation of the original verbal text is necessary for an allusion to function. There is an interesting passage where Bloom thematizes the balancing of the revealed and the hidden elements in allusions. Looking at a 'fellow ramming a knifeful of cabbage down as if his life depended on it' (*U*, 8. 682–3), Bloom thinks:

Born with a silver knife in his mouth. That's witty, I think. Or no. Silver means born rich. Born with a knife. But then the allusion is lost. (*U*, 8. 684–6)

This is one of the problems of allusion. Bloom cannot control the associations that 'silver' brings to the phrase 'silver knife in his mouth'. However, if he relinquishes 'silver', the allusion is lost. There needs to be enough from the original verbal text to suggest that connection, but not so much as to suggest irrelevant connections. The balance is hard to obtain.

The preponderance of allusions in *Ulysses* can hardly be overestimated. Symptomatically, the first spoken utterance in the novel, '*Introibo ad altare Dei*', is an allusion to the Mass. Hugh Kenner argues that there are multiple levels of distance separating the original from Buck Mulligan's parody:

Mulligan . . . is tastelessly pretending to be a Black Mass celebrant, who is going through the motions of an Irish priest, who is reciting from the *Ordo*, which quotes from St. Jerome's Latin version of Hebrew words ascribed to a Psalmist in exile: 'va-a-vo-ah mizbah elohim': 'I shall go up to the altar of God' (Psalm 42:4 Vulgate; 43:4 King James). So we might set the first words spoken in *Ulysses* inside six sets of quotation marks—
' " ' " ' " Introibo ad altare Dei" ' " ' " '
—a multiple integument of contexts to contain this Hebrew cry for help among persecution.[6]

This allusion therefore is the site of a multiple citation, a site of series of repetitions with different intentions and strategies. Within

---

[6] Hugh Kenner, *Ulysses* (London: George Allen & Unwin, Ltd., 1980), 34–5.

the text of *Ulysses*, this fragment is repeated again. In 'Circe', we find Mulligan performing a Black Mass: '*Introibo ad altare diaboli*' (*U*, 15. 4699). Earlier in 'Circe', Stephen alludes to the same text in '*ad deam laetificat iuventutem meam*' (*U*, 15. 122–3).

In these later occurrences of the allusion, we can find a complex textual strategy at work. These are independent allusions to the Vulgate, such as the first allusion in 'Telemachus'. However, they are also instances of verbal repetition from within the text. The problem is further complicated by the first occurrence itself being an allusion. The later occurrence of an allusion refers to two different sources, one within the text and one outside it.

In 'Telemachus', Mulligan's utterance makes intelligible the details that surround the passage. The description of his gestures, the shaving-bowl, the cross of mirror and razor, the rapid crosses that he subsequently makes in the air—all these require the allusion and its recognition to fall into place. The allusion here invokes the discursive universe of a ritual. This universe carries with it further connotations such as that of the foundation of ritual on faith and of the religious requirements to be observed when a Mass is performed. Mulligan's gestures, as described in the text, present another discursive universe, that of everyday activities.

These two discursive universes intersect in the allusion. The allusion brings to bear the horizon of intelligibility of the celebration of the Eucharist upon the world of Mulligan's activities. The intersection of the two discursive universes is at the same time a surface event and one that belongs to the deeper levels. At the surface level it is present as the lack of intelligibility of Mulligan's utterance which is in Latin and which, even if translated, does not make much immediate sense. (The utterance translates as 'I will go unto the altar of God.')[7] The intersection is deeper in the sense that a relationship of parody between the Mass and Mulligan's act is implied here.

If the apparent opacity of Mulligan's utterance refers us to a contemplation of the intersection of two discursive terrains, the discovery of this intersection brings our attention back to the surface. On our return to the surface the details fall into place—an elaborate pattern of parody is perceived. But the function of the

---

[7] See Weldon Thornton, *Allusions in 'Ulysses': An Annotated List* (Chapel Hill, NC: North Carolina University Press, 1968), 11.

allusion is not exhausted by this immediate act of making intelligible. It leaves its trace on our subsequent reading of the entire novel. For example, some of the patterns that emerge here and are subsequently brought to bear upon our reading of the novel are—(1) the opposition between the sacred and the profane, (2) the validation of ritual by faith and the possibility of repeating the ritual without its validation, and (3) the theme of the Eucharist. The sacred and the profane describe a set of antipodes which the novel takes up again and again. For instance, in 'Nausicaa' the scene oscillates between the celebration of the blessed sacrament within the church and a profane moment of ecstasy on the seashore. The relationship between ritual and faith takes us far deeper than the surface to Joyce's own use of structures of Christian order without subscribing to the grounds of their validation.[8] The theme of the Eucharist, as we are aware, evokes the notion of epiphany.

Later, when Mulligan performs a Black Mass in 'Circe', these elements are reactivated. In addition to all the effects that it generates as an allusion to the Vulgate, the passage also recalls its earlier use in 'Telemachus'. This latter aspect is part of the general strategies of repetition in 'Circe'. This can also be seen in the figure of 'Father Malachi O'Flynn', a name composed of Mulligan's name and other fragments from earlier parts of *Ulysses*.

The use of allusions seems to generate two contrary impulses in interpretation. On the one hand, the passage from 'Telemachus' confers intelligibility on the surrounding details, thus contributing to textual coherence. On the other hand, it opens up a deeper dissonance in highlighting the difference between the use of the fragment in the earlier text and in the present one. The repetition of allusion also seems to bring together both these aspects: it relies on a source from outside the text, but this does not lead to a totalizing interpretation since it is part of a series of repetitions with difference and variation. The same line from *Hamlet*, 'I am thy father's spirit' (I, v, 9) is misquoted in the same way in *Ulysses* by both Bloom (*U*, 8. 67) and Stephen (*U*, 9. 170). They are

---

[8] Umberto Eco considers this question in some detail in his *Aesthetics of Chaosmos: The Middle Ages of James Joyce*, tr. Ellen Esrock (Tulsa: University of Tulsa Press, 1982). William Noon discerns the same tendency in Joyce's treatment of Aquinas. See William T. Noon, *Joyce and Aquinas* (New Haven, Conn.: Yale University Press, 1957).

independent allusions that occur in different contexts. In Bloom's case it is in relation to poetic craft that the lines are invoked:

> That is how poets write, the similar sounds. But then Shakespeare has no rhymes: blank verse. The flow of the language it is. The thoughts. Solemn. (*U*, 8. 64–6)

Stephen's thoughts on the line designate a site where two scenarios intersect. One is familial and biographical, the other literary:

> —The play begins. A player comes on under the shadow, made up in the castoff mail of a court buck, a wellset man with a bass voice. It is the ghost, the king, a king and no king, and the player is Shakespeare who has studied *Hamlet* all the years of his life which were not vanity in order to play the part of the spectre. He speaks the words to Burbage, the young player who stands before him beyond the rack of cerecloth, calling him by a name:
> *Hamlet, I am thy father's spirit,* (*U*, 9. 164–9).

Both passages contain the same surface presentation of an allusion to *Hamlet*. This identity at the surface level draws attention to itself. Beneath the surface identity, the discursive contexts and the relation between text and allusion that confers meaning on the passage differ. In the repeated instance of the allusion, Stephen's primary aim is to illustrate his fragment by a concrete utterance from *Hamlet*. At the level of character, it can be appropriated into a coherent context easily. None the less, at the level of the text, this is also an event of self-focusing repetition.

In the repetition of allusions, as I have tried to show, there is a movement of transformation and recontextualization of the original text. The source of the allusion does not provide any unique authority that legislates over the production of meaning in the text. On the contrary, the original text is put into circulation within *Ulysses* with variable meaning. In this circulation, there is an implied questioning of notions of a full origin. The origins of a textual fragment do not seem to control its later itinerary or destiny. Once it gets involved in a chain of textual repetition within *Ulysses*, it becomes transformed and recontextualized. The notion of origin becomes devalorized by this process and functions as one element in a chain. It is this special use of allusion that takes it away from the notions of authority and validation with which it has traditionally been associated. This implies a radical attitude to tradition, as we shall see in the later chapters of this book.

## Jealousy and Curiosity

The repetition of similar situations is one of the noticeable features in Proust's *À la recherche*. The relationships of love, both Swann's and Marcel's, involve the same drama of possessiveness, jealousy, and suffering. Though each of these relationships is individual and inalienably specific, together they seem to recall one another and to constitute a series of repetitions that extends beyond the self-understanding of characters. Deleuze, while discussing *À la recherche* as an apprenticeship in signs, discerns an interplay of difference and repetition in this series:

Essence is incarnated in the signs of love, but necessarily in a serial, and hence a general, form. Essence is always difference. But in love, the difference has passed into the unconscious: it becomes in a sense generic or specific, and determines a repetition whose terms are no longer to be distinguished except by infinitesimal differences and subtle contrasts. In short, essence has assumed the generality of a Theme or an Idea, which serves as a law for the series of our loves.[9]

In Proust's text, it is the vocation of the artist to discover these laws. Swann's recognition of the impossibility of his love for Odette still does not reveal the law of his own love. Marcel's re-enactment of the same drama and his recognition of repetition reveals the prevalence of a law that provides intelligibility to this series.

This series of repetition is different from the modes we have examined so far. In contrast to repetition that takes place at the level of the verbal surface of the text, here repetition seems to occupy the level of a signified content, that of events or situations. However, it is rather misleading to attribute this recurrence to an objective and external reality that lies beyond the narrating consciousness. This is indeed because *À la recherche* is also a phenomenology, a story of progressive self-recognition, where a clear dichotomy between the subjective and the objective becomes difficult to maintain. In other words, if it is the narrating consciousness that *discovers* the laws of repetition, it is the same consciousness that forms the series of repetition too. There is another form of repetition in Proust that further underlines the role

---

[9] Gilles Deleuze, *Proust and Signs*, tr. Richard Howard (London: Allen Lane, 1973), 73.

of the narrating consciousness. Gérard Genette calls this the 'pseudo-iterative' and relates it to the distinction between the 'singulative' and the 'iterative' events in Proust's text.[10] Singulative events are unique and unrepeatable, while iterative events are repeated, like the walks on the Méséglise way or the Guermantes way. However, sometimes the narrator recalls an obviously singulative event as if it were iterative, thus transforming it into a pseudo-iterative event.

Joyce's work poses a different problem of distinction. As I pointed out earlier, repetition at the level of situations is often presented as verbal repetition. This is particularly the case in *Finnegans Wake* where the distinction between surface and deeper layers of narrative becomes problematic. Various events and character-identities seem to recall one another as if they were part of a serial organization. In the *Portrait* and *Stephen Hero*, such patterns of repetition are not immediately in evidence. One might be tempted to relate this to the aesthetic of epiphany that Joyce elaborates in these texts. At first sight, the epiphanic moment appears to be contrasted with moments of everyday perception:

The soul of the commonest object, the structure of which is so adjusted, seems to us radiant. The object achieves its epiphany. (*SH*, 218)

The epiphanic moment sets itself apart from mundane moments and appears similar to the singulative moments in Proust. However, on closer examination, the epiphanic seems to presuppose the mundane, even the iterative. Stephen speaks of the ballast office-clock and the movements of its hands as the groping of a spiritual eye. The monotonous repetition of the clock's temporality suddenly gives way to a moment of epiphanization. It has been suggested that in Joyce's later work, epiphany becomes the experience of the work of art, of its decentred structure. This is indeed supported by the evidence of an increased preoccupation with repetition and allusion in later Joyce.

*Ulysses* also presents instances of similarities in the configurations of events and situations, though this is less prominent than the repetition of verbal elements in the novel. Some aspects of this repetition can be related to character-subjectivities, but sometimes repetition traces a series that goes beyond a single character.

[10] Gérard Genette, *Narrative Discourse*, tr. Jane E. Lewin (Oxford: Basil Blackwell, 1980), 113 ff.

The sexual relations in the novel present such a series. Bloom's relations with Gerty and with Martha, and Molly's relations with several of her lovers, repeat the same elements in slightly different configurations. The relationship between Bloom and Molly is far more complex. None the less, many of these elements can be found to be operative there as well.

Martha's letter to Bloom and Gerty's fantasies about him show the dominance of fantasy—an indulgence in fantasizing about the other person, in imagining contexts of union with the other, rather than the experience of an actual relationship. 'Please tell me what you think of poor me,' (*U*, 5. 247–8) Martha writes:

Please write me a long letter and tell me more. . . . O how I long to meet you. Henry dear, do not deny my request before my patience are exhausted. Then I will tell you all. (*U*, 5. 251–4)

Nothing is really revealed in the game of signs that Bloom and Martha play with each other. All that matters and all that is aimed at is the pleasure of fantasy that this game provides. The signs that one inscribes, the intentions behind them, and the way the signs are presented to the public constitute different worlds. These are represented in Bloom's case by a play of proper names: the 'Henry Flower' of the letters, the nameless Bloom of the monologues, and the 'Mr Bloom' of the narration. The interplay of these realms can be seen in 'Sirens', where Bloom inscribes the signs of love, the signs that constitute him as Henry:

Bloom mur: best references. But Henry wrote: it will excite me. You know how. In haste. Henry. Greek ee. Better add postscript. What is he playing now? Improvising. Intermezzo. P.S. The rum tum tum. How will you pun? You punish me? Crooked skirt swinging, whack by. Tell me I want to. Know. O. Course if I didn't I wouldn't ask. La la la ree . . . I feel so sad today. La ree. So lonely. Dee. (*U*, 11. 888–94)

In Proust's world, as Deleuze demonstrates, love functions through a logic of jealousy that instigates the lover to explore the other person's complexities and to reduce the other to transparency. In *Ulysses*, by contrast, desire functions as a preoccupation with fantasy, not directed towards the other person but towards oneself. The world of the other lies concealed from vision but it inspires a depthless curiosity rather than jealousy. It is useful to recall here the dialectic of jealousy and disloyalty that Richard and Bertha undergo in the *Exiles*. The conclusion that Richard reaches in the play is an admission of the impossibility of resolving this dialectic in a certainty. The play ends with Richard recognizing the ultimate opacity of the other, a moment that takes him out of the problematic of jealousy and of the will to know.[11] In *Ulysses*, infidelity does remain a thematic concern, but jealousy loses some of its obsessive intensity and shows a far more complex pattern at work.

This is, to a large extent, due to the prevalence of self-indulgent fantasy as a mode of articulating desire. In contrast to jealousy and the will to interpret, I shall call this new complex 'curiosity'. Jealousy creates nightmares of apprehension—it bases itself on an unbearable uncertainty, the uncertainty of the loyalty of the other, the ultimate unknowability of the other's world. Curiosity, on the other hand, is preoccupied with the surface details of the other's world and produces fantasies where these details reconfigure pleasurably. If jealousy is negative and profound, curiosity is positive and superficial. If jealousy relies on a rhetoric of truth, curiosity is based on that of the fetish.

This distinction is illuminating in relation to both Martha and Gerty. In Proust's text, the lover reads and interprets the sign, but the sign progressively grows in complexity. Only half the sign is visible and available for interpretation while the other half remains inaccessible within the subject who emits the sign.[12] In *Ulysses*, Martha and Bloom produce signs so that they can be turned into fetish and thus appropriated into fantasy. There is no in-depth search for the ground of the sign's production. Curiosity is more concerned with producing more signs that can be turned into fetish. Here the word 'fetish' is not used in an exclusively psychoanalytical sense. The displacement of the usual function of the object and the relation of the object's relevance to its history are shared by many other uses of the term as well, as for example in psychology and anthropology. The emotional complex that I have called 'curiosity' is not defined primarily by ethical or epistemological concerns. It is rather indifferent to the problematic that can be characterized by

---

[11]  Richard: 'I can never know, never in this world. I do not wish to know or to believe. I do not care.' (*Exiles*, 162.)

[12]  'For each of our impressions has two sides: "Half sheathed in the object, extended in ourself by another half which we alone can recognize." Each sign has two halves: it *designates* an object, it *signifies* something different.' (Deleuze, *Proust and Signs*, 26.)

the oppositions: authenticity versus inauthenticity; truth versus falsehood. The agents here recognize that signs are artefacts, but they relate this element of fiction or deceptiveness to the game in which the signs are implicated.

If jealousy expresses itself in a vocabulary of dedication and betrayal, curiosity expresses itself in a language of fantasized intimacy. Martha's letter is coquettish, palely and prudishly so, and Gerty's monologue conveys an imagined intensity. Stylistically, 'Nausicaa' invokes cheap romantic fiction which provides moments of fantasy. This episode presents communication as silent speculation and an ocular relation that finally culminates in voyeurism and exhibitionism. For Bloom this communication evokes a fantasy centred around the perceived but unpossessed body of Gerty. For Gerty, it produces a fantasy that confers the context of her exhibition and Bloom's masturbation with signs of love:

She looked at him a moment, meeting his glance, and a light broke in upon her. Whitehot passion was in that face, passion silent as the grave, and it had made her his. At last they were left alone without the others to pry and pass remarks and she knew he could be trusted to the death, steadfast, a sterling man, a man of inflexible honour to his fingertips. (*U*, 13. 690–4)

But this was altogether different from a thing like that because there was all the difference because she could almost feel him draw her face to his and the first quick hot touch of his handsome lips. Besides there was absolution so long as you didn't do the other thing before being married ... (*U*, 13. 706–9)

This fantasy of union is the end, the rhetoric of love and trust merely a means for producing this fantasy. These elements are not confined to Gerty or Martha. Bloom's innumerable fantasies during the day belong to this series. Here one might be tempted to argue that curiosity and fantasy, the principles that seem to underlie the series, need to be located in Bloom's subjectivity. Curiosity seems to mark his attitude to various objects, ranging from popular science to Greek statues. Even Gerty's exhibitionism was already anticipated by other acts of voyeurism on Bloom's part (*U*, 5. 98–135). It can also be seen in some of the fantasies in 'Circe', especially when Virag discusses Bloom's sexual preferences (*U*, 15. 2311–467). Even Bloom's ideas on advertising show his preoccupation with a mystery that generates curiosity and induces the pleasures of fantasy:

I suggested to him about a transparent showcart with two smart girls sitting inside writing letters, copybooks, envelopes, blottingpaper. I bet that would have caught on. Smart girls writing something catch the eye at once. Everyone dying to know what she's writing. Get twenty of them round you if you stare at nothing. Have a finger in the pie. Women too. Curiosity. Pillar of salt. (*U*, 8. 131–6)

However, it is simplistic to suggest that the deployment of curiosity in *Ulysses* is psychologically determined and that it has Bloom as its sole source. As we saw earlier, the letter of Martha and the monologue of Gerty share the same elements and show a series that extends beyond a single character. Molly's monologue in 'Penelope' is also largely the presentation of a series of instances of sexual desire recollected and transformed into fantasy:

he was the first man kissed me under the Moorish wall my sweetheart when a boy it never entered my head what kissing meant till he put his tongue in my mouth his mouth was sweetlike young I put my knee up to him a few times to learn the way what did I tell him I was engaged for for fun to the son of a Spanish nobleman named Don Miguel de la Flora and he believed me that I was to be married to him in 3 years time theres many a true word spoken in jest there is a flower that bloometh ... (*U*, 18. 769–75)

Here, once again we find the fetishizing of details as grounds of fantasy and the production of signs as artefacts. Curiosity, as I suggested above, is less preoccupied with the identity of the object of desire than with the details. Molly's recollection has an abundance of such detail—of places, contexts, gestures, and conversations. The recurrent word that designates the other is always a 'he' and sometimes confusing as to the identity of the person being referred to.[13] In terms of grammar, there is a violation of the normal rules of pronominalization here. Repetition produces in this way a disturbance of textual coherence. A serial organization of elements which are partially substitutable underlies this recollection. Bloom seems to contemplate this series in 'Ithaca':

To reflect that each one who enters imagines himself to be the first to enter whereas he is always the last term of a preceding series even if the first term of a succeeding one, each imagining himself to be first, last, only and alone whereas he is neither first nor last nor only nor alone in a series originating in and repeated to infinity. (*U*, 17. 2127–31)

[13] See Robert Adams, *Surface and Symbol: The Consistency of James Joyce's 'Ulysses'* (New York: OUP, 1962), 40.

Molly's monologue is not exclusively dominated by curiosity. The strands of affirmation in 'Penelope', the gradual drift of the monologue around Bloom, and the final return of the text to Bloom—all these are indeed too obvious to need further elaboration. 'Penelope' is characterized as much by jealousy in relation to Bloom, showing a possessiveness and a search for the truth of Bloom's actions, as it is by curiosity. However, such jealousy does not appear to be present in her recollection of other characters, and at times her attitude to Bloom manifests a mixture of both jealousy and curiosity.

This is in some sense paralleled by Bloom's response to Molly. Boylan's impending visit to Molly insistently surfaces in Bloom's monologues several times during the day. As we saw, even 'Mrs Marion', originating in Boylan's 'bold hand' on the envelope, recurs many times in the text. This can be seen as a sign of jealousy, a preoccupation with loyalty and betrayal. However, it is also possible that Bloom is partially attracted by the possibility of betrayal. Perhaps Bloom's reluctance to go back home and his exhibition of Molly's photograph to Stephen can be understood as signs of this. This can be related to curiosity and to a gratification of desire through fantasy. In relation to Molly's adultery, this attitude does not appear directly in Bloom's monologues. Boylan's visit is thought of in Bloom's monologues largely through images of apprehension and loss. In 'Circe', however, this fantasy is presented in an image of voyeurism, combining elements of curiosity with Molly and Boylan. Bloom's look through the keyhole repeats the elements of exhibitionism and masturbation from 'Nausicaa'. It functions in a way that is very different from Swann's ransacking of Odette's room in À la recherche. Swann searches for a sign that will lead him to the discovery of a truth: the sign in itself is inconsequent. In 'Circe', Bloom does not look for a sign, but the activity of looking becomes a detail in itself that can be invested with fantasy. Elements of curiosity and fantasy are present in Bloom's relation to Molly in other parts of the novel as well, in his preoccupation with undergarments and in the pornography that both of them share.

It is this mixture of jealousy and curiosity that constitutes some of the complexity in the relation between Bloom and Molly. In 'Ithaca', jealousy is listed among the four emotions that Bloom feels when he returns to his bedroom. However, this is soon superseded by an attitude of 'abnegation' that recognizes a comic repetition in adultery:

Why more abnegation than jealousy, less envy than equanimity?

From outrage (matrimony) to outrage (adultery) there arose nought but outrage (copulation) yet the matrimonial violator of the matrimonially violated had not been outraged by the adulterous violator of the adulterously violated. (*U*, 17. 2195–9)

This attitude is similar to the one behind the contemplation of the series of Molly's lovers that I cited above (*U*, 17. 2127–31). The sense of detachment that arises here from a mixture of pleasure and pain can also be seen in *Exiles* and *Finnegans Wake*. Even though the relationship between Bloom and Molly is not dominated by either jealousy or curiosity, this distinction helps us in understanding it. An element of curiosity and the pleasures of fantasy seem to assuage the pain of jealousy, even if only partially.

I have tried to show above that there is the repetition of a configuration of elements in all these situations. They form a series of interpretatively significant connections. In this sense, one can speak of repetition at the level of signified content in *Ulysses*. Ellmann has pointed out similarities between Stephen's encounter with the soldiers and Bloom's encounter with the citizen.[14] He has also noted that 'Nausicaa' could be read as a parody of the episode of the wading girl in the *Portrait*.[15] Litz comments on Joyce's elaborate plans for parodying his earlier work in *Finnegans Wake*.[16] All these indicate that repetition as a compositional strategy in Joyce is at work at several levels, including that of the signified content.

There are two other forms that repetition assumes at the level of signified content in *Ulysses*. The first one concerns the presentation of the same events in different discourses, as for example in the recollection of the same event by different characters. The second form of repetition can be seen in the return of events and characters as fantasy in 'Circe'.

There are several events recalled from different perspectives in *Ulysses*. This includes the cloud seen by Stephen in 'Telemachus'

---

[14] Richard Ellmann, *Ulysses on the Liffey* (London: Faber & Faber, Ltd., 1972), 148–9.    [15] Id., *James Joyce*, (revd. edn., New York: OUP, 1982), 359.
[16] Walton Litz, *Art of James Joyce: Method and Design in 'Ulysses' and 'Finnegans Wake'* (London: OUP, 1961), 115.

(*U*, 1. 248–9) and by Bloom in 'Calypso' (*U*, 4. 218), the viceregal parade seen by various characters in 'Wandering Rocks', and certain incidents recalled by Bloom and Molly. One can see two different impulses at work here. One of them is the legendary Joycean ambition for naturalistic precision. The cloud, the meticulous ordering of time and simultaneity in 'Wandering Rocks', certain details first presented in narration and later recalled in monologue, such as Molly's giving money to the beggar (*U*, 10. 251–3, 18. 346–7)—these strategies seem to stabilize a fictional illusion of reality. The relation between *Ulysses* and *Thom's Directory* epitomizes this impulse. Distinct from this, one can see another tendency operating in some similar instances of repetition. This involves a process of relativization, where the same event is recalled differently by different characters. In 'Sirens', Bloom remembers:

> She looked fine. Her crocus dress she wore lowcut, belongings on show. Clove her breath was always in theatre when she bent to ask a question. Told her what Spinoza says in that book of poor papa's. Hypnotised, listening. Eyes like that. She bent. Chap in dress circle staring down into her with his operaglass for all he was worth. (*U*, 11. 1056–60)

Molly recalls the same incident:

> usual monthly auction isnt it simply sickening that night it came on me like that the one and only time we were in a box that Michael Gunn gave him to see Mrs Kendal and her husband at the Gaiety something he did about insurance for him in Drimmies I was fit to be tied though I wouldnt give in with that gentleman of fashion staring down at me with his glasses and him the other side of me talking about Spinoza and his soul thats dead I suppose millions of years ago I smiled the best I could all in a swamp leaning forward as if I was interested having to sit it out . . . (*U*, 18. 1109–17)

Even though it is the same event that is being recalled in both these passages, its significance changes from one to the other. In *Ulysses*, where recollection through interior monologue is a dominant form of self-presentation, the significance of an event becomes inseparable from its linguistic embodiment, the traces it leaves behind on the discourse of the person that recalls the event. Through the repetition of the same event with variable significance in different discourses, the text sets to work a process of relativization. The significance of an event needs to be seen here as constituted by discourse. Arguably, it is an extension of this principle that one finds in the use of a plurality of styles in the later chapters of *Ulysses*.[17]

The two impulses mentioned above are, to some extent, opposed to one another. One of them aspires to a validation of the text from outside, to the grounding of the text in a stable external world. The other impulse refers us to the set of discourses that circulate within the text. Fredric Jameson finds in such passages a process of 'dereification',

whereby the text itself is unsettled and undermined, a process whereby the universal tendency of its terms, narrative tokens, representations, to solidify into an achieved and codified symbolic order as well as a massive narrative surface, is perpetually suspended.[18]

Joyce's poetics is known for the prevalence of such contrary impulses. What one needs to be wary of, however, is the reduction of this play of contraries to a neat and overschematic ascending dialectic.[19] The strategies and intentions involved seem to be far too heterogeneous to be united in this way.

'Circe' enacts the extensive repetition of events from earlier parts of the text as fantasy. Paddy Dignam, Martha Clifford, the man in the mackintosh, Gerty MacDowell, and several other characters reappear. Groden argues that 'Circe' inaugurated a new compositional strategy whereby elements from earlier episodes were taken up and transfigured.[20] It might be tempting to see 'Circe' as a psychological re-enactment of the memories of Bloom and Stephen. On closer examination, the picture becomes far more complex. Several fantastic images seem inexplicable in terms of the recollection of characters. I shall examine a passage from 'Circe' in detail at the end of this chapter.

One of Joyce's models for 'Circe' was Flaubert's *La Tentation de saint Antoine*. In his discussion of this text, Foucault demonstrates the prevalence of the idea of the library underlying the fantasies.[21]

---

[17] For a detailed discussion of the plurality of styles in relation to the ethic of novelistic economy, see Karen Lawrence, *Odyssey of Style in 'Ulysses'* (Princeton, NJ: Princeton University Press, 1981).

[18] Fredric Jameson, *'Ulysses* in History' in W. J. McCormack and Alistair Stead (eds.), *James Joyce and Modern Literature* (London: Routledge & Kegan Paul, Ltd., 1982), 132–3.

[19] I find Ellmann's *Ulysses on the Liffey* an example of this tendency.

[20] Groden, *'Ulysses' in Progress*, 52.

[21] Michel Foucault, 'Fantasia of the Library', in id., *Language, Counter-Memory, Practice*, ed. D. F. Bouchard, tr. D. F. Bouchard and Sherry Simon (Oxford: Basil Blackwell, 1977), 87–109.

The fantasies of Saint Antony emanate from texts rather than from within. In other words, interiority is rendered as a library of texts here. Similarly, in 'Circe', the fantasies often recall a textual memory rather than a character's interiority in an immediate fashion. Gerty MacDowell's words in 'Circe' invoke, by way of memory, Gerty's own monologue in 'Nausicaa' rather than Bloom's perception of her. Her words are characterized by the same fantasy of sentimental love as in 'Nausicaa'. Bloom has no access to this monologue. The reader's own memory of the text, of the various discourses encountered earlier, is put into play here. One possible way to understand Joyce's use of Homer here is to see the Circean transformation as something that pertains to the narrative. It is the narrative, its elements and episodes, that is re-presented in a fantastic transformation in this episode.

### Readings: 'Sirens', 'Oxen of the Sun', and 'Circe'

To conclude, I shall examine three passages from *Ulysses* where repetition assumes diverse modes and functions at various levels. They serve as representative nodal points where motifs from different parts of the text are gathered together and where a number of series of repetition seem to converge. The passages I have chosen come from 'Sirens' (*U*, 11. 1–25), 'Oxen of the Sun' (*U*, 14. 288–308), and 'Circe' (*U*, 15. 293–357).

'Sirens', the episode where the art is music and the technic *fuga per canonem*, opens with an elaborate overture, the elements of which reappear subsequently in the episode.[22] Critics have often noted the resistance posed by this passage to easy intelligibility. However, it might still be simplistic to see in this a liberation of the signifier or of writing.[23] The overture relies on a strategy of verbal repetition that we have seen at work even in the earlier chapters of *Ulysses*. Here it operates at the level of the episode's organization rather than at the level of characters and their memory. The result is an increased focus on the activity of repetition. For the first time in the text, units of repetition are presented in themselves:

---

[22] Linati schema as cited in Ellmann, *Ulysses on the Liffey*, app.
[23] See Colin MacCabe, *James Joyce and the Revolution of the Word* (London: Macmillan, 1979), 80.

Bronze by gold heard the hoofirons, steelyringing.
Imperthnthn thnthnthn.
Chips, picking chips off rocky thumbnail, chips.
Horrid! And gold flushed more.
A husky fifenote blew.
Blew. Blue bloom is on the.
(*U*, 11. 1–6)

Five pages later, we come across the repetition of the 'chips' fragment: 'Into the bar strode Mr Dedalus. Chips, picking chips off one of his rocky thumbnails. Chips. He strolled.' (*U*, 11. 192–3). The 'horrid' fragment occurs in the conversation of the barmaids: 'O miss Douce! miss Kennedy protested. You horrid thing! And flushed yet more (you horrid!), more goldenly' (*U*, 11. 183–4). On the following page, we find 'He blew through the flue through two husky fifenotes' (*U*, 11. 217–18).

Thus the overture seems to succeed rather than precede the rest of the text in terms of composition: it seems to be reassembled from a more continuous discourse. The only ground for the coherence of the overture is the appearance of the elements later. Unlike some instances of repetition in the monologues where the prior history of the fragments ensures coherence, here it is the future use of the fragments that justifies their presentation in the overture. The passage functions as a textual prolepsis. To recognize the overture as an overture, one already needs a second reading or, more correctly, a double reading where the overture can preserve its fragmentary character as well as project its later use in the intelligible text.

None the less, even in the creation of the overture, a textual memory of the earlier episodes seems to be at work. Some phrases have already occurred before. In 'Wandering Rocks' we read:

Bronze by gold, Miss Kennedy's head by Miss Douce's head, appeared above the crossblind of the Ormond Hotel. (*U*, 10. 962–3)

Their watching the viceregal parade in 'Wandering Rocks' anticipates 'heard the hoofirons, steelyringing. Imperthnthn thnthnthn'. 'Bloom is on the' recalls Lenehan's '*Leopoldo or Bloom is on the rye*' (*U*, 10. 524). These instances seem to make it possible to read the overture in the context of a textual memory. To that extent, it does generate expectations of intelligibility in the reader. However, such expectations are questioned or qualified by the disjunctive nature of the overture and the arbitrariness of the ordering of elements in it. The order of fragments in the overture does not seem to follow any thematic or textual principle. Occasionally, one finds instances of verbal association such as 'Blew. Blue Bloom is on the' (*U*, 11. 6); here the phonic association provides a tenuous connection between the two fragments. Such links are not common in the overture. They seem only to highlight the pervasive sense of disconnectedness.

Similar processes are at work in the rest of the overture. 'A jumping rose of satiny breast on satin, rose of Castile' (*U*, 11. 8) takes up '*The Rose of Castile*' from 'Aeolus' (*U*, 7. 591), and unites it through a purely verbal association to the 'jumping rose'. These two elements are repeated subsequently in the episode in various ways. 'Jingle, jingle, jaunted, jingling' is repeated at least eight times in 'Sirens' in relation to Boylan. It is even repeated within the overture (*U*, 11. 19). The rest of the overture also shows instances of repetition from earlier episodes. 'Throstle' refers back to Bloom's monologues:

Beautiful on that *tre* her voice is: weeping tone. A thrush. A throstle. There is a word throstle that expresses that. (*U*, 6. 239–41)

'When he first saw' refers, through an allusion to Flowtow's opera *Martha*, to 'Aeolus', where the opera had been mentioned (*U*, 7. 58).

I have tried to show above that the overture of the 'Sirens' functions through a deployment of many devices of repetition, rather than by a simple opposition to the rest of the episode or to the intelligible text. Fragments of meaning and familiarity with motifs encountered earlier are played against the proleptic repetition that runs through the overture. It is more adequately understood as a textual nodal point which gathers together different strands of textual memory and various series of repetition than as the presentation of freely floating signifiers.[24]

The overture has generally been interpreted in terms of the

---

[24] The fragment that is not repeated subsequently and which MacCabe mentions, 'heard the hoofirons steelyringing' refers back to the 'Wandering Rocks' passage where Miss Kennedy and Miss Douce watch the viceregal parade (*U*, 10. 1197–9). It is significant that relevance here is established at the level of meaning and situation. See MacCabe, *James Joyce*, 80.

musical structure of the episode.[25] Indeed, it is the musical structure that makes the overture possible at all. However, interpretations that exclusively highlight this aspect overlook two other questions. Firstly, how does the musical structure affect the narrative? Secondly, is it not that the 'Sirens' overture employs a device that is used in several other parts of *Ulysses*, but perhaps in a more intense and self-focusing way? These questions do not invalidate the claims of a structural explanation of the overture in terms of music and leitmotif. They try to develop the reading to a further level in attempting to relate the overture to the textual strategies of *Ulysses* as a whole. Such an account needs to consider the general deployment of repetition in the novel.

The passage from 'Oxen of the Sun' (*U*, 14. 288–308) weaves together various motifs related to filiation from other parts of the text. It also repeats verbal fragments from earlier parts of the text. The relation of word and flesh, a strand that runs through the entire text and inaugurated in the mock Mass of Mulligan in its relation to the Eucharist is taken up by Stephen here. 'Scylla and Charybdis' had extended the theme of filiation beyond its original theological context to the problem of artistic creation. The relation established in this episode between creation and an experience of deprivation— of marital disloyalty in Shakespeare's case—can be seen in the allusion to Blake, 'Time's ruins build eternity's mansions'. In the complex scenario that unites Shakespeare to Hamlet, the natural logic of filiation is upset and we find a mystical notion of fatherhood. Here, in contrast, Stephen comments on the paradox of maternity, that of the virgin and the mother. The virgin-mother and Jesus are related through a unique paradox of creation:

> Or she knew him, that second I say, and was but creature of her creature, *vergine madre, figlia di tuo figlio*, or she knew him not and then stands she in the one denial or ignorancy with Peter Piscator . . . (*U*, 14. 302–4)

She is the mother as well as the creation of her son.

All these can be understood as repetition at the level of the signified content. They form a series with other moments in the text

---

[25] See e.g. Stuart Gilbert, *James Joyce's 'Ulysses': A Study* (Harmondsworth: Penguin, 1963); Frank Budgen, *James Joyce and the Making of 'Ulysses', and Other Writings*, ed. Clive Hart (London: OUP, 1972), 135–6; Anthony Burgess, *Joysprick: An Introduction to the Language of James Joyce* (London: André Deutsch, 1973), 83–8.

in terms of thematic concerns. The passage also shows the prevalence of two other modes of repetition—that of verbal fragments and of allusions. '*Omnis caro ad te veniet*', an allusion to the Psalms, had occurred in the 'Proteus' episode:

Behold the handmaid of the moon. In sleep the wet sign calls her hour, bids her rise. Bridebed, childbed, bed of death, ghostcandled. *Omnis caro ad te veniet*. He comes, pale vampire, through storm his eyes, his bat sails bloodying the sea, mouth to her mouth's kiss. (*U*, 3. 395–8)

Here the repetition operates at the level of the character's memory—or, to be more precise, the narrator's presentation of the character's memory—as well as of the textual memory. The continuity of the sense in which the phrase has been employed belongs more to Stephen's memory and the difference in the contexts that is highlighted belongs more to the level of the text.

The reference to Saint Bernard (*U*, 14. 297) recalls the reference in 'Nausicaa' (*U*, 13. 378). The network of associations in which the reference occurs is similar enough in both contexts to invoke the earlier occurrence. In both places, it is in relation to Virgin Mary that the name occurs. The idea that Stephen refers to is expressed in 'Memorae' which is invoked in 'Nausicaa'.[26] The reference to the 'house that Jack built' will be repeated later in the episode, in a different stylistic context: '*Behold the mansion reared by dedal Jack*' (*U*, 14. 405). 'Joseph the Joiner' takes us to Mulligan's song in 'Telemachus' (*U*, 1. 586). 'Léo Taxil' similarly refers us back to the earlier pages. It recalls the conversation in French that Stephen remembers in 'Proteus' (*U*, 3. 167). 'Consubstantiality', as we have already seen, refers back to 'Scylla and Charybdis' (*U*, 9. 481).

I mentioned earlier that this repetition was part of Joyce's schematic deployments in 'Oxen of the Sun'. The different series of developments that are unfolded as the episode progresses belong to different levels of textual organization.[27] For instance, the history of English prose style belongs to the stylistic surface; the theme of embryonic development indicates another level. This is symptomatically present at the narrative surface in certain words which correspond to features of the embryo at the relevant moment in

---

[26] Thornton, *Allusions in 'Ulysses'*, 311, 329–30.

[27] For a discussion of these levels, see J. S. Atherton, 'Oxen of the Sun', in Clive Hart and David Hayman (eds.), *James Joyce's 'Ulysses': Critical Essays* (Berkeley, Calif.: University of California Press, 1974), 313–39.

gestation. Joyce's recalling of the earlier events of the day is not done at the level of signified content. It is done through a series of internal allusions as in the passage we have been considering.

However, compared to the strategies of repetition in the 'Sirens', we can observe a marked change here. One might be tempted to say that the 'Sirens' overture is *predominantly* proleptic whereas 'Oxen of the Sun' is analeptic. As a broad distinction, I think this is valid. But this distinction proves inadequate if we use the terms in a strict and exclusive opposition. As we have seen, many of the elements in the 'Sirens' overture are already instances of repetition. And on the other hand, 'Oxen of the Sun' introduces new elements which are repeated susequently.[28] A more important difference lies in the way repetition fits in with the discursive context. In 'Oxen of the Sun' most of them are connected to their context by relations at the level of meaning. In 'Sirens' they seem to rely on association and in the overture, on arbitrary and explicitly disjunctive series.

The last passage I would like to consider is from 'Circe'. It depicts the encounter of Bloom with Molly in the nighttown. She is called 'Mrs Marion', an allusion to Boylan's envelope in 'Calypso' (*U*, 4. 244–5). The passage that speaks in parentheses throughout in 'Circe' in the language and format of stage directions describes her figure: '*Opulent curves fill out her scarlet trousers and jacket, slashed with gold*' (*U*, 15. 298–9). But this strange narrator is again relying on textual memory. If we turn back a couple of hundred pages, we will come across the pages of *Sweets of Sin* that Bloom was browsing through:

—*Her mouth glued on his in a luscious voluptuous kiss while his hands felt for the opulent curves inside her deshabille.* (*U*, 10. 611–12)

Here a peculiar relation is seen to prevail between the narrator and Bloom. The narrator in his invocation of the textual memory is invoking a passage from Bloom's memory as well. On the other hand, the narrator recalls objects which he had mentioned earlier in the fashion of recollecting repetition. Further down the page, Bloom is described as swallowing '*questions, hopes, crubeens for her supper, things to tell her, excuse, desire, spellbound*' (*U*, 15. 310–12). It is the same '*lukewarm pig's crubeen*' (*U*, 15. 158) that

---

[28] See William Schutte, *Index of Recurrent Elements*, 261–80.

was mentioned earlier by the narrator. Another 'stage direction' says, '*Fiercely she slaps his haunch, her goldcurb wristbangles angriling, scolding him in Moorish*' (*U*, 15. 316–17). This recalls Bloom's recollection where he thinks of Molly being Moorish:

Maybe the women's fault also. That's where Molly can knock spots off them. It's the blood of the south. Moorish. Also the form, the figure. Hands felt for the opulent. (*U*, 13. 967–9)

The status of the narrator's voice is again problematized by repetition and the collusion of Bloom's memory and the textual memory. This is further accentuated by the allusion to the passage from *Sweets of Sin* here. The relations between Bloom and the stage directions become more and more complex.

Another such instance where the distinction between the levels of character and the text becomes problematic is when Marion says, 'Nebrakada! Femininum.' This phrase had occurred in 'Wandering Rocks' and its explication there contributes to the intelligibility of the present context. It comes from a talisman that Stephen finds in a book called 'Charms and invocations of the most blessed abbot Peter Salanka to all true believers divulged' and which supposedly helps in winning a woman's love (*U*, 10. 849–51). Here it is Molly who utters the phrase and it does not refer back to any detail in the reader's knowledge of her or to Molly's memory as can be appropriated from the text. Here, repetition seems to break the frontier between the memories of two characters by playing them against each other at the level of the text.

There is repetition at the level of signified content happening all through 'Circe'. The earlier events in the day, the characters and the objects reappear, not on the level of the development of plot nor on a level that can be called fantasy and pitched against the real. 'Circe' combines both. One can see in this a transformation of earlier experience both at the levels of the characters and of the text.[29]

I had suggested, in relation to Gerty MacDowell's reappearance in 'Circe', that the episode resists a psychological interpretation

---

[29] Commenting on 'Oxen of the Sun', Karen Lawrence remarks: 'Increasingly, the characters' memory and the narrative memory fuse—at a certain level, all the "memories" in the book are fictions for the purpose of this fiction.' (Lawrence, *Odyssey of Style*, 141.)

based on personal fantasies. The soap that Bloom bought in 'Lotus-Eaters' reappears and so does Sweny the druggist. But this time he reappears in the disk of the soapsun (*U*, 5. 501–10, 15. 340–1). So do many other figures from the memory of Stephen and Bloom. Repetition at the level of signified content in 'Circe' does often allude to and rely on characters' memory. However, this is disturbed by instances such as the appearance of Shakespeare, a fantasy shared by both Bloom and Stephen. Further, the repetition of verbal elements problematizes the nature and status of different characters' memories as well as the textual memory.

We have seen, in our consideration of the three different passages, how the different modes of repetition discussed earlier in the chapter combine together in a variety of ways producing different kinds of effects. In 'Sirens', they were seen to produce a series based on disjunctions, arbitrariness, and occasionally phonic associations. In 'Oxen of the Sun', we found that repetitions actually constitute a specific level of textual organization. Belonging to the new discursive context in a relatively intelligible fashion, they recall earlier chapters on a different level of organization. In 'Circe', they seemed to function primarily to put to question the status of different discourses and to focus on acts of textual memory.

A common feature that all these repetitions share is their interference with the linear progress of the narrative.[30] A repeated sign always refers back and illuminates a play of identity and difference which cannot entirely be appropriated by a reading directed towards a totalizing meaning. In contrast to stabilizing repetition which aids such strategies of containment, the modes we have outlined above seem to rupture the sign in order to thematize the way it functions. This seems to me to have three important consequences. One is in relation to the experience of time and its implications for narrative organization. If the unilinear organization of narrative is continuously tampered with, would it not imply a consequent rupture of the experience of linear time too? The second consequence would pertain to the structure of the sign. Instead of a formal signifier/signified relationship, we have a machinery where the sign's discursive history plays an important part. What is the nature of this machinery? The third question

---

[30] For a discussion of the relation between the human experience of time and the narrative, see Paul Ricœur, *Time and Narrative*, tr. Katherine McLaughlin and David Pellauer, i. (Chicago: University of Chicago Press, 1984), 52 ff.

concerns Joyce's own poetics. How do the notions of creation and repetition figure in the poetics we can abstract from a reading of *Ulysses*? And how would it relate to Joyce's ideas of art, language, and tradition? I intend to take up these questions in the following chapters.

# 3

# The Structure of *Ulysses* and the Experience of Time

> Stephen closed his eyes to hear his boots crush crackling wrack and shells. You are walking through it howsomever. I am, a stride at a time. A very short space of time through very short times of space. Five, six: the *Nacheinander*. Exactly: and that is the ineluctable modality of the audible. Open your eyes. No. Jesus! If I fell over a cliff that beetles o'er his base, fell through the *Nebeneinander* ineluctably! (*U*, 3. 10–15)

In the opening of 'Proteus' Stephen contemplates the experience of space and time and their relation to the senses. The elements and concerns carefully deployed in this passage make it a useful point of departure for our discussion of the experience of time in *Ulysses*. In articulating some fundamental questions of narrative, the passage can be seen as symptomatic of the novel's encounter with time.

'Proteus' is dominated by the mode of interior monologue. In the passage cited above, the 'closing of the eyes' functions as a transition, as an opening to the world of interior experience. This world obeys a different logic for its articulation compared to the narrative that views events and objects from outside. The connections between the sentences here are associational. 'I am, a stride at a time' leads to 'A very short space of time through very short times of space.' The use of the word 'time' in these two sentences is not exactly identical. In the first, it forms part of the phrase 'at a time'. But it is disengaged from that context and made the topic of general philosophical reflection in the next sentence. This kind of associational connection is not peculiar to Stephen's monologues. The variety and richness of Bloom's monologues derive precisely from this impulse:

> Provost's house. The reverend Dr Salmon: tinned salmon. Well tinned in there. Like a mortuary chapel. Wouldn't live in it if they paid me. (*U*, 8. 496–7)

The 'Provost's house' leads to an evocation of his name. This further leads to 'tinned salmon,' but the 'tinned' leads back to a consideration of the house again. In this passage, the topic of discourse seems to be moving in a circle.

In Stephen's monologue which I cited earlier, there are two movements at work. One is the sequence of actions that Stephen performs, here presented through his perceptions of them. It begins with the onomatopoeia of 'crush crackling wrack and shells' and continues in the counting of steps 'five, six' and later in his listening to the sound of his boots: 'sounds solid' (*U*, 3. 17) and 'crush, crack, crick, crick' (*U*, 3. 19). In addition to these, there are other elements in the passage indicating Stephen's reflections on his actions. 'A very short space of time through very short times of space' is a clear instance of this. Another instance is 'Five, six' leading to '*Nacheinander*,' to a general reflection on temporal succession. Similarly, falling over (*U*, 3. 14) introduces 'a cliff that beetles o'er his base' (*U*, 3. 14), an allusion to *Hamlet* (1. iv. 71). This allusion transforms Stephen's ashplant into an 'ash sword'. The question of time is reintroduced in 'Am I walking into eternity along Sandymount strand?' (*U*, 3. 18–19) and in 'See now. There all the time without you: and ever shall be, world without end' (*U*, 3. 27–8).

The most noticeable characteristic that both these monologues share is their reluctance to fall into a linear sequence in terms of topic or coherent argument. The connections are verbal and associational. In Bloom's monologue, the topic moves in a circular manner from 'Provost's house' to his name to 'tinned salmon' to 'tin' to 'mortuary chapel' and then back to the house. In Stephen's case, distinct from the horizontal temporal sequence of actions, there is a vertical movement of his reflections, occasionally appropriating elements from the horizontal sequence, but developing them tangentially.

These strategies are different from the linear and external narration which we find often in the early episodes of *Ulysses*.

Solemnly he came forward and mounted the round gunrest. He faced about and blessed gravely thrice the tower, the surrounding land and the awaking mountains. Then, catching sight of Stephen Dedalus, he bent towards him and made rapid crosses in the air, gurgling in his throat and shaking his head. Stephen Dedalus, displeased and sleepy, leaned his arms on the top of the staircase and looked coldly at the shaking gurgling face that blessed him, equine in its length, and at the light untonsured hair, grained and hued like pale oak. (*U*, 1. 9–16)

The passage not only narrates the actions, but ensures the coherence of the narration by providing some connections between them as well: 'Then, catching sight of Stephen Dedalus . . .'; 'Stephen Dedalus, displeased and sleepy, . . . looked coldly . . .'. All the elements are organized to depict the unfolding of a linear sequence of actions. Elements of description provide a concreteness to the details involved but do not impede the progress of narration in any significant sense.

This distinction between interior monologue and narration has important bearings on our sense of temporal experience. The exterior perspective renders the reader an observer who has insight into the interconnections between the various actions that he observes. The discrete elements fall into place as he reads on and the emergent passage provides him with a continuous intelligible whole of temporal experience. The reader is not made aware of a relevant disjunction between the time of narration and the time of what is depicted.

However, in the monologues, the criteria of relevance are different from those in the narration. The reader is rendered an observer of the interior world, but the elements that ensure coherence need to be supplied by him. This certainly resists any easy identification between the experience of time implied in the monologue and that implied in the reader's appropriation of the monologue into an intelligible whole. But the problem extends even further. The nature of the intelligible whole that the reader reconstructs does not imply a linear horizontal organization of elements. In Bloom's monologue it seems to move in a circular way, and in Stephen's in disparate sequences, horizontally and vertically. This induces a certain lack of continuity in terms of temporal experience between exterior narration and interior monologue. In the monologues, there seems to have occurred a certain diffusion or dilation of temporal experience. In contrast with the organized linearity of the narration, we have in the monologue a flow of discrete elements connected associationally, but not integrated into a linear whole.

However, there is another aspect to the problems raised by this textual organization. Let us briefly look at the opening passage in 'Proteus' again. There one finds an allusion to *Hamlet* (*U*, 3. 14). The reader, later in the course of his reading, will realize that this unites with a large number of allusions to *Hamlet* present through the text. For example, the theme of paternity that is articulated in various ways in the text, is prominently raised in *Hamlet*.[1] Thus it unites with the theological discussions on the Trinitarian theme as well as the relation between Odysseus and Telemachus that informs the Homeric parallels. There is an articulation in the text of this connection between the theological and the Shakespearean connections with questions of paternity.

—I read a theological interpretation of it somewhere, he said bemused. The Father and the Son idea. The Son striving to be atoned with the Father. (*U*, 1. 577–8)

The production of a coherent whole which unites these diverse allusions and contexts, is certainly at odds with the temporal progress in the narrative outlined above. It seems to produce a unity akin to that in the spatial arts. The best example of this is provided in the idea of the human body that Joyce uses as a schematic principle in the organization of episodes. Different episodes are made to embody different organs of the human body. But the relation between the various organs of the human body is not temporal or sequential. The embodiment of the human body in the text thus involves the temporal presentation of a spatial image. Therefore, we have the distinction between the chronologically sequential narrative of events and actions, and a spatial reconstruction of schematic elements.

In the beginning of this chapter, I characterized the opening paragraphs of 'Proteus' as symptomatic of the novel's encounter with questions of temporal organization. The opposition between the spatial and temporal images outlined above is presented in 'Proteus' in the distinction between *Nebeneinander* and *Nacheinander*. Fritz Senn has argued that the source of these terms is Lessing's *Laocoön*, where they signify arts in the spatial and temporal modes—i.e. plastic arts and poetry.[2] Lessing wrote:

if it is true that in the imitations painting uses completely different means or signs than does poetry, namely figures and colors in space rather than articulated sounds in time, and if these signs must indisputably bear a

---

[1] See William M. Schutte, *Joyce and Shakespeare: A Study in the Meaning of 'Ulysses'* (New Haven, Conn.: Yale University Press, 1957); William T. Noon, *Joyce and Aquinas* (New Haven, Conn.: Yale University Press, 1957), ch. 6.

[2] Fritz Senn, 'Esthetic Theories', *JJQ* 2: 2 (1965), 134–6.

suitable relation to the thing signified, then signs existing in space can express only objects whose wholes or parts coexist, while signs that follow one another can express only objects whose wholes or parts are consecutive.[3]

In our examination of the text, I have tried to identify two kinds of complication to the temporal progress of the narrative. The first functions by the use of an associational connection between elements in the monologue and the second by a spatial unification of elements deployed throughout the novel.

These two aspects have dominated the discussions of time in the critical literature on *Ulysses* so far. One can discern two distinct tendencies in *Ulysses* criticism depending on the dominance of either of these aspects. This has resulted in two apparently opposing characterizations of the novel. One tendency describes *Ulysses* as a 'time-novel'. The other emphasizes the novel's 'spatial form'. The former focuses on the subjective experience of time in *Ulysses*. The latter stresses the schematic aspects of the novel's construction. I shall briefly examine these two tendencies by a consideration of two texts—Wyndham Lewis's treatment of *Ulysses* in *Time and Western Man* and Joseph Frank's comments in 'Spatial Form in Modern Literature'.[4] I shall not try to provide a comprehensive critique of these texts; my aim here is rather to identify their salient characteristics.

### 'Time-Mind' and 'Spatial Form'

Wyndham Lewis's response to *Ulysses* has two major aspects. One of them, which occupies a large part of the essay on Joyce, makes specific judgements on *Ulysses* without any clear relation to the theme of time. An example of this is Lewis's characterization of Joyce as a craftsman rather than as a creative writer. This aspect shall not concern us here. On the other hand, the position that the essay occupies in *Time and Western Man* indicates Lewis's

---

[3] Gotthold Ephraim Lessing, *Laocoön: An Essay on the Limits of Painting and Poetry* (1766), tr. Edward Allen McCormick (Indianapolis: Bobbs-Merrill, 1962), 78.

[4] Wyndham Lewis, *Time and Western Man* (London: Chatto & Windus, Ltd., 1927), esp. 'An Analysis of the Mind of James Joyce', 91–130; Joseph Frank, 'Spatial Form in Modern Literature', in id., *Widening Gyre: Crisis and Mastery in Modern Literature* (New Brunswick, NJ: Rutgers University Press, 1963), 3–62.

consideration of *Ulysses* as an example of a certain emphasis on temporal experience in literature and philosophy which he characterizes as the 'time-mind' or 'time-philosophy'.

I regard *Ulysses* as a time-book; and by that I mean that it lays its emphasis upon, for choice manipulates, and in a doctrinaire manner, the self-conscious time-sense, that has now been erected into a universal philosophy.[5]

In his preface, Lewis tries to specify what the 'time-mind' or 'time-philosophy' is:

The main characteristics of the Time-mind from the outset has been a hostility to what it calls the 'spatializing' process of a mind *not* the Time-mind. It is this spatializing capacity and instinct that it everywhere attacks. In its place it would put the Time-view, the flux. It asks us to see everything *sub species temporis*. It is the criticism of this view, the Time-view, from the position of the plastic or the visual intelligence that I am submitting to the public in this book.[6]

The philosophical exposition of the time-philosophy, for Lewis, is to be found in the work of Bergson[7]—in his critique of the conversion of inner temporal experience into measurable spatial categories and in his distinction between *temps* and *durée*.[8] *Temps* designates the measurable, homogeneous time that man speculatively imposes upon his inner temporal experience. In contrast to this, for Bergson, the pure and original intuition of time is heterogeneous. It is this realm of inner multiplicity, discontinuous and qualitative, that Bergson terms *durée*.[9] In his attempts to articulate *durée*, Bergson came up against a paradox. He recognized that such an articulation always entailed a reliance on spatial metaphors. The language of philosophy and of social intercourse always effects a translation of *durée* into spatial terms. 'Outside us mutual externality without succession; within us succession without mutual externality.'[10]

---

[5] Lewis, *Time*, 100.     [6] Ibid. 3–4.

[7] Henri Bergson, *Matter and Memory*, tr. Nancy Margaret Paul and W. Scott Palmer (London: Swan Sonnenschein & Co., Ltd., 1911); id., *Creative Evolution*, tr. Arthur Mitchell (London: Macmillan, 1960); id., *Time and Free Will: An Essay on the Immediate Data of Consciousness*, tr. F. L. Pogson (London: George Allen & Unwin, Ltd., 1910).     [8] See id., *Time and Free Will*, esp. 90–9.

[9] 'What is duration within us? A qualitative multiplicity, with no likeness to number; an organic evolution which is yet not an increasing quantity; a pure heterogeneity within which there are no distinct qualities.' (ibid. 226.)

[10] Ibid. 227.

Lewis argued that the 'torrent of matter' which one finds in *Ulysses* is a literary representation of *durée*.

In *Ulysses* you have a deliberate display, on the grand scale, of technical virtuosity and literary scholarship. What is underneath this overcharged surface . . . is rather an apological than a real landscape; and the two main characters, Bloom and Dedalus, are lay-figures . . . on which such a mass of dead stuff is hung, that if ever they had any organic life of their own, it would speedily have been overwhelmed in this torrent of matter, of *nature-morte*.

This torrent of matter is the einsteinian flux. Or (equally well) it is the duration-flux of Bergson—that is its philosophic character, at all events.[11]

This presentation of *durée* or 'Bergsonian fluidity' is occasioned by the method of 'telling from the inside'. Lewis's critique of Joyce's method is twofold. On the one hand, he argues that all that the interior monologue provides you with is an encounter with the author's mind:

once down in the middle of the stream, you remain the author, naturally, inside whose head you are, though you are sometimes supposed to be aware of one person, sometimes of another . . . generally speaking, it is *you* who descend into the flux of *Ulysses*, and it is the author who momentarily absorbs you for that experience. That is all the 'telling from the inside' amounts to. All the rest is literature, or dogma; or the dogma of time-literature.[12]

This leads to a criticism of characterization: Lewis complains of the lack of variety and the lack of concreteness in the presentation of characters. He contends that the figures offered to us in the opening of *Ulysses*, on closer scrutiny, betray the utmost conventionalism in characterization. And so does the presentation of Bloom, whom Lewis regards as a stage Jew.

The second aspect of Lewis's critique pertains to a related but distinct point. There is, according to Lewis, an underlying conventionalism of method in *Ulysses*. This method, Lewis argues, is that of obsessive nineteenth-century naturalism. The technical virtuosity of the novel, for Lewis, is evidence of the progressiveness of Joyce the craftsman. Beneath the surface of *Ulysses*, Lewis finds a dead preoccupation with the 'last stagnant pumpings of Victorian Anglo-Irish life'.[13] 'Proust *returned* to *temps perdu*,' says Lewis,

---

[11] Lewis, *Time*, 119.     [12] Ibid. 120.     [13] Ibid.

'Joyce never left them. He discharged it as freshly as though the
time he wrote about were still present, because it was *his* present.'[14]
Though he argues that Joyce wrote a time-book to some extent by
accident, Lewis is not hesitant to propose a general connection
between time-philosophy and a mechanical view of the world:

> The inner meaning of the *time-philosophy*, from whatever standpoint
> you approach it ... is the doctrine of a mechanistic universe; periodic,
> timeless, or nothing but 'time', whichever you essentially prefer; and,
> above all, essentially dead ...[15]

> The theoretic truth that time philosophy affirms is a mechanistic one. It
> is the conception of an aged intelligence, grown mechanical and living
> upon routine and memory, essentially; its tendency, in its characteristic
> working, is infallibly to transform the living into the machine, with a small,
> unascertained, but uninteresting margin of freedom.[16]

The validity of Lewis's philosophical argument is disputable.
One could argue against a facile identification of the Bergsonian
and the Einsteinian notions of time. Similarly, the confusions
regarding the relation of Bergson's philosophy to a mechanical
universe, of the notion of *durée* to the notions of timelessness:
these, too, require rigorous analysis and greater specification before
being considered as philosophically reliable. However, it is not my
purpose to examine these explicitly philosophical aspects of Lewis's
argument. I shall confine myself to outlining those aspects of the
narrative structure of *Ulysses* that Lewis relies on.

These are primarily of two types. The first one relates to an
opposition between interior monologue and the obsessive naturalistic precision in *Ulysses*. The interior monologue, for Lewis,
occasions the presentation of flux and this destroys the concreteness of the usual uses of naturalism. The second concerns the
progressiveness of Joyce's methods, the immense machinery of
allusions and parody. For Lewis, this is in tension with what he
calls the underlying conventionalism—whether it be the use of
clichés in expression or in characterization or, again, the obsessive
naturalistic preoccupation with the world of 1904.

Some other attempts to establish connections between Bergson's
philosophy and *Ulysses* emphasize the same aspect of the narrative
organization as Lewis. For example, Shiv K. Kumar bases his
argument on the distinction that Bergson makes between two ways

[14] Ibid. 109.        [15] Ibid. 110.        [16] Ibid.

of knowing reality.[17] The first involves the adoption of a point of view in relation to the object: the knowledge this leads to can only be relative.[18] The second involves intuitive identification with the object. The stream-of-consciousness novel, for Shiv Kumar, is an attempt to render reality in its original aspect through such an intuitive identification. Shiv Kumar's distinction relates to that between *durée* and *temps*—between the multiple and heterogeneous reality of the original subjective experience and its later conversion into representation. Shiv Kumar relates this not only to the interior monologue of *Ulysses* (which he finds constantly informed by *mémoire involontaire*) but also to Joyce's attitudes towards his literary past and to history. 'Joyce is primarily engaged,' he says, 'in an attempt to relive his past away from the locale and recreate it in a medium that may be called *la durée*.'[19]

Whereas the *Portrait* and *Ulysses* treat time as *durée réelle*, as a process of interblending of the past, present and future, *Finnegans Wake* attempts to present the entire historical consciousness of man.[20]

If, for Shiv Kumar, the authenticity of Joyce's work lies in the presentation of *durée* through the disruption of ordinary modes of representation, for Robert Klawitter, it is rather in the depiction of the unreality of the modes of representation that this authenticity needs to be sought.[21]

Several analysts have made the mistake of supposing that Bergson's philosophy can lead to a novel of *durée réelle*. But there can be no representation of reality as Bergson describes it because reality for Bergson is always falsified by representation.[22]

Klawitter's assumption is that the world depicted in *Ulysses* is 'formal, mechanical, determinate and uncreative'.[23] However, Klawitter argues, Joyce not only depicts this mechanical world, but calls attention to its status as a product of false representation—the intellectual representation that imposes a homogeneous time on the multiplicity of *durée*. Thus the point of concurrence between Bergson and Joyce needs be sought rather in the method of 'antiliterature'.

---

[17] Shiv K. Kumar, *Bergson and the Stream of Consciousness Novel* (London: Blackie & Son, Ltd., 1962).    [18] Ibid. 21.    [19] Ibid. 118.
[20] Ibid.
[21] Robert Klawitter, 'Henry Bergson and Joyce's Fictional World', *Comparative Literature Studies*, 3 (1966), 429–37.    [22] Ibid. 435.    [23] Ibid. 433.

Antiliterature I take to be literature that not only accepts, but seeks not to cover up, the fictionality of representations . . . Bergson's philosophy analyses the shape of the fictional world of all representations and so explains the relation between the theme of the anti-novel's fiction and the shape of its world.[24]

Thus Kumar's and Klawitter's studies express the two strategies emerging from the paradox of *durée*. *Durée* is the only authentic temporal experience worth expressing. But once the attempt to express it begins, its authenticity disappears. Thus Kumar moves towards an articulation of *durée* in terms of disrupted temporal sequences—'interblending of past, present and future'—while Klawitter argues for a deconstructive pattern, a portrayal of the world depicted as fictional.

All the three critics mentioned above, in articulating the Bergsonian distinction in *Ulysses*, seem to move beyond the periphery of the stream-of-consciousness technique. For Lewis, naturalism and the literary repertoire provided the point of complication. In Kumar, the notions of the literary past and of the history of human consciousness signify a movement beyond the realm of subjective experience for the presentation of *durée*. In Klawitter, it is the comedy of repetitions that show the world of representations to be absurd:

Repetition is a form of the comic, such as vice in the curvature of the soul, a moving circle of reincarnations; and the reciprocal interference of series . . . or partial superposition as in ambiguity . . . Bergson's *Laughter* begins to describe the world of *Finnegans Wake*.[25]

Thus, for an adequate characterization of the temporal experience in terms of stream of consciousness, we have to move out of that realm into other patterns of textual organization. The obsessive naturalism, Homeric analogues, attitudes to one's own literary past, tradition, or history—all these constitute trans-individual principles of textual organization. It is precisely such patterns that the theory of the spatial form chooses as objects for close attention.

Joseph Frank, who introduced the concept of spatial form into discussions of modernist texts, notes:

Joyce composed his novel of a vast number of references and cross references that relate to each other independently of the time sequence of

[24] Ibid. 430.        [25] Ibid. 436.

the narrative. These references must be connected by the reader and viewed as a whole before the book fits into any meaningful pattern.[26]

The mode of reading that such a novel demands is similar to that of modern poetry. The reader is required to read *Ulysses*, 'by continually fitting fragments together and keeping allusions in mind until, by reflexive reference, he can link them to their complements.'[27] This aspect of spatial unification is certainly opposed to the mode of temporal unfolding in the novel. A paradox of reading practice opens up from this tension.

A knowledge of the whole is essential for an understanding of any part; but unless one is a Dubliner such knowledge can be obtained only after the book has been read, when all the references are fitted into their proper place and grasped as a unity.[28]

Frank admits that this is 'the equivalent of saying that Joyce cannot be read—he can only be reread.'[29]

This interesting question concerning the mode of reading of *Ulysses* is treated by Frank in an ambiguous way. Frank recognizes that there are numerous meaningful spatial patterns deployed in the novel. How does the reader judge which of the several patterns he recognizes are relevant?

Ultimately, if we are to believe Stuart Gilbert, these systems of reference form a complete picture of practically everything under the sun, from the stages of man's life and the organs of the human body to the colors of the spectrum; but these structures are far more important for Joyce . . . than they could ever possibly be for the reader.[30]

Frank proposes to concern himself, not with these patterns in their empirical particularity, but with the perceptual form of the novel. Hence it appears that he is concerning himself with a theoretical question—what are the conditions of the possibility of meaning in a novel that relies on spatial form? However, the promise is betrayed in the ensuing pages. Frank relies solely on one pattern of such identification—the naturalistic presentation of Dublin.

Joyce desired . . . to build up in the reader's mind a sense of Dublin as a totality, including all the relations of the characters to one another and all the events that enter their consciousness . . . At the conclusion it might almost be said that Joyce literally wanted the reader to become a Dubliner

---

[26] Frank, *Widening Gyre*, 16.     [27] Ibid. 18.     [28] Ibid. 19.
[29] Ibid.                                             [30] Ibid. 16–17.

. . . It is this birthright that, at any one moment of time, gives the native a knowledge of Dublin's past and present as a whole; and it is only such knowledge that would enable the reader, like the characters, to place all the references in their proper context.[31]

Thus being a Dubliner, for Frank, exempts the reader from the paradox of rereading. In adopting this position, there is a lapse into an empirical treatment of the question of spatial form. The perceptual form of the novel can be disregarded, Frank seems to argue, if you have sufficient empirical information concerning Dublin.

That this lapse is unselfconscious is indicated by Frank's privileging of Dublin as the most relevant and most indispensable ground of unification. No adequate reasons are given as to why one such organizational element should have priority over others which, Frank assures us, the readers are at liberty to ignore. The exclusive privileging of Dublin as the spatial form implies the most empirical interpretation of the notion of space and indicates a preference for a naturalistic reading of *Ulysses*.

A critique of the notion of spatial form implicitly informs Frank Kermode's *The Sense of an Ending*.[32] Kermode argues that spatial form is a mistaken characterization of 'temporal integration'.

When Augustine recited his psalm he found in it a figure for the integration of past, present, and future which defies successive time. He discovered what is now erroneously referred to as 'spatial form'. He was anticipating what we know of the relation between books and St. Thomas's third order of duration—for in the kind of time known by books a moment has endless perspectives of reality.[33]

This third order of duration is *aevum*, distinct from linear time and eternity, the duration Aquinas assigned to angels. This duration participates in both the temporal and the eternal. Kermode argues that spatial form is a figure for *aevum*.

*Aevum*, you might say, is the time-order of novels. Characters in novels are independent of time and succession but may and usually do seem to co-operate in time and succession; the *aevum* co-exists with temporal events at the moment of occurrence, being, it was said, like a stick in a river. Barbant believed that Bergson inherited the notion through Spinoza's *duratio*, and

[31] Ibid. 18–19.
[32] Frank Kermode, *Sense of an Ending: Studies in the Theory of Fiction* (New York: OUP, 1967).                    [33] Ibid. 71.

if this is so there is an historical link between the *aevum* and Proust; furthermore this *durée réelle* is, I think, the real sense of the modern 'spatial form', which is a figure for the *aevum*.[34]

There are two interesting moments in this argument. The first is the contention that spatial form does not abolish time. It coexists with temporal unfolding and participates in it. The second moment is the relation Kermode suggests between *durée réelle* and spatial form. This makes possible a non-psychological reading of *durée*—a structural understanding of the two distinct modes of temporal experience. However, here too the relations work in a vague and general, rather than in a clear, way. The analogy with the characters poses new problems. Characters are affected by the temporal events in which they participate and novels usually depict their temporal experience. Frank's notion of spatial form is different from this. It is the reorganization of disparate moments from a temporal sequence, as if in a jigsaw, that Frank seems to be concerned with. And he is characterizing a certain aspect of literary modernism through the notion of spatial form. Kermode's example of the character takes away the specific theoretical and historical relevance of this notion. However, the argument that needs closer attention is the one concerning the relation of spatial form to temporal unfolding.

In Kermode's view, the experience of time in modern novels derives its specificity from the introduction of contingency and from the disruption of prevalent norms of concord in fiction.[35] Thus a simple opposition between space and time seems untenable. Kermode points out a relevant aspect of this complication when he indicates the limits of spatial unification in *Ulysses*:

Joyce's day in *Ulysses* retains plenty of skin; it seems very doubtful that he 'proceeded on the assumption that a unified spatial apprehension of his work would ultimately be possible,' as Joseph Frank claims, for the book is full of coincidences that are non-significant, and there is a real indeterminacy in character which can only imply . . . 'a thickening of the web of contingency'.[36]

Not all the elements in the novel are amenable to spatial unification. Even instances of coincidence and correspondence, where such a unification is apparently called for, may not

---

[34] Ibid. 72.    [35] See ibid., chs. 4 and 5.    [36] Ibid. 176–7.

contribute to the understanding of the novel in any meaningful way. Thus there is an indeterminacy concerning the validity of spatial syntheses.

Both the lines of argument we followed in the earlier pages elaborated a distinction, but ended in revealing limits. The notion of Bergsonian *durée*, articulated in terms of subjective experience, eventually seemed to move into a consideration of transindividual patterns in the novel. The theory of spatial form, on the other hand, started off with a distinction between temporal unfolding and spatial patterns, but had problems in determining the validity of the pattern established. Both characterizations ultimately share, I believe, a recognition of the heterogeneous organization of time in *Ulysses*. It is this heterogeneity that I shall seek to examine in the following pages. The oppositions proposed by the critics we discussed above are indeed operative in *Ulysses*, but in a discontinuous and asymmetric way. It is this complex deployment of narrative expectations and their frustration that constitutes the experience of time in *Ulysses*.

## Impediments to the Narrative

In the previous chapter I considered the legendary Joycean impulse towards naturalistic fidelity. This can be seen in the precision of the spatial and temporal details furnished in the text. Each episode is assigned a specific hour of the day. This generates the possibility of simultaneous perception of an event or object by several characters, as in the case of the cloud seen by both Stephen and Bloom. The chronometric precision in the organization of various sequences and their intersection in 'Wandering Rocks' has been commented on by critics. The accuracy of the topographical details too is conspicuous. One need only look at *A Topographical Guide to 'Ulysses'* for evidence of the systematic use of Dublin maps in the organization of the text.[37] Joyce himself claimed that the city could be reconstructed from his book if it ceased to exist.[38]

But this impulse is not unequivocally allowed to dominate the

[37] Clive Hart and Leo Knuth, *A Topographical Guide to 'Ulysses'*, 2 vols. (Colchester: A Wake Newslitter Press, 1975).

[38] Frank Budgen, *James Joyce and the Making of 'Ulysses', and Other Writings*, ed. Clive Hart (London: OUP, 1972), 69.

structure of *Ulysses*. It is always in tension with other patterns of organization. I shall illustrate this first in relation to the notion of space. The use of Dublin maps, as I mentioned above, shows the naturalistic impulse in play here. The fictional space, presented by the text for the reader to imagine, is equated with or approximated to the empirical space of Dublin as it existed in 1904. The continuous queries Joyce made to 'Aunt Josephine' during the composition testify to this attempt at empirical approximation:

I want that information about the Star of the Sea Church, has it ivy on its seafront, are there trees in Leahy's terrace at the side or near, if so, what, are there steps leading down to the beach?[39]

Is it possible for an ordinary person to climb over the area railings of no 7 Eccles Street, either from the path or the steps, lower himself from the lowest part of the railings till his feet are within 2 feet or 3 of the ground and drop unhurt. I saw it done myself but by a man of rather athletic build. I require this information in detail in order to determine the wording of a paragraph.[40]

This appears like an attempt to reproduce the Dublin map in as much detail as possible so that the empirical reality of the city functions not only as a general and guiding background to the experience of space in the novel, but as a model that is followed in great detail.

However, the map of Dublin determines only one level of the topographical organization in the novel. As Michael Seidel convincingly argues, Joyce worked with two sets of maps—one of Dublin and the other of the Mediterranean, the geographical setting of the *Odyssey*.[41] Joyce seems to have superimposed the Mediterranean map on that of Dublin so that the itinerary of Bloom and Stephen reproduces the routes of Odysseus and Telemachus. The spatial experience of the protagonists reproduces that of their epic predecessors. Thus there is the coexistence of two forms of topographical organization in *Ulysses*—the naturalistic and the schematic. The space of the novel is thus both empirical space and epic space. This ambiguity in the significance of spatial detail is

---

[39] *Letters*, i. 136.
[40] Ibid. 175.
[41] Michael Seidel, *Epic Geography: James Joyce's Ulysses* (Princeton, NJ: Princeton University Press, 1976), maps on pp. 132–7, 149, 176–81, 218–27, 248–51.

only one example of the pervasive tension between the naturalistic and the schematic impulses throughout the novel.[42]

Robert Adams has investigated some aspects of this tension in his *Surface and Symbol*.[43] He rightly argues that in spite of the precision in the reproduction of real details, in many cases a naturalistic element can function as a non-naturalistic or purely fictional element. In some cases, this is caused by the purely private nature of the information and in some others, by the lack of completeness in the information made available to the reader. In such cases, the reader converts a 'surface' element into a 'symbol'.[44]

The problem that underlies this lack of stability of the distinction between 'surface' and 'symbol' is that of relevance. Can the details be appropriated into a significant sequence? The relevance of many of the purely naturalistic elements is internal—they are there just to indicate the approximation of fictional details to real ones. However, the reader attempts to integrate them into the significant unities he constructs. Even purely naturalistic elements—e.g. 'Erin's King'—are subjected to symbolic interpretation. This again points to the ongoing tension between the naturalistic and the schematic impulses.

This has direct relevance for the experience of time in the novel. The two antipodes of this dialectic, in terms of time, are constituted by (1) the chronometric time that informs the naturalistic organization of temporal details, and (2) the spatial unities suggested in the two schemata—e.g. colours, organs, etc. But between these two extremities, in the actual experience of reading, we find various degrees of mediation. In other words, the reader forms significant unities which show the influence of these impulses to various degrees. I shall consider some of these unities.

We have seen that the interior monologue organizes elements in a different way from the narration. The criteria of relevance that the reader brings to bear on the monologue are different from those of the narration. In the monologue a certain latitude is allowed concerning coherence. The elements presented in the monologues

---

[42] A similar instance can be found in the superimposition of the figure of a sleeping male human body on the map of Dublin in *Finnegans Wake*. See John Bishop, *Joyce's Book of the Dark: 'Finnegans Wake'* (Madison, Wis.: University of Wisconsin Press, 1986), map A and relief map B, pp. 32–5.

[43] Robert Adams, *Surface and Symbol: The Consistency of James Joyce's 'Ulysses'* (New York: OUP, 1962).　　　　　　　　　[44] Ibid. 83–6.

usually retain their discreteness and participate in a loose and associational connection. The elements in the narration, on the other hand, present a more organic and logically integrated sequence. The relation between reading time and fictional time certainly differs in the monologue and in the narration. The monologue is free to present material that is apparently irrelevant from the point of view of plot. We find such elements in the narrative too, occasionally, as in the case of elements creating a 'reality effect'.[45] In such cases the relevance of the element derives from its exceptionality. Beyond a certain degree such elements can impede the progress of the narrative. There are many instances of this in *Ulysses* as we shall see shortly. In the meantime, let us return to the case of the monologue.

Sometimes the monologue intrudes into the external action presented by the narrative and presents another sequence, apparently unconnected to this action.

> He hummed, prolonging in solemn echo the closes of the bars:
> —*Don Giovanni, a cenar teco*
> *M'invitasti.*
> Feel better. Burgundy. Good pick me up. Who distilled first? Some chap in the blues. Dutch courage. That *Kilkenny People* in the national library now I must.
> Bare clean closestools waiting in the window of William Miller, plumber, turned back his thoughts. They could: and watch it all the way down, swallow a pin sometimes come out of the ribs years after, tour round the body changing bilary duct spleen squirting liver gastric juice coils of intestines like pipes. But the poor buffer would have to stand all the time with his inside entrails on show. Science.
> —*A cenar teco.*
> What does that *teco* mean? Tonight perhaps. (*U*, 8. 1039–52)

Here the interior monologue breaks away from the humming and eventually returns to it. The whole monologue forms a parenthesis framed by the humming of the words from *Don Giovanni*. The time taken by the monologue cannot be clearly determined. It is even possible that it occurred at the same time as the humming. Even within the monologue, continuity is violated. The transition to the *Kilkenny People* is abrupt. Another break is introduced by the return of the narrative: 'Bare clean closestools waiting in the

---

[45] See Roland Barthes, 'L'Effet du réel', *Communications*, 11 (1969), 84–9.

window of William Miller, plumber, turned back his thoughts'. When the monologue returns, the transitions are again missing: 'They could'. What is this a response to? It could relate to the paragraph where Bloom thinks about digestion and inventions.

First sweet then savoury. Mr Bloom coasted warily. Ruminants. His second course. Their upper jaw they move. Wonder if Tom Rochford will do anything with that invention of his? Wasting time explaining it to Flynn's mouth. Lean people long mouths. Ought to be a hall or a place where inventors could go in and invent free. (*U*, 8. 1033–7)

'They could' also relates to 'you could' (*U*, 8. 1030).

Thus the monologues can function as a sequence of disjunctions framed by external actions. This way of introducing a different mode of perception or action is something that Joyce uses several times in *Ulysses*. For example, Bloom's fantasies of grandeur in 'Circe' occupy such a position. This particular sequence of fantasies is introduced by Zoe's remark: 'Go on. Make a stump speech out of it' (*U*, 15. 1353). They conclude with the litany of the 'Daughters of Erin' and with Bloom's becoming '*mute, shrunken, carbonized*'. The earlier narrative takes over again with Zoe saying, 'Talk away till you are blue in the face' (*U*, 15. 1958). The nature of the temporal lapse is, once again, indeterminate. These fantasies could have a real temporal duration if we consider them as a dramatic substitute for an utterance by Bloom which is not presented in the text. Or we could understand Zoe's 'Talk away till you are blue in the face' as coming immediately after her 'Go on. Make a stump speech of it.' According to this second reading the sequence of fantasies does not have real temporal duration. In other words, the fantasies cannot be located in the temporal scheme of external events with precision. Their temporality is not translatable into that of the events.

The case of the monologue we considered is structurally very similar. The monologue may or may not have a real temporal duration. One significant aspect of this problem is that we cannot institute a unilinear time based on the narration and then locate the monologues within it. They can be located as happening between two events, two moments in the narration, or two acts of perception. But their duration cannot be specified in greater detail. This causes a temporal indeterminateness or dilation in the monologues.

The narrative roots of the Bergsonian studies on *Ulysses* can be located here. The subjective discourses suggest a different temporality. Shiv Kumar considers them as the literary presentation of *durée*. However, the distinction between the monologue and the narration gets increasingly complicated as we progress. There is some radical equivocation about the status of discourses, even in the early chapters of *Ulysses*. I shall consider its implications for the notion of the sign in the next chapter. For the time being, I shall indicate the nature of the problem by examining one such instance.

His shadow lay over the rocks as he bent, ending. Why not endless till the farthest star? Darkly they are there behind this light, darkness shining in the brightness, delta of Cassiopeia, worlds. Me sits there with his augur's rod of ash, in borrowed sandals, by day beside a livid sea, unbeheld, in violet night walking beneath a reign of uncouth stars. I throw this ended shadow from me, manshape ineluctable, call it back. Endless, would it be mine, form of my form? Who watches me here? Who ever anywhere will read these written words? (*U*, 3. 408–15)

The monologue commences by 'Why not endless . . .'. It is triggered off by the 'ending' introduced by the narrative. It appears as if Stephen is reading the very written words of the narrative. This could be related to 'read these written words' at the end of the passage, where Stephen is considering the poem that he has written. The opposition between 'ending' and 'endless' is taken up again in the monologue, this time in relation to the distinction between body and soul, through allusions to Aristotle's *De Anima*.[46] The shadow thrown by the body is contrasted with the soul, the 'form of forms'. The shadow created by the external and tangible aspect of the corporeal being is finite—'ending', 'manshape ineluctable'. The soul, interiority, is described as 'endless'. In a way, this reproduces the distinction between the narration that depicts the external states and events and the monologue that presents an interior discourse. As we have seen, the relation between the narration and the monologue was, in this passage, the opposition between 'ending' and 'endless': 'His shadow lay . . . ending' of the narration and 'Why not endless . . .' of the monologue. In this network of connections, the text can be read as thematizing its own procedures.

---

[46] 'Form of forms' is an allusion to Aristotle's characterization of the soul in *De Anima*, 432$^a$1–3. See *Complete Works of Aristotle: The Revised Oxford Translation*, ed. Jonathan Barnes, i (Princeton, NJ: Princeton University Press, 1984), 686.

However, this entire reading has been made possible by the ambiguity of the status of 'ending' in the first sentence. Formally, it belongs to the narration. However, since its repetition informs strongly the ensuing monologue, it seems to be part of Stephen's perception. Thus there is an equivocation about the discursive status of 'ending'. The repetition of the 'ending'/'endless' opposition seems to highlight this and destabilize the sharp distinction between narration and monologue.

This makes it difficult to sustain an interpretation of time based on the opposition of the categories 'subjective' and 'objective'. Indeed Joyce makes use of such a distinction, but the inconsistency of its use renders the resultant experience of time all the more heterogeneous. Part of the passages we assign to narration seems to slide into the temporal dilation characteristic of the monologues.

There is another sort of temporal dilation in the narration of *Ulysses*. This does not arise from the insertion of subjective perceptions of characters into the narration. It has to do with an abandoning of the usually prevalent criteria of relevance. For example, the last section in 'Wandering Rocks' recounts the itinerary of the viceregal parade, the way several characters perceive the parade, and how the viceroy exchanges salutes with many of them. Since in the composition of 'Wandering Rocks', Joyce aimed at creating a section disconnected from the earlier and the later parts of the novel, the episode itself makes it necessary to redefine the novel's overall economy. Since Joyce eventually abandoned the symmetric counterparts for this section in the beginning and the end of the novel, structurally it creates a peculiar disjunction in the novel, a disjunction that prepares the reader for the more conspicuous disjunctions in the later chapters. However, even within the episode, 'Wandering Rocks' possesses an inner diversity, consisting of fragments from different worlds of perceptions. In such an episode continuity and connection are ensured mainly through external means—by the prevalence of temporal and spatial contiguity in an external sense. The last section of the episode is a narrative manifestation of these external connections. The viceregal parade passes through the fragments recounted before, thus uniting them in an external, contingent manner. It is this contingency that determines the economy of narration here. It accumulates details of how the parade passed through one point after another. In contrast with the diverse temporalities recounted in the earlier sections of the episode, here we find a narration that mimes the pseudo-objective discourse of reports. The contingent connections between the details and the proliferation of elements produce a slackening of narrative progress, a betrayal of the inability of chronometric time to subsume the diverse temporal sequences of the previous sections in the episode.

This method—that of connecting sequences contingently or externally—recurs in Joyce's later work. One prominent form that this prolific accumulation of elements takes is that of lists. In 'Cyclops' we have several such lists, ranging from that of the Irish heroes to that of trees that attend the wedding. Lists involve an uncoupling of the temporality of reading from that of action. They are analogous to descriptions in their contrast with narration. However, descriptions allow the reader to organize a series of perceptions into an integrated whole. The principle that lies behind lists is empirically exhaustive of a set or a group. Furthermore, the lists in 'Cyclops' are pseudo-lists: we find Patric W. Shakespeare, Mohammed, and Dante Alighieri among Irish heroes. The list of trees too could be extended infinitely. This again puts into question the criteria concerning the selection of elements. No hierarchy prevails in these lists in terms of significance, and this differentiates lists from descriptions even more. The presentation of lists in the narrative thus results in a temporal halt. The exaggerated narrator of 'Cyclops' is a strategy for such constant obstruction of narrative progress. He presents documents, detailed descriptions, and re-writing of events from the other narrative.

Steven Connor, while examining the role of lists in Beckett's work, treats them as a form of repetition.[47] In contrast with the horizontal progress of the narrative, lists present a certain verticality—one element in a chain is developed vertically by being presented alongside several substitutes. Thus one element in the chain becomes too inflated to be included in the chain at all. The sense of abundance and looseness of language that arises here is, to a large extent, a result of the violation of a horizontally organized narration.

A variation of this strategy can be seen in another instance in 'Cyclops'. The entry of Alf Bergan, Dennis Breen, and Breen's wife

---

[47] Steven Connor, *Samuel Beckett: Repetition, Theory and the Text* (Oxford: Basil Blackwell, 1988).

into Barney Kiernan's pub is first presented in the discourse of the solemn narrator. Immediately after that, we are given a new presentation of the same event in the nameless narrator's language. Similarly, Bloom's exit is presented from the point of view of both the narrators. The two narrations tend to run parallel to each other on these occasions, but their sequential presentation enters into tension with this. This creates a sense of parody and of repetition that complicates the experience of narrative progress.

However, these strategies are not confined to 'Cyclops'. The following passage from 'Aeolus' shows the same impeding of narrative progress:

> Grossbooted draymen rolled barrels dullthudding out of Prince's stores and bumped them up on the brewery float. On the brewery float bumped dullthudding barrels rolled by grossbooted draymen out of Prince's stores. (*U*, 7. 21–4)

The exaggerated scientific precision of 'Ithaca', the headlines in 'Aeolus', the overture of 'Sirens', many of the parodies in 'Oxen of the Sun'—all partake in this interruption of narration and the consequent complication of temporal experience. Many of these devices are occasioned by Joyce's reliance on external patterns for organizing the narrative. The 'Aeolus' headlines indicate reliance on the format of the newspaper; the 'Sirens' overture, on musical composition; 'Ithaca', on catechism. The passage from 'Aeolus' cited above was part of Joyce's attempt to present as many rhetorical figures as he could in the episode. In addition to these, we have certain patterns of organization which affect the monologue as well as the narration. Examples of this would include the Homeric analogues and the patterns of colours, organs, and symbols. The reliance on such external patterns is not an entirely new literary device. It is argued that the episodes in the *Odyssey* are 'related by their correspondence with a cyclic ritual'.[48] If that is the case, Homer also relies on external patterns for the organization of narrative and Joyce's use of such patterns could be considered as an allusion to Homer.

What are the implications of such patterns for the experience of time in *Ulysses*? So far we have examined only some individual

---

[48] See Kermode, *Sense of an Ending*, 5. See also Georg Roppen and Richard Sommer, *Strangers and Pilgrims: An Essay on the Metaphor of Journey* (Oslo: Norwegian Universities Press, 1964), 19–20.

instances where these patterns are at work. We found different ways of impeding the temporal progress of the narrative. This, it was argued, results in the heterogeneity of temporal experience. The question is whether these various strategies occupy positions in a unified system—whether their diversity can be unified at a deeper level.


Odyssey: *Schema and Asymmetry*

The most widely known and the most widely discussed aspect of this unification is the presence of the *Odyssey* as a structural source. This seems to have provided Joyce with a set of interpretative tasks. The writing of the text of *Ulysses* was also an act of interpretative mediation between the levels of the novel and the epic. This can be seen, for instance, in Joyce's discussions of the problems of writing 'Oxen of the Sun' and 'Circe'.

I am working now on the *Oxen of the Sun* the most difficult episode in an odyssey, I think, both to interpret and to execute . . .[49]

Am working hard at *Oxen of the Sun*, the idea being the crime committed against fecundity by sterilizing the act of coition.[50]

I am sorry you do not think your ideas on *Circe* worth sending. As I told you a catchword is enough to set me off. *Moly* is a nut to crack. My latest is this. Moly is the gift of Hermes, god of public ways, and is the invisible influence (prayer, chance, agility, *presence of mind*, power of recuperation) which saves in case of accident. This would cover immunity from syphilis (σνφιλις = swine-love?).[51]

The establishment of connections between the two texts here involves the use of analogy and interpretation. Interpretation seems to determine the ground on which the analogy is built. However, once the analogy is worked into the text during the composition, its self-evidence disappears. Joyce's decision to suppress the Homeric titles of the episodes is best seen in this light. The Homeric correspondences have to be discovered by the reader. Since the only way the reader can go about this task is through an act of interpretation, discovery here amounts to construction. The acts of interpretative mediation that Joyce established between the *Odyssey* and *Ulysses* are not necessarily the ones that the reader establishes

[49] *Letters*, i. 137.    [50] Ibid. 139.    [51] Ibid. 147.

through his interpretative judgements. In short, the use of the *Odyssey* becomes a gesture on the author's part to provide a ruse for the reader's search for unities.

However, problems arise at this stage. Relying on a text as a unifying strategy for another text brings into play the very unity or disunity of the original text. This indirectly raises questions about the kind of unification that *Odyssey* itself can be submitted to. Furthermore, do the relations between the Homeric episodes and their Joycean counterparts display homogeneity?

Critics, from Stuart Gilbert to Michael Seidel, have explored these parallels to an amazingly rich extent. Such parallels do indeed provide a preliminary ground for raising questions concerning the effect of these elements on our reading of the novel, or concerning the discursive status of these parallels in relation to other elements in the text. But critics who tend to use these elements as an interpretative key for the novel tend to stop short of raising these questions. Fredric Jameson recognizes this when he observes that the *Odyssey* parallel is one of the organizational frameworks of the narrated text, but 'it is not itself the interpretation of that narrative, as the ideologues of myth have thought. Rather it is itself—qua organizational framework—what remains to be interpreted.'[52] One of the preliminary problems faced by a critic who uses Homer as an interpretative key to *Ulysses* concerns Joyce's tone: is *Ulysses* a parody of *Odyssey*, or is it an act of positive, heroic imitation? Without identifying the tone, the significance of the events in the novel in relation to the epic becomes obscure. However, the tone does not remain consistent through the novel. Bloom's general similarity to Ulysses is positive in so far as the theory of the all-round hero goes. But the gravity of the parallels between Molly and Penelope is more difficult to determine. Bloom's cigar in the 'Cyclops' episode, in itself richly humorous, brings forth a tension between the ironic tone in relation to the details and the generous sympathetic tone in relation to Bloom. Richard Ellmann, in response to the argument that *Ulysses* is a great joke on Homer, suggests that the joke, in this context, has a double aim:

The first aim is mock-heroic, the mighty spear juxtaposed to the twopenny cigar. The second, a more subtle one, is what might be called the

---

[52] Fredric Jameson, '*Ulysses* in History', in W. J. McCormack and Alistair Stead (eds.), *James Joyce and Modern Literature* (London: Routledge & Kegan Paul, Ltd., 1982), 128.

ennoblement of the mock-heroic. This demonstrates that the world of cigars is devoid of heroism only to whose who do not understand that Ulysses' spear was merely a sharpened stick, a homely instrument in its way, and that Bloom can demonstrate the qualities of man by word of mouth as Ulysses by a thrust of a spear.[53]

It is true that the relations between the Homeric text and *Ulysses*, the interpretative mediation between them, determine our under-standing of *Ulysses* to a large extent. However, this in its turn is not an issue where there is any critical consensus. Interpreters who regard the Homeric text as some kind of key to *Ulysses* attribute consistency to the interpretative mediation between these two texts—whether it be through the notion of the 'mock-heroic' or through its 'ennoblement' or through both. However, it is precisely the consistency of these parallels that is open to question. The very asymmetry of the parallels, the different kinds of analogy that have gone into their production, refuse to be unified under such a single tone. The Homeric text that the reader recovers from *Ulysses* is widely heterogeneous in its levels of proximity to the novel. It is a text subjected to discrete acts of interpretation at different points. Thus the incitement to unification produces a radical heterogeneity in our reading of the original text, let alone of *Ulysses*.

This further implies that instead of a temporal synthesis which unites the entire text, we have discrete syntheses which refuse to be united at any further level. If all the parallels had occupied the same level, we could have talked about an epic realm of significance beyond the novel's unfolding. However, the epic itself is disunited by its use in the novel. Instead of a consistently meaningful parallel, one finds discrete encounters of both texts, producing zones of meaning in the novel.

The presence of such zones is all the more evident in the schematic patterns that Joyce used. Joyce seems to have considered the co-presence of these various patterns in the text as significant. This can be seen in the two schemata that Joyce circulated among his friends—the Linati schema and the Gilbert–Gorman plan. For each episode, the Linati schema shows eight levels: time, colour, persons, technic, science/art, sense, organ, and symbol. The Gilbert–Gorman plan does not have persons and sense among the levels. Instead, there are two new columns: that of correspondences

[53] Richard Ellmann, *James Joyce* (revd. edn., New York: OUP, 1982), 360.

and of the scene. Ellmann has provided a comparison of the two schemata in *Ulysses on the Liffey.*

One can recognize in this schematic impulse the narrative problem that theorists of the spatial form specified rather inadequately. The strongest threat to the linearity of the narrative does not arise, as Joseph Frank believed, from the scattering of naturalistic detail. These details can be integrated temporally by the reader through a narrative of perceptions. The scattered details about Dublin can indeed be put together at the end of the book to produce a unified vision of the city. But they are presented in a fragmented way precisely because Joyce wanted to subordinate them to a narrative of characters' perceptions. However, it is much more difficult to appropriate the external patterns of organization—for example, colour, organ, etc.—into a narrative.

Joyce's understanding of the schema seems to be evident in the letter to Linati of 21 September 1920:

I think that in view of the enormous bulk and the more than enormous complexity of my three times blasted novel it would be better to send you a sort of summary—key—skeleton—scheme (for your personal use only). Perhaps my idea will appear clearer to you when you have the text. . . . I have given only catchwords in my scheme but I think you will understand it all the same. It is an epic of two races (Israelite–Irish) and at the same time the cycle of the human body as well as a little story of a day (life). . . . It is also a sort of encyclopaedia. My intention is to transpose the myth *sub specie temporis nostri.* Each adventure (that is, every hour, every organ, every art being interconnected and interrelated in the structural scheme of the whole) should not only condition but even create its own technique. Each adventure is so to say one person although it is composed of persons—as Aquinas relates of the angelic hosts.[54]

We find two distinct impulses here. The first is to designate realms of unification of the text—'an epic of two races', 'cycle of the human body', 'a little story of a day (life)', 'a sort of encyclopaedia'. Each of these phrases is a characterization of the text as a whole. However, the text is all these at the same time. Each of those descriptions provides a way of unifying the text without attempting to account for all its elements. Certain details in the text would make possible the attempt to unify the text under any of the phrases

[54] *Letters,* i. 146–7.

cited above. But such unities are only partial and non-inclusive. The elements which submit to the unifying category are produced, at the level of the composition, by the category itself. We shall return to this question later. For the moment, let us consider the other impulse displayed in Joyce's letter.

This impulse is directed towards a new object—a new unity other than that of the text. That unit is 'adventure'. Joyce's clarification of this term is instructive. It designates a site where the hour, organ, art, etc. get interconnected in the structural scheme of the whole. The adventure, to put it crudely, is to the syntagmatic level what the unifying phrases are to the paradigmatic level. This would appear all too obvious from the tabular structure of the Gilbert–Gorman plan. However, on closer examination, this apparent self-evidence seems to disappear.

The adventure seems to be a nodal point on which several series converge. At the same time, it seems to be an instance of transversal connections made across several vertical lines. If one wants to push this geometrical metaphor further, one could say that the adventure presents, in terms of conceptualization, a tension between the point and the line.[55] That is why the parallel with the syntagmatic level seems inadequate. It is clear that Joyce designates it to a realm prior to textual unfolding: 'Each adventure . . . should not only condition but create its own technique.' In that sense, it refers to a point of simultaneous presence of different elements. But when the adventure is defined in terms of interconnection between elements of a series which was already defined (namely hour, elements of the human body, etc.), then the simultaneous point-like character seems to break down. Joyce seems to have been aware of this aporia when he invokes the Aquinian concept of angels, unified and multiple at the same time.

If one examines Joyce's compositional devices, they seem to vary in different episodes. The Homeric parallels seem abundant, for instance, in the notesheets of 'Ithaca'. But, as Phillip Herring has observed, they are less prominent in the case of 'Cyclops', 'Nausicaa', and 'Oxen of the Sun': 'the reason for this may well lie in the fact that these episodes have self-contained structural

---

[55] This makes it difficult to see the schema as another narrative. It has as its constitutive tension, the opposition between the adventure and the different levels of progress. The asymmetry in its organization can be seen also in the absence of certain elements for some episodes.

rationales that propel them along clearly defined lines.'[56] At the level of the text, the schematic aspects are manifest, most often in the careful deployment of semantemes which exegesis can pick up, connect, and elucidate. However, these semantemes often do not attract our attention if we do not look for them. This is most clearly evident for the schematic aspect of colour. There is no necessary relation that takes the reader from the empirical level of the text to an identification of the schema. There is a disparity between the actual occurrence of colours in the episodes and the colours schematically designated. In some cases, the connection between the schema and the text becomes accessible for the reader only through the schema. On the other hand, in some episodes, there are less arbitrary relations among the various schematic aspects, and between them and the text. 'Sirens' is one such episode, where the connection between ear, music, *fuga per canonem*, and barmaids as the sirens seems less arbitrary than, for instance, the connection in 'Calypso' between kidney, economics, orange, nymph, and narrative as mature. This makes Joyce's claims about the adventure, about the interpenetration of various elements therein, a disuniting factor for interpretation.

By combining with one another in a different fashion for each episode, the schema produces discursive terrains. In contrast to the linear unfolding of the narrative, these provide spatial territories where the production of literary meaning happens under specific norms. Elements in the episode demand a double interpretation: one at the level of narrative unfolding and another at the level of the discursive regularities particular to the episode. Thus a duality of interpretative levels opens up again. I shall examine this in greater detail in the next chapter in the context of the discussion of the sign in *Ulysses*. For the moment, it is enough to recall one example:

—Metempsychosis, he said, is what the ancient Greeks called it. They used to believe you could be changed into an animal or a tree, for instance. What they called nymphs, for example.

Her spoon ceased to stir up the sugar. She gazed straight before her, inhaling through her arched nostrils.

—There's a smell of burn, she said. Did you leave anything on the fire?

—The kidney! he cried suddenly. (*U*, 4. 375–81)

[56] James Joyce, *Joyce's 'Ulysses' Notesheets in the British Museum*, ed. Phillip F. Herring (Charlottesville, Va.: University of Virginia Press, 1972), 50.

We know, from an examination of the schema, that Joyce attributes special significance to 'kidney' and to 'nymph'. However, this does not have any immediate bearing for the reader's understanding of the passage. Joyce's weaving of various semantemes, especially at a later stage in the composition, therefore introduces the possibility of making interpretative connections that are difficult to unify. Attention to the schema sets up a process of differentiation of the text, the emergence of a large number of possible connections. This seems to render interpretation an unending task. This, however, is different from the dream of an undifferentiated discourse and of freely floating signifiers that the critic might want to read into Joyce. It is arguable that there is no moment in *Ulysses* where discourse is thought of except as produced within grids of regularities.

Michael Groden's study of the compositional history has emphasized the incidence of changing intentions and techniques which cannot be accommodated into a unifying understanding of the novel's aesthetic. The transition from 'stream of consciousness' through 'parody' to the 'creation of new styles', the composition of 'Eumaeus' very early and the rest of 'Nostos' much later, the revision of the earlier chapters at the proof stage—all these complicate the identification of an all-encompassing and at the same time unified aesthetic. This has, I think, its implications for the schema too. Far from being an Archimedean point of judgement, the schema is caught up in the flux it is trying to control and order. The atemporal moment of temporal synthesis has already fallen into time.

Since Joyce uses the model of interior monologue pervasively in *Ulysses*, it is tempting to argue that the continuity that informs the novel is a continuity of consciousness, as is exemplified in the notion of 'stream of consciousness'. However, to understand the method in terms of a psychological subjectivity or of continuity of fictional characters is, to a large extent, to miss some profounder aspects of Joyce's experiment. Among them is Joyce's treatment of memory and the specifically linguistic or discursive turn that he gives to it.

In 'Oxen of the Sun', there is an ironic formulation of this:

> There are sins or (let us call them as the world calls them) evil memories which are hidden away by man in the darkest places of the heart but they abide there and wait. He may suffer their memory to grow dim, let them be

as though they had not been and all but persuade himself that they were not or at least were otherwise. Yet a chance word will call them forth suddenly and they will rise up to confront him in the most various circumstances, a vision or a dream, or while timbrel and harp soothe his senses or amid the cool silver tranquility of the evening or at the feast, at midnight, when he is now filled with wine. (*U*, 14. 1344–52)

In *Ulysses*, it is mainly the 'chance word' that generates recollection, predominantly through the recollection of verbal fragments. Sometimes the consciousness of the subject is rendered purely as a collection of such verbal fragments:

O sweety all your little girlwhite up I saw dirty bracegirdle made me do love sticky we two naughty Grace darling she him half past the bed met him pike hoses frillies for Raoul de perfume your wife black hair heave under embon *señorita* young eyes Mulvey plumb bubs me breadvan Winkle red slippers she rusty sleep wander years of dreams return tail end Agendath swoony lovey showed me her next year in drawers return next in her next her next. (*U*, 13. 1279–85)

However, the repetition of these verbal fragments does carry with it associations in the form of contexts and of other verbal fragments. It is these traces and the play of difference that arises between the previous use and the present context, that constitute memory in *Ulysses*. Memory does not represent here an organic whole with an unchanging meaning, but a series of repetitions that lead on to other series. An element that was combined with certain other elements in a previous episode brings with it traces of these combinations. Thus recollection is predominantly explored through repetition in the interior monologue.

In the last chapter, I argued that these acts of repetition sometimes go beyond the boundaries of character-subjectivities and form patterns that exceed psychological associations. This points to the limits of an interpretation based on the notion of stream of consciousness in a psychological sense. However, the presentation of consciousness in terms of discourses and repetition does have some similarities to Bergson's notion of *durée*. In his study of Bergson, Deleuze argues that *durée* is inseparable from the movement of actualization. For 'actualization comes about through differentiation, through divergent lines, and creates so many differences in kind by virtue of its own movement'.[57] The profound

---

[57] Gilles Deleuze, *Bergsonism*, tr. Hugh Tomlinson (New York: Zone Books, 1988), 43.

relation between *durée* and stream of consciousness is based on the continuous process of differentiation that informs them. It is through the use of different discourses and of repetition that this differentiation operates in Joyce's text. Each verbal fragment recalled induces a difference, an interplay between its former and present discursive connections.

Therefore, the notions of repetition and of a textual memory that goes beyond individual characters are central to the experience of time in *Ulysses*. We have seen how repetition functions to upset sharp distinctions between narration and monologue and, indirectly, those between the presentation of subjective and objective experiences of time. Furthermore, instances of repetition constitute an interruption of linear time, making complex recapitulations essential to the narrative. This retrospective arrangement, however, does not lead to a totality—each fragment is always open to further repetition, a point that Joyce emphasizes in *Finnegans Wake* through its circularity. Through repetition, we get series—expanding, differing from themselves, intersecting with one another. This leads to disparate temporal syntheses which cannot be further totalized. Such a process escapes the rather simple models of linear or cyclical time.

I shall consider below, as in the previous chapter, three passages from *Ulysses* in relation to the differentiation of levels and to the problems of unification. The passages are from 'Cyclops' (*U*, 12. 1–205), 'Oxen of the Sun' (*U*, 14. 1–17), and 'Circe' (*U*, 15. 4054–245).

*Readings: 'Cyclops', 'Oxen of the Sun', 'Circe'*

The opening pages of 'Cyclops' (*U*, 12. 1–205) present an interesting example, a noticeable feature of the episode being the prevalence of two contrasting narrative voices. The first narrator is modelled on techniques of conventional story-telling. The story opens by fixing the place, the context and then moves on to a recalling of incidents, details of conversation, etc. The range of the story in terms of characters and voices expands. This is done through a process of citation. First the narrational context involves the narrator and one narratee. Then it becomes complex by the inclusion of Joe Haynes. The direction of the narrator's voice shifts from the first addressee to Joe.

A bloody big foxy thief beyond by the garrison church at the corner of Chicken lane—old Troy was just giving me a wrinkle about him—lifted any God's quantity of tea and sugar to pay three bob a week ... (*U*, 12. 13–16)

There is a continuous shift in the narrational context—a movement at the level of the source of the story or at the level of the addressee. In the next paragraph the same strategy is repeated when the narrator's utterance includes other people's utterances through citation. But this narrational expansion can still be contained in terms of the linear narrative progress. The main controlling logic of the entire passage is that of progressive story telling. But already, at the level of fictional organization, one finds elements of a different kind. In the first sentence, we hear of a 'bloody sweep that came along and he near drove his gear into my eye' (*U*, 12. 2–3). This introduces the 'Cyclops' theme by alluding to Ulysses' blinding of Cyclops by a burning olive-stake in the *Odyssey*. However, the schema, in the set of correspondences, mentions cigar in relation to Ulysses' stake. This occurs later in the episode when Bloom speaks in an agitated fashion to the citizen, still holding his cigar (*U*, 12. 1469). There is a textual connection at the level of motifs between the two instances. Similarly, 'collector of bad and doubtful debts' (*U*, 12. 24–5) introduces a theme pertinent to Ulysses and obliquely to Bloom. These instances reveal the emergence of the levels of fictional organization and of the text which cannot be strictly appropriated into the linear narrative in terms of character or incidents. Moreover, the references to the schema and to Homer on the one hand, and the level of textual repetition on the other, do not converge. If one set of correspondences relies on character as its ground, the level of textual repetition violates that: it makes the theme of blinding a leitmotif that can be united to any character and be deployed in several parts of the episode.

The apparent simplicity and the deep asymmetry of levels in this first passage are countered by a second narrative strategy. After introducing the story of Herzog and Geraghty, the voice changes. The new voice provides a transcript of the agreement signed between Herzog and Geraghty. Against the surface texture of the unilinear narrative of the earlier passage, we are here presented with a document. This document does not carry the story forward. It does not even give us any significant information. The parodic intent of the passage becomes more and more obvious as the

episode progresses. In the pseudo-heroic presentation of the citizen
(*U*, 12. 151–73), we have evidently a humorous parody of epic
exaggeration. However, in terms of narrative organization, these
passages constitute a resistance to the linear progress of the story.
Sometimes the passages are static as in the list of the Irish heroes (*U*,
12. 176–99), in the list of the clergy (*U*, 12. 927–38), or in the list
of trees in the tree-wedding passage (*U*, 12. 1268–78). The mock
scrupulous exactitude concerning details creates an accumulation
of elements that defies laws of relevance inherent in any linear
narrative unfolding.[58] This seems to create two important effects.

The first of them can be characterized as a spatialization of
discourse—the sudden emergence of a new territory of discourse
which cannot be accounted for in terms of sequential narration.
However, it must be remembered that there is a contextual
justification for the introduction of these passages. The second
narrative voice is introduced by the first through a contextual
connection. For example, the document is introduced by the first
narrator's actual mention of the case. However, once the second
voice takes over, the text does not conform to the hierarchies of
relevance instituted by the earlier voice. The second voice describes
or recites. The first voice predominantly narrates. The result of this
disjunction is primarily an emphasis on the artificiality of the text.
The second voice cannot, in any strict sense, be designated as a
voice. It could be argued that it is rather a series of independent
passages which cannot be contained under a single narrative voice.
The telling of the same event according to both narrative
strategies—the solemn pseudo-epic narration of the entry of Denis
Breen and its immediate retelling in the plebeian voice (*U*, 12. 244–
8, 12. 249–56)—highlights the discursive diversity. This diversity
or, as I called it earlier, instances of narrative disjunction, cannot be
recuperated in a unifying single narrative.

Secondly, this disjunction can be seen to introduce a remarkable
difference in tempo. In trying to connect the two disjunctive realms
of discourse, the reader gets involved in a process of translation—in
trying to determine what exactly is happening in terms of the

[58] The opposition of descriptive detail to narrative hierarchy is examined in
Lukács: Georg Lukács, 'Narrate or Describe', in id., *Writer and Critic and Other
Essays*, ed. and tr. Arthur Kahn (London: Merlin, 1970), 110–48. But the parodic
accumulation of details has, at its core, the opposition between different norms of
hierarchization rather than the absence of hierarchy. MacCabe also underplays the
presence of diverse hierarchies behind the proliferation of detail in *Ulysses*.

narrative he was following. This process is only partially successful. He might be able to work out vague parallels in description, working on principles of analogy. But passages such as

> Love loves to love love. Nurse loves the new chemist. Constable 14A loves Mary Kelly. Gerty MacDowell loves the boy that has the bicycle. (*U*, 12. 1493–5)

refuse such reappropriation. The only connection of this passage to the preceding text is the theme of love that had come up in Bloom's discussion with the citizen. The reference to Gerty MacDowell here operates at the level of the text as an instance of textual prolepsis. Even where the translation is partially successful, as in the description of the journey to the pub and the meeting with the citizen, the accumulation of narratively irrelevant elements creates a radical slackening of tempo. The temporal progress of the narrative is inhibited and bogged down by a spatialization of discourse in description.

These effects in 'Cyclops' demonstrate the irreducibility of the various levels in the narrative organization of the episode. However, the levels are connected to each other in a non-unifiable and tenuous way. In the Linati schema, Joyce designated the technique of the episode as 'alternating asymmetry'. I have tried to show how this is related to a general production of asymmetries and of instances of disunity throughout *Ulysses* and to the production of a differentiated narrative and a non-unifiable experience of time.

The next passage I shall consider occurs in the 'Oxen of the Sun' episode. It is well known that this episode abounds in levels of organization. Joyce's letter to Budgen testifies to this:

> Am working hard at *Oxen of the Sun*, the idea being the crime committed against fecundity by sterilizing the act of coition. Scene, lying-in hospital. Technique: a nineparted episode without divisions introduced by a Sallustian–Tacitean prelude (the unfertilized ovum), then by way of earliest English alliterative and monosyllabic and Anglo-Saxon . . . then by way of Mandeville . . . then Malory's *Morte d'Arthur* . . . then the Elizabethan chronicle style . . . then a passage solemn, as of Milton, Taylor, Hooker, followed by a choppy Latin-gossipy bit, style of Burton-Browne, then a passage Bunyanesque . . . after a diarystyle bit Pepys–Evelyn . . . and so on through Defoe—Swift and Steel—Addison—Sterne and Landor—Pater— Newman until it ends in a frightful jumble of pidgin English, nigger

English, Cockney, Irish, Bowery slang and broken doggerel. This progression is also linked back at each part subtly with some foregoing episode of the day and, besides this, with the natural stages of development in the embryo and the periods of faunal evolution in general. The double-thudding of the Anglo-Saxon motif recurs from time to time . . . to give the sense of the hoofs of oxen. Bloom is the spermatozoon, the hospital the womb, the nurse the ovum, Stephen the embryo.[59]

Patterns of conception, gestation, and birth are emphasized at each level of the episode's organization. As the episode progresses, a certain evolutionary process gets enacted on each of these levels. The most noticeable of such levels are the human body, the earth, and language.

The invocation in the opening lines displays several interesting elements in the textual machinery. It produces the tension we encountered earlier between discreteness and contiguous connections, the problem of linguistic series, and the paradoxical logic of prefiguration on which textual repetition is based. The first sentence presents three different languages, not related to one another except through their participation in the same sentence.[60] This combination of connectedness at one level and disconnectedness at another is repeated with respect to the relations between the three sentences that constitute the invocation. Their contents, concerns, and rhetorical tropes differ. However, they partake in the exclamatory tone of the entire invocation and provide a brief drama of affirmative decision, prayer, and exultation.

The presence of different languages in the opening sentence brings in another significant concern. The recapitulation of the history of the English prose style is one of the structural principles of continuity in the episode. The invocation has to be outside the series—it even precedes the original element in the series. This is accomplished through the contingent juxtaposition of different languages. The second sentence of the invocation occupies a different level in its invocation of the sun and, thus, of the schema. And the third and the last sentence, in recording the midwife's exultant cry when she identifies the child's sex, creates the structure of prefiguration with which we are familiar by now. The midwife

---

[59] *Letters*, i. 139–40.
[60] Don Gifford and Robert J. Seidman, *Notes for Joyce: An Annotation of James Joyce's 'Ulysses'* (New York: E. P. Dutton, 1974), 136.

has not appeared in the text yet. Thus the invocation becomes already a retrospection, occupying the level of a second reading.

In organizing the 'Oxen of the Sun', Joyce worked with an embryonic chart which is in fact a catalogue of differences that appear with each month in the embryo's growth.[61] The growth of the embryo culminates in the human body through a process of increasing differentiation. This is made present in the body of the text by a deployment of semantemes. Similarly, faunal evolution is also suggested in the text at times. But neither of these series is consistently visible. The parallels between the characters and the agents in the microcosmic drama of fertilization occupy a different level altogether. All these point to an asymmetry in the operation of the schematic deployments in the 'Oxen of the Sun' episode as well. I shall, for the moment, concern myself with the most visible of all series—that of English prose style.

Stuart Gilbert, in his exegetical work on *Ulysses*, points out that Joyce seems to have abandoned the Sallustian–Tacitean prelude as representative of the unfertilized ovum.[62] The unfertilized ovum precedes figuration but, if represented in terms of this figure, would occupy the inner space of the innermost ring. The problem of representing the unfertilized stage in the evolution of English prose style is analogous. It is outside and inside the language of the Anglo-Saxon series. Joyce represents this stage in the 'Oxen of the Sun' as a 'chaos'. Gilbert describes this passage (*U*, 14. 7–32) as an imitation of the style of the English translations of some medieval Latin tracts on childbirth. The convolution of the style is evident:

Universally that person's acumen is esteemed very little perceptive concerning whatsoever matters are being held as most profitably by mortals with sapience endowed to be studied who is ignorant of that which the most in doctrine erudite and certainly by reason of that in them high mind's ornament deserving of veneration constantly maintain when by general consent they affirm that other circumstances being equal by no exterior splendour is the prosperity of a nation more efficaciously associated than by the measure of how far forward may have progressed the tribute of its solicitude for that proliferant continuance which of evils the original if it be absent when fortunately present constitutes the certain sign of omnipollent nature's incorrupted benefaction. (*U*, 14. 7–17)

---

[61] See Joyce, '*Ulysses*' *Notesheets*, 162–5.

[62] Stuart Gilbert, *James Joyce's 'Ulysses': A Study* (Harmondsworth: Penguin, 1963), 257 n.

Just as the unfertilized ovum can be represented in a space surrounded by the convolutions of its own potential history, the pre-series language can be represented in terms of the convolutions— the product of later moments in the series. The equivocal relation of this moment to the rest of the series is captured in the choice of the translated text as model. Instead of going back to the origins of English prose, it goes to the translations of medieval Latin texts for models. The translation occupies a later moment within the series of evolutionary stages in the history of English prose. But Latin is outside the series. One can see a problematization of the notion of origin in this choice. What is presented here is not an undifferentiated plenitude but the conscious disruption of a series. This implies a non-linear and complex organization of temporality.

This aspect of 'Oxen of the Sun' is accentuated by the pervasive use of textual repetitions. As mentioned earlier, 'Oxen of the Sun' makes this into a schematic aspect. Through a repetition of verbal fragments that we have already encountered within the text of the episode, it is connected to the earlier episodes in the novel. Examples of this, amply available in the episode, would include 'Zarathustra' (*U*, 14. 363, 14. 1431, 1. 728), 'wheatkidneys' (*U*, 14. 155, 3. 119), 'whatness' (*U*, 9. 84–5, 14. 399–400). In the preceding chapter, I examined the prevalence of such repetition and the emergence of a textual memory, and tried to show how this level of textual memory complicates an interpretative attempt to contain the narrative in terms of fictional organization or of the schema. Instead it facilitates the emergence of newer levels on which continuity needs to be traced, thus resisting the linearity of the narrative progress.

The last paragraph I shall consider in this chapter concerns the presentation of the theme of time in 'Circe' (*U*, 15. 4054–245). This includes the 'Dance of the Hours' and Stephen's breaking of the chandelier. I have discussed above the variety and inconsistency in the interpretative unifications in *Ulysses* and the resultant non-totalizable nature of its temporal organization. In relation to the opposition between public time that pertains to the naturalistic impulse of *Ulysses* and the stasis implied in the schematic impulse, it can be argued that there is an ultimate subordination of the former to the latter. This submission of the naturalistic to the schematic is symptomatically represented in the presentation of specific hours for the episodes in the schema. 'Penelope' is kept outside this determination in the Gilbert–Gorman plan and the Linati schema assigns infinity as its time. Thus public, measurable time is made into a determined aspect attributed to some specific episodes. 'Circe' seems to reaffirm this in that this element is fantastically objectified in the 'Dance of the Hours' that happens there. Elements represented at different levels in the text are re-presented in 'Circe', not in relation to the logic of a continuous narrative as in many other episodes, but to various sequences of fantasy.[63] These fantastic repetitions, as I tried to show in the last chapter, cannot always be contained in terms of characters' memories. The 'Dance of the Hours', seen in this light, could be characterized as the textual presentation, in terms of fantasy, of a structural element. What could this time of fantasy be, when all hours could dance? Would it be some 'beyond' or some extra-temporal terrain? The schema assigns an hour to 'Circe' and at the level of public time, the episode fits into the sequential continuity of preceding and succeeding episodes. This implies that the thematiza-tion of time pertains to specific different levels and that no single level would give us complete access to this concern. The above discussions point in that direction. Another complication in relation to the context under discussion is provided by the connection, at the level of textual memory, between Bloom's musings on Ponchielli's 'Dance of the Hours' (*U*, 4. 525–36) and the present passage (*U*, 15. 4054–101). This would bring in two additional levels—verbal repetition and allusion free from character.

Similarly, the smashing of the chandelier, at the level of its concern with time and in relation to Stephen, recalls the opening of 'Proteus' where time is related, without any conceptual resolution, to a whole network of ideas—the modalities of the visible and the audible, space and time, Hamlet, Lessing, the Christian conceptions of eternity and change. Both 'Proteus' and 'Circe', being episodes of transformation, concern themselves thematically with the tension between identity and flux. It may not be accidental that the explicit textual moments where time as a concern is presented in *Ulysses* should occur in these episodes. As an allusion, 'time's livid final flame' recalls Blake. In terms of textual memory, it recalls the earlier occurrence of the phrase in 'Nestor' (*U*, 2. 8–10). In addition

---

[63] See John Paul Riquelme, *Teller and Tale in Joyce's Fiction: Oscillating Perspectives* (Baltimore: Johns Hopkins University Press, 1983), app. 2, pp. 235–42.

to all these connections, this moment signifies a halt in the fantasy sequence, when a different order of temporality takes over.

In this chapter, I have examined problems of temporal synthesis in *Ulysses*. We saw the disuniting effects of an ambitiously unifying schematic impulse. We also saw the effects of repetition, of memory, and of the monologue in creating differential temporality. How does this complex experience of time relate to the notion of language and of the literary sign in *Ulysses*? Does the sign conceal an inner temporality, an essential incompleteness and openness, beneath its apparent solidity? It is to these questions that we shall turn in the next chapter.

# 4

## *Ulysses* and the Notion of the Sign

THERE is a fundamental ambiguity about the sign that Joyce manipulates throughout his fiction. It can be described in two ways: (1) by pointing to the function of the sign, and (2) by pointing to its origin. If one describes the ambiguity in terms of function, it can be characterized as a tension between the denotative and the expressive; in terms of origin it is a tension between the public and the private. The sign could represent something in accordance with the public discursive context into which it is inserted. At the same time, it could be expressive of a private intention at variance with the public context of enunciation. In *Ulysses*, two such instances, both productive of light-hearted humour, concern Leopold Bloom:

> Watch! Watch! Silk flash rich stockings white. Watch!
> A heavy tramcar honking its gong slewed between.
> Lost it. Curse your noisy pugnose. Feels locked out of it. Paradise and the peri. Always happening like that. The very moment. Girl in Eustace street hallway Monday was it settling her garter. Her friend covering the display of. *Esprit de corps*. Well, what are you gaping at?
> —Yes, yes, Mr Bloom said after a dull sigh. Another gone.
> —One of the best, M'Coy said. (*U*, 5. 130–7)

Here Bloom's utterance could be inserted into the earlier interior monologue or into the context of the conversation with M'Coy. The variance in the contexts, by thematizing implicitly the disjunction between the internal and the external contexts, produces humour.

> —I was just going to throw it away, Mr Bloom said.
> Bantam Lyons raised his eyes suddenly and leered weakly.
> —What's that? his sharp voice said.
> —I say you can keep it, Mr Bloom answered. I was going to throw it away that moment.
> Bantam Lyons doubted an instant, leering: then thrust the outspread sheets back on Mr Bloom's arms.
> —I'll risk it, he said. Here, thanks. (*U*, 5. 534–41)

Here the insertion of 'throw it away' into a different discursive context is presented explicitly.

If these examples provide us with two distinct discourses, one internal to the speaker's mind and the other external to him, in the *Portrait* and in the early chapters of *Ulysses* one gets another mode of encounter of discourses, this time an instance of conflation. Hugh Kenner has invited attention to this phenomenon under the name 'the Uncle Charles Principle'.[1] It consists in the conflation of first-person interior content and third-person exterior narrative form. In Kenner's example, the word 'repair'[2] in the narrative concerning Uncle Charles is justified only in relation to Uncle Charles's own vocabulary. The object of the narrative overbrims and starts colouring the form of that narrative itself. Similarly, in the *Portrait*, we have Stephen's thoughts in a third-person narrative and the idiom of the narrative changes from section to section, indicating the stage of development of Stephen's sensibilities. This gives rise to a certain irony as well, resulting from the difference between the two levels within the same utterance. In the preceding chapter, I examined some instances of the same kind of conflation and the resultant ambiguity of tone in certain passages of *Ulysses*. There it was seen to have given rise to certain sets of disjunctions which would resist interpretative reunion. In *Finnegans Wake*, a pervasive flux, apparently with greater homogeneity, replaces these disjunctions and conflations. But the nature of this flux implies frequent changes in the speaking voice as well as in the stratification of discourses into internal and external.

What I have tried to say concerns a certain preoccupation in Joyce's texts with the ambiguity of signs. This ambiguity is seen to pull the sign in two contrary directions. On the one hand, the sign is meant to represent the external world; on the other hand, it is meant to express how this reality is perceived in the pure privateness of the character's mind:

---

[1] Hugh Kenner defines the principle in *Joyce's Voices* (London: Faber & Faber, Ltd., 1978), 18: 'So let us designate the Uncle Charles Principle: *the narrative idiom need not be the narrator's.*'

[2] 'It would be Uncle Charles' own word should he chance to say what he was doing. ... Not that he does so speak in our hearing. Rather, a speck of that characterizing vocabulary attends our sense of him. ... This is apparently something new in fiction, the normally neutral narrative vocabulary pervaded by a little cloud of idioms which a character might use if he were managing the narrative.' (Ibid. 17.)

The [reader] would be installed in the thought of the main character from the first lines on, and it is the uninterrupted unfolding of that thought which substituting for the customary forms of narrative, [would] apprise us of what the character does and what happens to him.[3]

Against this aspiration of the stream-of-consciousness method, it has been argued that the characters' private thoughts are not linguistic all the time.[4] However, literary discourse necessitates the representation or expression of the characters' inner life in language—in finding verbal formulas for their thoughts, perceptions, and actions. Not only that. In externalizing the characters' thoughts in the form of discourses that circulate within the text, the author already accomplishes a conversion of those thoughts into the public realm. Whatever private discursive world the sign belongs to can only be inferred from an external investigation of the sign. The world that the sign comes from has to be constituted retrospectively through a reading of signs.[5]

We are familiar with some of the devices that Joyce uses in order to indicate the sources of signs. The discursive norms that organize the monologues of various characters are different. We have a difference in rhythm, concerns, and content. One would be arguing in a circle if one started from these worlds as givens and then moved on to consider the linguistic rendering of them. The world of each character is constituted as a repertoire of signs and of particular ways of combining them. However, at the same time, some signs keep recurring in all the different repertoires and make a conceptualization of external reality possible. In the chapter on the modes of repetition in *Ulysses*, I referred to the role of a certain kind of repetition in stabilizing this sense of reality. Thus the sign points in two contrary directions. One is that of the external world

[3] Reported by Valery Larbaud, preface to Edouard Dujardin's *Les Lauriers sont coupés* (Paris: Bibliothèque 10/18, 1968), 9.

[4] Wyndham Lewis, *Time and Western Man* (London: Chatto & Windus, Ltd., 1927), 121–2. Lewis cites from his *Art of being Ruled* (ch. 4, pt. 12): 'He had to pretend that we were really surprising the private thought of a real and average human creature, Mr Bloom. But the fact is that Mr Bloom was abnormally *wordy*. He *thought in words*, not images, for our benefit, in a fashion as unreal, from the point of view of the strictest naturalist dogma, as a Hamlet soliloquy.'

[5] An interesting instance for illustration would be Erwin R. Steinberg's reading of 'Penelope' in his *Stream of Consciousness and Beyond in 'Ulysses'* (Pittsburgh: University of Pittsburgh Press, 1973), where inferences about the character are made from a textual analysis of the monologue and of the recurrent syntactic structures in it.

and the other, that of the repertoires of signs, internal to the text.

*And no more turn aside and brood.*
   His gaze brooded on his broad toed boots, a buck's castoffs *nebeneinander.* (*U*, 3. 445–7)

The second occurrence of the word 'brood' refers, at the same time, to an action in the denotative way and refers us to the previous occurrence of 'brood'—a word that is expressive here of Stephen's private world. The *'nebeneinander'* breaks from the third-person narrative and refers to the group of signs that constitutes Stephen's world. In referring to these groups, the text makes present some traces which are indicative of the origin of the sign. These traces are present, not by replacing the referential use of the signs of question, but as additional points of suggestion, pointing to a new level in the narrative.

   The real point at issue here is a transgression of the classical distinction between 'mimesis' and 'diegesis'. In Plato's use of this distinction, 'diegesis' involves the author speaking in his own voice and 'mimesis', the imitation of the character's discourse.[6] The distinction implies a value-judgement in terms of truth and authenticity since mimesis involves a masking of real identities. The philosophical underpinnings of this could indeed be traced to the theory of forms. Gérard Genette has reintroduced these terms into critical vocabulary, where mimesis and diegesis define the proportion of elements in the text that give information, to the elements that indicate the presence of the informer (narrator) in the narration:

Finally, therefore, we will have to mark the contrast between mimetic and diegetic by a formula such as: *information* + *informer* = *C*, which implies that the quantity of information and the presence of the informer are in inverse ratio, mimesis being defined by a maximum of information and a minimum of the informer, diegesis by the opposite relationship.[7]

The diegetic narrative is presented as contaminated by the mimetic material it is meant to circumscribe and command. Once this

   [6] See Plato's *Republic*, 392c–395: ' "Is not everything that is said by fabulists or poets a narration of past, present, or future things?" "What else could it be," he said. "Do not they proceed either by pure narration [*diegesis*] or by a narrative that is effected through imitation [*mimeseos gegenomenei*] or by both?" ' (Plato, *Republic*, tr. Paul Shorey (Cambridge, Mass.: Harvard University Press, 1953), 225.)
   [7] Gérard Genette, *Narrative Discourse*, tr. Jane E. Lewin (Oxford: Basil Blackwell, 1980), 166.

contamination starts undermining the hierarchical dominance of a diegetic discourse, the very foundation of that distinction is put into question. The privileging of the diegetic over the mimetic is grounded on a principle of translatability. The mimetic would be amenable to a process of translation and integration to a higher level, as is evidenced in Plato's attempt to rewrite parts of Homer. This process of ascending integration can be seen to have been put to use to a bewildering extent in such works as *A Thousand and One Nights*, Flaubert's *La Tentation de saint Antoine*,[8] Proust's *À la recherche*,[9] and many of Borges's stories. This gives rise not only to the distinction between mimetic and diegetic discourse, but also between different diegetic levels in these texts. Gérard Genette has studied the stratification of these levels in Proust's narrative. He comments:

any intrusion by the extradiegetic narrator or narratee into the diegetic universe (or by diegetic characters into a metadiegetic universe, etc.) or the inverse . . . produces an effect of strangeness that is either comical or fantastic.[10]

For example, as Borges remarks,

those inversions suggest that if the characters in a story can be readers or spectators, then we, their readers or spectators, can be fictitious.[11]

The adulteration of the diegetic by the mimetic does not have this as an immediate result. But by blurring the elementary distinction which would open up a hierarchy of diegetic levels, it makes such a hierarchy impossible. There is no pure diegesis that is totally free from the mimetic impulse. Diegetic discourse too displays a complicity with what it seeks to depict. This makes it difficult for a higher level of diegesis to emerge, either within the text or at the level of the 'arranger'. If the diegetic is already mimetic, the act of arranging would not be entirely free from the same contagion.

A comparison with Proust would not be out of place here. Proust manages a coalescence of extreme mimetic depiction and extreme

---

[8] See Michel Foucault, 'Fantasia of the Library', in id., *Language, Counter-Memory, Practice*, ed. D. F. Bouchard, tr. D. F. Bouchard and Sherry Simon (Oxford: Basil Blackwell, 1977), 87–109.

[9] See Genette, *Narrative Discourse*, esp. the sections on 'Mood', 161–211, and 'Voice', 212–62.      [10] Ibid. 234–5.

[11] Borges, *Other Inquisitions 1937–1952* (New York: Simon and Schuster, 1965), 46.

diegetic commentary by resorting to the 'mediated intensity' of the remembered image.[12] What is remembered is, even after a temporal lapse, modally immediate. This actually comes about by locating the mimetic and the diegetic levels as two phases of maturity within the narrator. The moment of the experience recalled and the moment of the enunciation are mediated by a redemptive memory and a generosity[13] characteristic of autobiographical narratives.

Joyce's fiction, even with the *Bildungsroman* affinities of the *Portrait*, resists such an autobiographical unification. The mediating elements are made to produce a conflation of levels that would create ambiguity and disjunction rather than unity. What Proust accomplishes through an evocative use of the past imperfect[14] which would simultaneously play upon the intensity of the past experience and the adequacy of present reflection, Joyce resists and denies by a use of the simple present and a diegetic simple past[15]

---

[12] Genette, *Narrative Discourse*, 168. Genette observes, 'But the marvel of the Proustian narrative (like that of Rousseau's *Confessions*, which here again we must put side by side with it) is that this *temporal distance* between the story and the narrating instance involves no *modal distance* between the story and the narrative: no loss, no weakening of the mimetic illusion. Extreme mediation, and at the same time utmost immediacy. That too is perhaps symbolized by the rapture of reminiscence.' (Ibid. 168–9.)

[13] Jay Bernstein in his study of the emergence of the concept of self in the novel, defines 'generosity' as 'self esteem deriving from the autonomous operation of the will' and argues that 'as generosity transforms autobiography from history into fiction, autobiography transforms generosity from an ethic of self-possession into an epistemological quest for lost times and past selves.' (Id., *Philosophy of the Novel: Lukács, Marxism and the Dialectic of Form* (Brighton: Harvester Press, 1984, 171, 177.)

[14] Proust commenting on Flaubert noted 'how a particular use of the past definite, the present participle and of certain pronouns and prepositions has renewed our vision of things almost to the same extent as Kant, with his categories renewed our theories of knowledge and of the reality of the external world.' (Marcel Proust, *A Selection from his Miscellaneous Writings*, ed. and tr. Gerard Hopkins (London: Allan Wingate, 1948), 224.)

[15] This is not true about the later chapters of the novel. However, in the earlier chapters one does find a preponderance of these tenses, though probably not to the same extent as the past imperfect dominates the Proustian narrative. It is interesting to note that the complication of the technique by the intrusive presence of the narrative in episodes from 'Sirens' onwards, also parallels a frequent use of more complex syntactic forms. Groden's thesis about the three compositional stages could find an echo there in so far as the beginning of the second phase marks this phase of complication. Joyce himself valued the role of syntax very highly, as evidenced in the remark he made to Budgen: 'I have the words already. What I am seeking is the perfect order of words in the sentence.' (Frank Budgen, *James Joyce and the Making of 'Ulysses', and Other Writings*, ed. Clive Hart (London: OUP, 1972), 20.)

which, as I have tried to show, refuses assignment to the status of reflective or diegetic unification.

If this is true about the early chapters of *Ulysses*, the picture becomes obviously more complex in the later ones. In the later chapters, instead of referring to the external world and to a group of signs which indicates a character, the sign refers to many groups at the same time. The sign bears on its surface the traces of diverse worlds. The reference to the subjective origin of the sign by using an inventory attached to a particular character continues. But along with it, there emerge the inventories of episodes, of allusions, and of internal repetitions. Thus the origin, the grounding of the sign, gets ruptured and fragmented. The sign seems more to be the product of its circulation, of the history of its alliances. I shall first examine this in relation to repetitions and literary allusions.

## Sign: History and Meaning

One may recall the examples of verbal repetitions that I discussed in my first chapter. The example of 'metempsychosis' (*U*, 4. 339) would suffice to illustrate the case. It gives rise to a series of uses of the word and its supposed mispronunciation by Molly. However, as we saw, these repeated instances are not necessarily contained by the meaning of the word in the first instance of its use.

Mrs Marion. Met him pike hoses. Smell of burn. Of Paul de Kock. Nice name he. (*U*, 11. 500–1)

Here the sign 'Met him pike hoses' bears the trace not of a character's private psychological world. It refers us rather to the earlier instances of the use of the word. It is this history of the uses of the sign that is made present as a trace here. The original sense in which 'metempsychosis' was used is alluded to in a later context:

Nature woman half a look. God made the country man the tune. Met him pike hoses. Philosophy. O rocks! (*U*, 11. 1061–2)

I suggested that this passage invokes an earlier instance in the text where 'metempsychosis' was thematized (*U*, 3. 477–9). Here too, the history of the sign is mobilized for the generation of meaning. However, for a reader who encounters 'Met him pike hoses' here, its history includes 'Mrs Marion. Met him pike hoses.' This use is again invoked in 'Up the quay went . . .' (*U*, 11. 1187–9). The history that is remembered here is not one of ideal repetition with the same sense being realized every time. In each occurrence, something new is added in terms of contextual experience, and traces of the earlier context form part of this new element.

These traces are traces of differences between the various worlds that the sign has passed through. The passage in 'Sirens' (*U*, 11. 1187–9) indeed invokes the earlier occurrence of 'Met him pike hoses' in the same episode, but if we attempt to determine what the phrase means in 'with met him pike hoses went Poldy on', we can only point to this network of traces and remembered contexts. The closest we can get to a substantive meaning of the word is by relating it to *Ruby, Pride of the Ring* or *Sweets of Sin*. However, this relation is mediated through associations evoked and established through the use of the word in the context of erotica.

How can we characterize the traces of the context in which a sign is used? Some of the significant elements in a discursive context include the addresser, addressee, the nature of the enunciative act, etc. In fact, often we infer many of these elements from the way signs are organized in discourse.

Behold the handmaid of the moon. In sleep the wet sign calls her hour, bids her rise. Bridebed, childbed, bed of death, ghostcandled. *Omnis caro ad te veniet.* He comes, pale vampire, through storm his eyes, his bat sails bloodying the sea, mouth to her mouth's kiss. (*U*, 3. 395–8)

This is indeed within the limits of the interior monologue. But one can discern a movement towards the self-consciously poetic, towards the lyrical. Northrop Frye has suggested that the lyric has the mode of an utterance being overheard.[16] Not only is the addressee left indeterminate here, but the question of his existence is also left undecided. It is a discourse which is meant and not meant for the other, which constitutes the speaking subject as the listener as well. A self-conscious literariness manifests itself in the allusions to the Bible, Shakespeare, and the Requiem Mass. The

---

[16] 'The lyric is, to go back to Mill's aphorism referred to at the beginning of this book, pre-eminently the utterance that is overheard. The lyric poet normally pretends to be talking to himself or to someone else: a spirit of nature, a Muse . . . a personal friend, a lover, a god, a personified abstraction . . . The lyric is, as Stephen Dedalus says in Joyce's *Portrait*, the poet presenting the image in relation to himself: it is to *epos*, rhetorically, as prayer is to sermon.' (Northrop Frye, *Anatomy of Criticism* (Princeton, NJ: Princeton University Press, 1957), 249.)

first two lines are exercises in literary composition rather than meaningful allusions. This whole movement culminates in the production of the last two lines which are free of literary echoes but preserve the lyricism of the preceding lines and accentuate it by assonance and alliteration. The act of scribbling it down that happens a few lines later (*U*, 3. 406–7) completes the transition: the monologue has become a lyric, an objectified work of art. Thus there is a movement from the internal to an objectification of the internal, from monologue to lyric, that organizes this piece of discourse. This involves a stratification of levels here if we consider the levels that pertain to memory, meditation, and poetic composition. Comments which are insightful about one level need not be valid in relation to another. The way in which each sign relates to the others is specific to the level they occupy.

Now let us turn to another passage where the same sign occurs:

Then spake young Stephen orgulous of mother Church that would cast him out of her bosom, of law of canons, of Lilith, patron of abortions, of bigness wrought by wind of seeds of brightness or by potency of vampires mouth to mouth or, as Virgilius saith, by the influence of the occident or by the reek of moonflower or an she lie with a woman which her man has but lain with, *effectu secuto*, or peradventure in her bath according to the opinions of Averroes and Moses Maimonides. (*U*, 14. 241–7)

Here the elements that constitute the context are almost entirely different. The status of the addresser and addressee is much more problematic than in the earlier context. The voice is that of the narrator, a concept that we have learnt not to take for granted through our reading of the 'Sirens', 'Nausicaa', 'Cyclops', and the preceding pages of the 'Oxen of the Sun'. The narrator uses Stephen's words and, as in other parts of the 'Oxen of the Sun', keeps repeating elements from the earlier episodes. The phrase 'vampires mouth to mouth' invokes Stephen's poem in two ways. One is at the level of Stephen's memory and of his own allusion, albeit private, to his verse. The other concerns the narrator's repetition of elements. What is invoked here is not memory in a psychological sense, but a context of the use of the sign. The way in which 'mouth to mouth' relates in this passage to the surrounding elements is different from the case in the earlier passage. What is highlighted is the difference in the way signs are organized in these two passages. And it is this difference that opens up the sign's history.

Thus we have the sign's ostensible use and its history differing from each other. In the example under consideration, 'mouth to mouth' ostensibly refers to a spurious medieval theory of impregnation. Its history, on the other hand, would point to the lyricism of the earlier context of its use and invite attention to the different discourses into which the sign has been inserted. The present use of the sign—i.e. its ostensible meaning—does not contain the history of its previous uses. In other words, the lyricism of the earlier use is not contained by the present context. The metaphysical associations of 'metempsychosis' are not contained by its occurrence in the context of erotica. I have suggested, in the second chapter, that the intersection of different discourses beneath the sign opens up an infinite play of identity and difference. This play between history and the present points to the non-totalizable nature of the sign's history within the text. Or, once the repetition of a sign invites attention to itself as an event of repetition, the unification of its history under any single occurrence becomes impossible.

One could argue that this reduction of the sign to contexts extends to some of the situations narrated in the novel as well. The reappearance of images from earlier episodes in 'Circe' is an example of this. For instance, when Bello is auctioning the female-metamorphosed Bloom:

A BIDDER

A florin.
(*Dillon's lacquey rings his handbell.*)

THE LACQUEY

Barang!

A VOICE

One and eightpence too much. (*U*, 15. 3092–8)

This is an allusion to a passage in 'Hades':

—And Reuben J, Martin Cunningham said, gave the boatman a florin for saving his son's life.
    A stifled sigh came from under Mr Power's hand.
—O, he did, Martin Cunningham affirmed. Like a hero. A silver florin.
—Isn't it awfully good? Mr Bloom said eagerly.
—One and eightpence too much, Mr Dedalus said drily. (*U*, 6. 286–91)

The repetition of the sign 'a florin' invokes its earlier context which is presented again. Another example, this time not related to verbal signs, concerns Bloom's potato, Joyce's equivalent for '*Moly*'.

BLOOM

(*with feeling*) It is nothing, but still, a relic of poor mamma.

ZOE

Give a thing and take it back
God'll ask you where is that
You'll say you don't know
God'll send you down below

BLOOM

There is a memory attached to it. I should like to have it. (*U*, 15. 3512–20)

The significance derives from the memory attached to it, from the traces of the contexts in which it was implicated. There is no internal validation of significance—no validation at all except through the series of these alliances. Joyce's own interpretation of this element invokes the question of signhood. He wrote to Budgen in 1920:

*Moly* is a nut to crack. My latest is this. Moly is the gift of Hermes, god of public ways, and is the invisible influence ... which saves in case of accident ... Hermes is the god of signposts: i.e. he is, specially for a traveller like Ulysses, the point at which roads parallel merge and roads contrary also. He is an accident of providence.[17]

'*Moly*' is, schematically, the sign that points in the right direction. In terms of fictional detail in *Ulysses*, its (i.e. Bloom's potato's) significance accrues from its prior history alone. It would not be far-fetched to conceive a similarity between this implication of the sign's significance in its history and the concept of the sign I was describing above. Just as the position of a signpost involves the concurrence of 'roads parallel' and 'roads contrary', the sign involves the confluence of divergent discourses.

   The neutralization of the sign that results from considering signification as a product of the sign's history within the text would, I think, relate to the theme of the fetish and of curiosity for surfaces that we find in Joyce's writings. This theme recurs in Bloom's preoccupation with stockings and undergarments, in Martha's letter, in Gerty's exhibitionism, and in the sexual fantasies of all these characters and of Molly. In the second chapter I pointed out a contrast between 'curiosity' and 'jealousy', the principles underlying the sexual relationships in the fictional worlds of Joyce and Proust respectively. 'Curiosity', in the sense in which I defined

[17] *Letters*, i. 147–8.

the term, concerns itself with surfaces and their mystification so that they can be productive of fantasy. 'Jealousy', on the other hand, relies on a problematic of truth and interpretation so that the other person's private subjective world can be rendered predictable and transparent. If the sign is regarded as an object of depth interpretation in jealousy, in curiosity it is rendered as a fetish, devoid of all innate meaning but open to mystification and appropriation in fantasy. The relationship of the fetish to desire is non-natural and based on a prior context where the object was implicated in desire. The fetishized object is emptied of its usual function. At the same time it is not projected as a symbol of transcendent meaning. The potato does not mean anything; nor do the 'rich stockings'. However, their material presence is absolutely essential for desire to operate. The object, or the fetish, is reduced to a pure surface. This surface is then endowed with a sensual significance that arises from the history of its use. This significance serves as the occasion for the fantasy. My purpose is not to impose a psychological typology on Joyce's use of signs, but to point out a certain similarity of structure and a common reliance on history for the production of meaning in the case of the fetish and in the case of the sign.

The reduction of the signs to their surface is manifested symptomatically in several parts of *Ulysses*. One example of this is indeed the 'man in the macintosh'. The secrecy that surrounds him is essentially a history of curiosity and of investment. All that we know of him for sure, all that his identity in the novel is based on, is a pure surface, a mackintosh. He appears several times in the text, never giving us much more than the sheerest surface details. A deepening of the mystery here is accomplished through repetition— each time he comes up, the history of his appearance extends in complexity. A new invitation for investment or for interpretative speculation is made.

Another moment where the logic of curiosity or of the fetish operates in Joyce is in relation to language itself. Bloom recounts:

Girl in the Meath street that night. All the dirty things I made her say. All wrong of course. My arks she called it. (*U*, 13. 867–9)

There is a specific gratification of desire in its articulation itself. Language here becomes a fetish, like a shoe or a foot, generating its effects through association with the body and with desire. It is not merely that language makes you imagine a certain experience—it constitutes that experience. There are other similar fantasies of language in 'Circe' as well.

All these recall the 'tell me all' motif that recurs several times in *Ulysses* as well as in *Finnegans Wake*. This motif is related in *Ulysses*, not only to the correspondence between Martha and Bloom; it also underlies the meditations on confession in the text:

Confession. Everyone wants to. Then I will tell you all. Penance. Punish me, please. Great weapon in their hands. More than doctor or solicitor. Woman dying to. And I schschschschschsch. And did you chachachachacha? And why did you? Look down at her ring to find an excuse. (*U*, 5. 425–9)

In 'Penelope', Molly recounts the priest's curiosity during confession. This is in some sense anticipated by one of Joyce's early stories, 'The Sisters', where once again there is a configuration of desire, religion, and language. In all these cases, articulation has an intimate relation to desire, the pleasure arising from the use of language as fetish.

The notion of the sign that we have been considering implies a certain primordiality on the part of the sign's history relative to its meaning. Here history means the various uses to which the sign has been put in the history of its repetitions. In other words, repetition is the very condition of the sign's possibility. However, as we saw, certain forms of repetition work to destabilize the sign's meaning. This resistance to totalization becomes an originary character of the sign. This resistance arises from the diversity of the discursive terrains through which the sign passes. In each terrain it acquires a different value which gets imprinted on its surface and which it carries to other terrains. The image that emerges is topographical: different territories where different discursive norms hold.

The *Odyssey* itself has the structure of an adventure in space. The uniqueness of each adventure is reinforced by the specificity and enclosure of each episode. Michel Serres points to this aspect of the epic—that of establishing connections between disjunctive spaces:

The plurality of the disjointed spaces, all different, is the primal chaos, the condition of the series that assembles them. Ulysses' journey, like that of Oedipus, is an itinerary. And it is a discourse the prefix of which I can now understand. It is not at all the discourse (*discours*) of an itinerary (*parcours*), but, radically, the itinerary (*parcours*) of a discourse (*discours*), the course, *cursus*, route, path that passes through the original disjunction, the bridge laid down across crevice ... The global wandering, the mythical adventure, is, in the end, only the general rejoining of these spaces, or as if the object or target of discourse were only to connect, or as if the junction, the relation, constituted the route by which the first discourse passes ... Thus we have Penelope at the theoretical position: the queen who weaves and unweaves, the originally feminine figure who, become male, will be Plato's Royal Weaver ... In the palace of Ithaca, Ulysses, finally in the arms of the queen, finds the finished theory of his own *mythos*.[18]

In *Ulysses*, each site creates its own technique by combining a set of elements specific to itself. Each episode demands a different set of norms for reading, a different way of connecting signs, a different allocation of priorities. Just as the narrative of 'Sirens' is influenced by the model of the fugue, that of the 'Oxen of the Sun' is determined by the passage under pastiche, and that of 'Ithaca' by the structure of catechism. However, as I suggested in the previous chapter, there is no symmetry in the deployment of the schematic elements in different episodes. The preponderance of such elements, their visibility on the surface, their influence on the reading process—all these elements vary from episode to episode, or probably even from one part of the episode to another. The episode appears a convenient unit to go by, primarily because of the importance attributed to it during the novel's composition. The lack of homogeneity in the presence of these elements in various parts of the novel would make it difficult to effect an interpretative unification among all these disjunctive spaces. But, at the same time, one should remember that the schema is symptomatic of an impulse towards totality. The elements charted out in the schema fall into vertical columns designated under the titles colour, technique, hour, organ, etc. Similarly, at the other end of the spectrum, the naturalistic impulse of the novel would also suggest some kind of continuity. This raises the questions of the homogeneity of spaces established by the novel.

Can we translate all the stylistically different episodes into one style, some stylistic *telos* that would have command over all the individual styles and confer specific degrees of intelligibility and value on them? In other words, can the textual diversity of *Ulysses* be ameliorated through a process of translation? We found that the

---

[18] Michel Serres, 'Language and Space: From Oedipus to Zola', in id., *Hermes: Literature and Philosophy* (Baltimore: Johns Hopkins University Press, 1982), 48–9.

repetition of signs in different discursive contexts would resist such a unification. A pure discourse, a homogeneous space, would require the possibility of ideal repetition, repetition of the same as the same.[19] That would imply the reappearance of the sign with the same signification, irrespective of context and of history. One mode of repetition in *Ulysses*, as argued in the second chapter, aspires to this aim and contributes to a stabilization of the experience of reality, whether it be internal as in the case of memories and experiences attributable to psychological subjects or external as in the case of events and the spatio-temporal details shared by different characters. It is this process of stabilization that the other, more disquieting mode of repetition puts into question. At the level of the sign too there are thus two contradictory impulses at work.

It might be more useful to characterize even the relations that obtain between the different discursive spaces in *Ulysses* as contradictory. What unites them, however, is the fact that all of them rely on external determinations of discourse—external principles of organization of the text. Discourse in each episode is produced under a specific grid. This grid is not exhausted by the two schemata that Joyce devised. We find additional schematic elements in his letters, notesheets, etc. The theme of linguistic history in the 'Oxen of the Sun' and the use of correspondences between female genitalia and certain words in the composition of 'Penelope' do not appear in the schemata.[20] However, this does not exclude them from functioning as principles of organization specific to an episode. One finds a proliferation of such principles during the composition of *Ulysses*.

The other element that various discursive spaces share in common is the group of signs that travel through them. These signs evoke the memory of their previous occurrences in the reader's mind. What disunites the episodes, what makes it impossible to produce a homogeneous space by uniting them are: (1) the different ways in which the organizational principles function in different parts of the novel and (2) the disunity I have tried to explore above,

[19] One could relate this to a similar notion in Husserl's concept of language and to Derrida's interpretation, which focuses on the sign's relation to the possibility of ideal repetitions in Husserl. See Jacques Derrida, *Speech and Phenomena and Other Essays on Husserl's Theory of Signs*, tr. David B. Allison (Evanston, Ill.: Northwestern University Press, 1973).

[20] See Richard Ellmann, *Ulysses on the Liffey* (London: Faber & Faber, Ltd., 1972), app.

occasioned by the disjunction between the sign's previous history and its present meaning. Thus the journey of Ulysses, to use the metaphor of the *Odyssey*, leaves each site of adventure inalienably specific, but united through the memory of the adventure and its telling—i.e. the epic. John Paul Riquelme notes that the styles of *Ulysses* are the styles of its teller as Ulysses, as *polytropos*. Here *tropos* means trope, identifying adventure in life with adventure in articulation.[21]

## Mimesis and Diegesis

Let us return to the question of how the signs are combined in various discourses in *Ulysses* and what effects they generate. In 'Ithaca' we find a text that tries to give very detailed answers to all the questions asked. Commenting on the episode, Joyce wrote to Budgen that, in 'Ithaca',

All events are resolved into their cosmic physical, psychical etc. equivalents, e.g. Bloom jumping down the area, drawing water from the tap, the micturition in the garden, the cone of incense, lighted candle and statue so that not only will the reader know everything and know it in the baldest coldest way, but Bloom and Stephen thereby become heavenly bodies, wanderers like the stars at which the[y] gaze.[22]

One can find two distinct orientations in this passage. One of them is towards pseudo-scientific precision in description, the particularity of details reconceptualized in a discourse which aspires to extreme objectivity and generality. It is this translation of particular experience into a jargon of generality that makes the description cold and bald. The second orientation is towards a reinstatement of subjective experience. This is suggested in the transformation of Bloom and Stephen into 'stars' and in the final anthropomorphism which transforms stars into 'wanderers'. The subtle opposition between the subjective and objective can be felt in the tension between affective and pseudo-scientific moments in the answers.

---

[21] John Paul Riquelme, *Teller and Tale in Joyce's Fiction: Oscillating Perspectives* (Baltimore: Johns Hopkins University Press, 1983), 133. See also Fritz Senn, *Joyce's Dislocutions: Essays on Reading as Translation*, ed. J. P. Riquelme (Baltimore: Johns Hopkins University Press, 1984), 128–9.

[22] *Letters*, i. 159–60.

Alone, what did Bloom hear?

The double reverberation of retreating feet on the heavenborn earth, the double vibration of a jew's harp in the resonant lane.

Alone, what did Bloom feel?

The cold of interstellar space, thousands of degrees below freezing point or the absolute zero of Fahrenheit, Centigrade or Réaumur: the incipient intimations of proximate dawn. (*U*, 17. 1242–8)

The phonic imitation of 'reverberation' and 'resonant' in the first answer and the exaggeration of actual information ('thousands of degrees below the freezing point or the absolute zero of Fahrenheit, Centigrade or Réaumur') clearly disregard the aspiration for objective precision.

However, this tension introduces a complication of narrative hierarchies in 'Ithaca'. This episode is written in the form of pure diegesis. No character is allowed his own voice. In this respect 'Ithaca' can be contrasted with 'Penelope' which is presented exclusively as mimetic discourse, where the narrator does not speak at all. But the tension between the affective and the objective introduces some notion of subjectivity into the discourse. However, the subjective moment that colours the language of 'Ithaca' cannot always be attributed to a character. For example, 'The heaventree of stars hung with humid nightblue fruit' (*U*, 17. 1039) and 'Sinbad the Sailor and Tinbad the Tailor and Jinbad the Jailor and Whinbad the Whaler . . .' (*U*, 17. 2322–6) cannot clearly be attributed to Bloom. The presence of subjective perceptions here is rather a principle in the organization of discourse. This creates, as Walton Litz maintains, 'a rhythmic alternation between mythic or "epiphanic" moments and longer stretches of realism which validate these moments'.[23] This alternation is indeed a complication of the apparently diegetic discourse of 'Ithaca'. Diegesis itself imitates some actions or perceptions, trying to imitate their voice.

There are other elements in 'Ithaca' which complicate the diegetic discourse even further. The tone, the degree of complexity, the rhetorical strategies—all these vary from one part of the episode to another.

---

[23]  Walton Litz, 'Ithaca' in Clive Hart and David Hayman (eds.), *James Joyce's 'Ulysses': Critical Essays* (Berkeley, Calif.: University of California Press, 1974), 402.

What did Bloom do at the range?

He removed the saucepan to the left hob, rose and carried the iron kettle to the sink in order to tap the current by turning the faucet to let it flow.

Did it flow?

Yes. From Roundwood reservoir in county Wicklow of a cubic capacity of 2400 million gallons, percolating through a subterranean aqueduct of filter mains of single and double pipeage constructed at an initial plant cost of £5 per linear yard by way of the Dargle, Rathdown, Glen of the Downs and Callowhill to the 26 acre reservoir at Stillorgan, a distance of 22 statute miles, and thence, through a system of relieving tanks, by a gradient of 250 feet to the city boundary at Eustace bridge, upper Leeson street . . . (*U*, 17. 160–70)

This sudden change in the mode of description thematizes the status of the narrator's voice. There is no continuity or homogeneity of attitude on the part of the narrator throughout the episode. This renders the notion of pure diegesis problematic. Moreover, the rules concerning the economy of information in diegetic discourse are violated very often in 'Ithaca'.

A more important complication occurs at the structural level. There are moments in the episode where an extra-diegetic element is introduced under the guise of diegesis.

What universal binomial denominations would be his as entity and nonentity?

Assumed by any or known to none. Everyman or Noman.

What tributes his?

Honour and gifts of strangers, the friends of Everyman. A nymph immortal, beauty, the bride of Noman. (*U*, 17. 2006–11)

Here, the word 'Noman' suggests the correspondence between Bloom and Ulysses. Thus a relationship to the schema is introduced here. Since the schema contains the principles of organization of diegesis in the episode, it can be argued that a violation of diegetic levels occurs here. An element from a higher level of organization seems to be intruding into what we called diegesis. These disturbances of hierarchies render the continuity of the narrative voice even more open to question.

All these discontinuities are, in a sense, anticipated by the catechistic technique of the episode. The catechism of 'Ithaca' produces its effects by sudden changes in discursive contexts. Most questions point to immediate objects of experience while the answers present an immensely mediated discourse of knowledge. There is a sudden change of discursive norms between the questions and the answers. This produces a rift between the discursive expectations that the questions raise in the reader and their actual realizations in the answers. Like the alternating asymmetry of the two discourses in 'Cyclops', here too Joyce employs a dialectical technique to produce disjunctions.

How can one characterize this relationship of the diegetic discourse to the schematic technique that organizes it? I would suggest that this relation displays a strong mimetic impulse. The diegesis of 'Ithaca' imitates catechism. This is one of the prominent aspects of Joyce's complication or disturbance of narrative hier-archies and of the distinction between diegesis and mimesis. Could this be extended to other parts of *Ulysses*? We shall briefly examine some aspects of the narrative organization in 'Sirens'. In this episode, one strong mimetic impulse is evidenced in the interior monologue. The thoughts of the character, his perceptions, memories, and actions, the entire interior drama of the psyche is presented in an immediate fashion, i.e. unmediated by diegesis. But how does diegesis or narration function in 'Sirens'?

Bald deaf Pat brought quite flat pad ink. Pat set with ink pen quite flat pad. Pat took plate dish knife fork. Pat went. (*U*, 11. 847–8)

Bloom heard a jing, a little sound. He's off. Light sob of breath Bloom sighed on the silent bluehued flowers. Jingling. He's gone. Jingle. Hear. (*U*, 11. 457–8)

Compare these passages to the following:

Wish I could see his face, though. Explain better. Why the barber in Drago's always looked my face when I spoke his face in the glass. Still hear it better here than in the bar though farther. (*U*, 11. 721–3)

The syntax of the first two passages shows a manipulation of language different from the last one and unfamiliar in the earlier episodes. The accumulation of adjectives, the inversion of noun and adjective, or object and subject, the repetition of monosyllables with the same phonemic structure—all these details point to this. Critics tend to explain these syntactic and phonic deviations in relation to the theme of music and to the structure of the fugue. But Bloom's monologue does not betray these characteristics. The

broken fragments of sentences which constitute it show a closeness
to the monologues in the earlier episodes.

Something new and easy. No great hurry. Keep it a bit. Our prize titbit:
*Matcham's Masterstroke*. Written by Mr Philip Beaufoy, Playgoers' Club,
London. (*U*, 4. 501–3)

The monologues of Bloom are less unfamiliar than the narration in
this episode. It is the narration that is imitating the musical
structure. But narration, as we saw earlier, occupies the position of
diegesis as opposed to mimesis. But here, as in the case of 'Ithaca',
diegesis seems to be mimetic of the technic. This is an instance of
transgression of the distinction between the mimetic and the
diegetic. The narration mediates between the mimetic passage that
depicts Bloom's thoughts or the conversations of characters, but it
is itself mimetic of the schematic technique that dominates the
episode.

Now let us examine a passage from 'Penelope':

frseeeeeeeefronnnng train somewhere whistling the strength those
engines have in them like big giants and the water rolling all over and out
of them all sides like the end of Loves old sweeeetsonnnng the poor men
that have to be out all the night from their wives and families in those
roasting engines stifling it was today . . . (*U*, 18. 596–600)

Here, as in the monologue of Bloom that we cited earlier, mimesis
happens at the level of the depiction of character's thoughts. But a
second level, that of the interconnection of mimetic details, is also
provided by the monologue. The schematic technic in the Linati
schema is 'Monologue Resigned Style' and in the Gilbert–Gorman
plan 'Monologue (female)'.[24] However, here too, both in conception and in technique, Joyce resorts to other non-mimetic elements.
In a letter to Harriet Shaw Weaver after the publication of *Ulysses*,
Joyce remarked:

I have rejected the usual interpretations of her [Penelope] as a human
apparition—that apparition being represented by Calypso, Nausikaa and
Circe, to say nothing of the pseudo-Homeric figures. In conception and
technique, I tried to depict the earth which is pre-human and presumably
post-human.[25]

During the composition of 'Penelope', Joyce had already compared it to 'the huge earth ball slowly and surely and evenly round

---

[24] See Ellmann, *Ulysses on the Liffey*, app.     [25] *Letters*, i. 18.

and round spinning', its four cardinal points being parts of the female body, expressed by the words, 'because', 'bottom', 'woman', and 'yes'.[26] Thus the impulse towards mimetic fidelity in 'Penelope' works in conjunction with external regularities that form a discursive grid. This grid does not depict anything in a mimetic way. It is a set of correspondences Joyce designed for imposing order on the monologue. The correspondences are not self-evident; Joyce did not derive them from any prior texts. They regulate the interconnections between elements at the mimetic level by providing some signs with an additional dimension.

Is not the relation of the diegetic discourse to the schema realized by first reducing the technic to a set of abstract and sometimes arbitrary principles or regularities? Does not the 'Sirens' narration imitate the fugue structure by reducing it through a process of abstraction? Bloom thematizes such a process in his monologue:

> Numbers it is. All music when you come to think. Two multiplied by two divided by half is twice one. Vibrations: chords those are. One plus two plus six is seven. Do anything you like with figures juggling. Always find out this equal to that. Symmetry under a cemetery wall. He doesn't see my mourning. Callous: all for his own gut. Musemathematics. And you think you're listening to the etherial. But suppose you said it like: Martha, seven times nine minus x is thirtyfive thousand. Fall quite flat. It's on account of the sounds it is. (*U*, 11. 830–7)

Such a reduction happens in 'Ithaca' too. Catechism is converted into a series of strategies of exaggerated precision. In 'Oxen of the Sun' the history of English prose style is reduced to a finite number of authors and a finite number of stylistic features of certain texts. In 'Aeolus' rhetoric is presented as the realm of interrelations by the deployment of a number of rhetorical figures.[27] But the regularities such a reduction engenders vary from case to case. The mode of operation of these regularities, as we have seen in our examination of passages from 'Ithaca', 'Sirens', and 'Penelope', also varies. All they have in common is the possession of discursive regularities which are external to the mimetic impulses of the passages. In the episodes which rely on the monologue as the primary strategy of

[26] Ibid. 170.
[27] See, for a list of rhetorical figures deployed in 'Aeolus', Don Gifford and Robert J. Seidman, *Notes for Joyce: An Annotation of James Joyce's 'Ulysses'* (New York: E. P. Dutton, 1974), app., pp. 519–25.

mimesis, this involves a manipulation of the style of the monologue ('Nausicaa'), a careful manipulation of some signs within it ('Penelope') or a distinction in terms of stylistic strategies between the narration and the monologue ('Sirens'). In the earlier chapters the strategy seems to be more thematic. In 'Lestrygonians', Joyce relies on a continuous use of motifs of food.

> Poor Mrs Purefoy! Methodist husband. Method in his madness. Saffron bun and milk and soda lunch in the educational dairy. Y.M.C.A. Eating with a stopwatch, thirtytwo chews to the minute. And still his muttonchop whiskers grew. (*U*, 8. 358–61)

> At Duke lane a ravenous terrier choked up a sick knuckly cud on the cobblestones and lapped it with new zest. Surfeit. Returned with thanks having fully digested the contents. First sweet then savoury. . . . Their upper jaw they move. Wonder if Tom Rochford will do anything with that invention of his? (*U*, 8. 1031–5)

It is interesting to notice that the motifs of food in these passages were introduced later during the revisions. Joyce once told Budgen:

> Walking towards his lunch my hero, Leopold Bloom, thinks of his wife, and says to himself, 'Molly's legs are out of plumb.' At another time of day he might have expressed the same thought without any underthought of food.[28]

In 'Nestor' history is presented as a thematic concern in the monologue. Here the words that relate to the second level, that of interrelations, are not related to it through arbitrary correspondences but through direct thematization.

This way of generating inference which we called the second level is different from the strategies we found in 'Sirens', 'Nausicaa', and 'Penelope'. It is different from the strategies of the later non-monologic episodes. For example, in 'Oxen of the Sun', the mimetic level is abandoned. We have, instead, a series of narrative voices mimicking the prose styles of different ages and authors. Does a continuous perception of the real in the form of a linear narrative emerge from this? If it does, what kind of transformations of these styles will produce that narrative? I shall examine these questions at the conclusion of this chapter by an analysis of a passage from the 'Oxen of the Sun'. Similarly, the oscillation of contrary narrative voices in the 'Cyclops' and of a theatrical arrangement of fantastic

---

[28] Budgen, *James Joyce*, 21.

images in the 'Circe' point to new forms of interrelation of levels. The tiredness of 'Eumaeus' is produced at the level of stylistic rhythm and of the length of sentences in the narrative. All these point to a use of distinct discursive regularities in different episodes, thus determining the alliance of signs variously.

The tensions between the interior monologue and narration and the peculiar set of problems they give rise to, seem to make it necessary to speak of an essential heterogeneity in Joyce's understanding of language. Language seems to occupy a space, fluid and indeterminate, between the interior monologue and narration. The opposition which the text initially relies on—namely mimesis and diegesis—is progressively violated. Each site of adventure is left specific: the norms of one do not apply in the same way in another. But is this entirely true of the earlier chapters? There is an asymmetry in the use of schematic impulses, in the interrelations between mimesis and diegesis or monologue and narration, in the earlier episodes and in the later ones. Groden's comments on this asymmetry are instructive:

From the start of his work on *Ulysses*, Joyce's interior monologue technique produced a gradual revelation of characters through their fragmentary thoughts and memories, but much of the 'spatial' aspect of the book resulted from his 1921 revisions. During his last six months of work, he intensified the pattern of symbols, motifs and personal histories. His work on the symbols relates to the schema that he prepared in late 1921; that plan essentially reflects this aspect of his work. In some cases he took elements already in the book and found symbolic and schematic values for them.[29]

This may account for the thematic presentation of the 'art' in the earlier episodes. And it can help us understand the continuity of the narrative in the early chapters in contrast to the episodic disjunction in the later ones. But the later revisions render this distinction anything but absolute. The process of 'spatialization', a term Groden borrows from Joseph Frank,[30] affects the earlier chapters also. It has been argued, in relation to 'Ithaca', that the object of

[29] Michael Groden, *'Ulysses' in Progress* (Princeton, NJ: Princeton University Press, 1977), 196–7.

[30] Joseph Frank, 'Spatial Form in Modern Literature', in id., *Widening Gyre: Crisis and Mastery in Modern Literature* (New Brunswick, NJ: Rutgers University Press, 1963), 8–9. See Ch. 3, above, for a discussion of the theory of spatial form.

pastiche is the episodic technique itself.[31] This relates, in my opinion, to the implicit thematization of the discursive regularities in the disjunction of levels and their interrelation, in each episode.

If episodes are discursive spaces ruled by different norms, what kind of narrative does *Ulysses* constitute? It certainly points to different levels of continuity in the schema—the structure of a day, historical detail pertaining to 16 June 1904, Dublin, the human body, the encyclopaedia, the *Odyssey*. It preserves the heterogeneity of terrains but establishes the only kind of continuity possible, that of the adventures of discourse. One could argue that this is the position of the author, the arranger. But the arranger is only the origin of so many asymmetries and disjunctions that no interpretation can unify.

### Sign and Tradition

Joyce's encounter with the tradition of representation is all too evident in the preponderance of literary allusions in *Ulysses*. I considered some aspects of the structure of allusions under the more general category of repetition. To connect that discussion to our present consideration of the literary sign, we shall first reconsider the contextual traces that the sign bears. In the case of allusions, these traces come from a world that is external to the text of *Ulysses*. The inventory of signs that an allusion refers to is another text with its own specific ways of aligning signs together. However, traces of its original context of use are carried to the text of *Ulysses* by the sign. To give an example,

The good bishop of Cloyne took the veil of the temple out of his shovel hat: veil of space with coloured emblems hatched on its field. (*U*, 3. 416–18)

There is an allusion to Bishop Berkeley and one to Mallarmé here. The first allusion takes shape through Stephen's earlier reference to Berkeley and through the discussion of optics present generally in the episode and particularly in the lines that follow the passage.

Hold hard. Coloured on a flat: yes, that's right. Flat I see, then think distance, near, far, flat I see, east, back. Ah, see now! Falls back suddenly, frozen in stereoscope. (*U*, 3. 418–20)

[31] Harold D. Baker, 'Rite of Passage: 'Ithaca', Style and the Structure of *Ulysses*', *JJQ* 23: 3 (1986), 277.

The interpretative possibilities this opens up can be illustrated by Thornton's gloss on this passage:

Father W. T. Noon suggests that Stephen's allusion to Berkeley 'grows out of his own optical experiments as he walks beside the sea, and suggests some familiarity on Joyce's part with Berkeley's 'Essay Toward a New Theory of Vision', in which Berkeley sets out to establish that the sense qualities are 'inside the head' (*JA*, p. 113). Stephen's remark about the bishop does seem to go to the core of Berkeley's philosophy. The veil of the temple which separated the holy from the most holy . . . probably refers to Berkeley's going beyond Locke in saying that not only secondary qualities but reality itself is mental. Stephen's statement about the veil and the shovel hat means that Berkeley found reality inside his head.[32]

What I intend to suggest does not concern the validity of any of these remarks. It concerns, rather, a process that the allusion sets in motion. A sign (here, 'bishop of Cloyne') that carries traces from outside the text puts into motion an attempt to connect it with the neighbouring signs. This involves, on the critic's part, an effort to bestow new significance on these signs so that they relate better to the traces from outside the text. Here, for example, Thornton attributes a new significance to the 'veil of the temple' by taking it as symptomatic of the distinction between the positions of Locke and Berkeley. Similarly, the 'shovel hat', referring ostensibly to Berkeley's protestantism, is made to suggest the discovery of reality 'inside one's head'. A similar search for suggestive details goes on in relation to the world where the sign comes from. The neighbouring signs that point to experiments in optics make possible a relation to one specific text that Berkeley wrote: 'Essay towards a New Theory of Vision'.

Thus the traces from outside the text that an allusion carries trigger off a process of reading which bestows new significance on the neighbouring signs. A proliferation of traces results from putting one trace into play. The interesting result of this is that the text that is alluded to remains implicitly present, tacit, and available for reactivation during the reading of the entire novel. When Bloom experiments with his vision, the range of interpretative possibilities includes making connections to Berkeley's text and its earlier use in *Ulysses* (*U*, 8. 564–70, 15. 1841).

[32] Weldon Thornton, *Allusions in 'Ulysses': An Annotated List* (Chapel Hill, NC: North Carolina University Press, 1968), 63. For another discussion of the passage, see Pierre Vitoux, 'Aristotle, Berkeley and Newman in "Proteus" and *Finnegans Wake*', *JJQ* 18: 2 (1981), 161–75.

Thus allusion occasions the dissemination of traces from another text onto signs in the present text. For the reader or for the critic, it makes sense to speak of a collection of the texts alluded to. This collection or repertoire forms the background of a reading of *Ulysses*, rendering it open to remembrance at any point. It is this repertoire that I called the tradition of representation. What is the function of such a collection? In my opinion, it indicates in an asymptotic fashion, the site of the prior alliances of all signs within the text. If so much of what is said in the novel consciously demands that attention be given to its previous use inside or outside the text, if paying attention to such a demand has implications for our reading, it indicates the profound complicity of the sign's signification with the history of its use. What relationship to history would involve such a complicity?

Derrida's comparison of the projects of Husserl and Joyce provides us with a certain way of addressing these questions. An examination of this text will not be out of place here because it takes up many of our present concerns: the sign, repetition and historicity.

Since equivocity always evidences a certain depth of development and concealment of a past, and when one wishes to assume and *interiorize* the memory of a culture in a kind of *recollection (Erinnerung)* in the Hegelian sense, one has, facing this equivocity, the choice of two endeavours. One would resemble that of James Joyce: to repeat and take responsibility for all equivocation itself, utilising a language that could equalize the greatest possible synchrony with the greatest potential for buried, accumulated and interwoven intentions within each linguistic atom, each vocable, each word, each simple proposition, in all worldly cultures and their most ingenious forms (mythology, religion, sciences, arts, literature, politics, philosophy and so forth). And, like Joyce, this endeavour would try to make the structural unity of all empirical culture appear in the generalized equivocation of a writing that, no longer translating one language into another on the basis of their common cores of sense, circulates through all languages at once, accumulates their energies, actualizes their most secret resonances, discloses their furthermost common horizons, cultivates their associative syntheses instead of avoiding them, and rediscovers the poetic value of passivity.[33]

This manipulation of radical equivocity is more characteristic of *Finnegans Wake* than of *Ulysses*. The circulation of sense through

[33] Jacques Derrida, *Edmund Husserl's 'Origin of Geometry': An Introduction*, tr. J. P. Leavy (Brighton: Harvester Press, 1978), 102.

many languages at the same time and the use of 'buried, accumulated ... intentions within each linguistic atom' are pervasively present in *Finnegans Wake*. But these tendencies are not entirely absent in *Ulysses*. Derrida characterizes Joyce's project as having proceeded from 'a certain anti-historicism and a will to "awake" from the "nightmare" of "history", a will to master the nightmare in a "total and present resumption"'.[34] This aspiration is present in *Ulysses* in its attempt to present the *Odyssey*, the epic of two races, the human body, a medieval encyclopaedia, and all these under the empirical rubric of a day in Dublin.

However, if the pun is the epitome of the strategies of *Finnegans Wake*, that of *Ulysses* is the allusion. The pun or portmanteau word complicates the sign by conflating two different signs, thus making it resonate with a surplus of signification. The allusion, on the other hand, refers to a specific context within the history of the sign, thus complicating its structure by putting into play the history of its use. In a reading of *Finnegans Wake*, a knowledge of the languages it uses, or at least of the senses in different languages that are put to use, becomes essential for intelligibility. A reading of *Ulysses*, on the other hand, does not always require a knowledge of allusions for elementary intelligibility. As we have seen, one can follow the ostensible contextual sense of signs. However, the strategies used in organizing the text—such as the division of discourses into heterogeneous episodic spaces, repetition, asymmetry of schematic structuring—invite attention to the history of the sign, the diversity of ways in which it gets determined. This confers an additional dimension that complicates the structure of the sign and opens up the possibility of interpretations. The tension that occurs between history and context within the sign is so fundamental that iterability or the presentation of the site of repetition—i.e. history— becomes the pre-condition of all univocity. It is by presenting this historical dimension, by thematizing the heterogeneity of discourse, that *Ulysses* engages with the tradition of representation.

### 'Oxen of the Sun' and Questions of History

I shall conclude this chapter with some comments on the 'Oxen of the Sun' episode. I have already examined passages from this

---

[34] Ibid. 103.

episode in the previous chapters to show how schematic deployment causes an unceasing production of disjunctions which resist
synthetic interpretations. Here, I shall try to show how the
questions of sign and history are implicitly taken up in this episode.
Joyce considered the 'Oxen of the Sun' as concerned with birth, as
is evidenced by his letter to Budgen.[35] He outlines three parallel
series of genesis happening at the level of organization. They are:
(1) faunal evolution, (2) embryonic development, and (3) the
history of English prose style. These are in addition to the event of
birth narrated in the episode, the birth of Mrs Purefoy's baby.
However, the 'Oxen of the Sun' occupies a peculiar position in the
structure of the novel. In spite of being the chapter of birth, it does
not mark the beginning of anything new. It does not announce the
beginning of a new discourse or new textual strategies. Nor does it
mark the origin or end of the novel. In terms of Joyce's
compositional strategies too, it marks the 'middle stage', as Groden
characterizes the phase of Joyce's reliance on parody.[36]

However, the three historical series indirectly indicate the
conditions of possibility of nature, human body, and the text.
Among these three series, textual evidence concerning faunal
evolution is not as convincing or conspicuous as the evidence for
the other two.[37] It has been argued that Joyce possibly abandoned
this project after his letter to Budgen.[38] I shall not consider this
series in detail here for two reasons: (1) there is relative lack of
textual evidence for this series, and (2) the model of history that
faunal evolution implies approximates to the embryological model
discussed in detail below.

---

[35] *Letters*, i. 139–40. The letter is quoted at length in Ch. 3.

[36] I follow Michael Groden in his distinction between the initial, the middle, and
the last stages in the composition of *Ulysses*: 'In the first stage ("Telemachus" to
"Scylla and Charybdis") he developed an interior monologue technique to tell his
story. In the middle stage ("Wandering Rocks" to "Oxen of the Sun"), he
experimented with the monologue and abandoned it for a series of parody styles that
act as translations of the story. He balanced his growing interest in the stylistic
surface with a continuing interest in the human story. Finally, in the last stage
("Circe" to "Penelope"), he created several new styles and revised the earlier
episodes.' (Groden, *'Ulysses' in Progress*, 4.) For an alternative, rather bipartite,
division of the compositional history, see Walton Litz, *Art of James Joyce: Method
and Design in 'Ulysses' and 'Finnegans Wake'* (London: OUP, 1961).

[37] See Robert Janusko, *Sources and Structures of James Joyce's 'Oxen'* (Essex:
Bowker Publishing Co., 1983), 4.

[38] Ibid.

In some novels of maturation, the event of maturity sometimes concludes the novel, thus making the entire text the result of this process of maturation. In some other cases, the advent of maturity marks the opening of a new section, a new organization of elements, stylistic or otherwise, that marks the transition. Joyce had used a complex version of the first model in the *Portrait*. There the history that the novel traces is indeed the process of maturation that eventually leads to the composition of the novel. However, the specificity of each phase of experience is preserved not only in terms of the events narrated or the details described, but also in terms of style. Each section delineates a stylistic universe different from the others.

His mother had told him not to speak with the rough boys in the college. Nice mother! The first day in the hall of the castle when she had said goodbye she had put up her veil double to her nose to kiss him: and her nose and eyes were red. But he had pretended not to see that she was going to cry. She was a nice mother but she was not so nice when she cried. And his father had given him two fiveshilling pieces for pocket money. And his father had told him if he wanted anything to write home to him and, whatever he did, never to peach on a fellow. (*P*, 9)

He closed the door and, walking swiftly to the bed, knelt beside it and covered his face with his hands. His hands were cold and damp and his limbs ached with chill. Bodily unrest and chill and weariness beset him, routing his thoughts. Why was he kneeling there like a child saying his evening prayers? To be alone with his soul, to examine his conscience, to meet his sins face to face, to recall their times and manners and circumstances, to weep over them. (*P*, 140)

The selection of details ('her nose and eyes were red', 'two fiveshilling pieces', 'hands were cold and damp', 'chill and weariness'), of words ('nice mother', 'not so nice', 'peach on a fellow', 'Bodily unrest', 'conscience', 'sins face to face', 'alone with his soul'), and of syntactic constructions (short sentences, sentences beginning with 'but' or 'and' in the earlier passage, long sentences with many clauses in the latter)—all these are determined by the particular phase they characterize. This mimetic impulse, as I have suggested at the beginning, contaminates the narration too. There is a careful conflation of third-person forms and first-person content in both the passages. However, in this careful organization of selected details and in that of narration and depiction, lies hidden the ambiguous presence of a Flaubertian artist paring his finger-nails.[39] The continuity of the narrative relies on the presence of this attitude throughout the novel. It is the continuous presence of a non-intrusive authorial consciousness. And the story that the novel recounts is the prehistory of this non-intrusive consciousness. Arguably, that is why there is no need to present the style of the matured artist explicitly at the end. Stephen's diaries are also part of the history prior to the emergence of the artist of the *Portrait*. The style of this artist is a certain disappearance of style. Thus there is no final vantage-point from which a perspective can be obtained, where all phases will fall into place. The author's perspective is present all the way through in the play of the first and the third persons, as a way of observing, of recreating the moment of experience in language.

This attempt to render specificity to each phase by letting it speak its own language relates to the theory of epiphany Joyce seems to have held early in his life. Each phase has an epiphanic revelation which unites the temporal phase by giving it a unitary significance. Everything in discourse is submitted to that epiphany, and it is in the submission of language to the epiphanic moment, in this particular authorial attitude, that the continuity of the narrative is established. And it is in this attitude that we should locate the result of the history that the novel recounts. But Joyce leaves the actual moment of emergence of this attitude unspecified. There is a temporal gap and a distance in terms of artistic maturity between the hero of the last pages of the *Portrait* and the author of the first pages. The rendering absent or suppression of this moment of emergence is crucial to the organization of history in the *Portrait*. If the phase of artistic maturity could be represented, the twin levels of mimesis and diegesis would have to become exactly identical for that phase. And since the authorial consciousness is indicated by a disappearance of style, it probably could not be represented in substantive terms, like the moments in his prehistory.

One may remember that Stephen and the early Joyce use quasi-

[39] 'The esthetic image in the dramatic form is life purified in and reprojected from the human imagination. The mystery of esthetic like that of material creation is accomplished. The artist, like the God of the creation, remains within or behind or beyond or above his handiwork, invisible refined out of existence, indifferent, paring his fingernails.' (*P*, 219.)

biological terms to describe aesthetic processes.[40] The metaphors of conception, gestation, and birth indicate the trajectory of aesthetic process too. 'Oxen of the Sun' in its organization takes up two themes I have mentioned in relation to the *Portrait*.[41] The first is, indeed, contained in the metaphor of embryological development. The second is manifested as the arrangement of a series of stylistic universes. However, in the 'Oxen of the Sun', these phases are liberated from the different phases in the character's history. If, in the *Portrait*, the theme of maturation unifies both these strands, in the 'Oxen of the Sun' they produce an interesting tension.[42] I shall argue that in spite of their common concern with narrative continuity and consequently with history, the theme of embryonic development and that of the history of English prose can be viewed, in a certain sense, as radically different from each other.[43]

Embryonic and stylistic evolution offer two distinct models of historical and narrative organization. The embryological model describes the history of an organic, teleological development. The anterior phases give way to more perfect posterior phases. The embryo of the seventh month is more complete and perfect than that of the third month, since it is closer to childbirth. The

[40] This is evident in the *Portrait* when Stephen explains his theory to Lynch: 'Mac Alister . . . would call my esthetic theory applied Aquinas. So far as this side of esthetic philosophy extends Aquinas will carry me all along the line. When we come to the phenomena of artistic conception, artistic gestation and artistic reproduction I require a new terminology and a new personal experience' (*P*, 214). It comes up again in the sentence 'The mystery of esthetic like that of material creation is accomplished' (*P*, 219). Ellmann and Mason point out a passage in 'The Paris Notebook' anticipating this: '*e tekhne mimeitai ten physin*—This phrase is falsely rendered as 'Art is an imitation of Nature.' Aristotle does not here define art; he says only, 'Art imitates nature' and means that the artistic process is like the natural process.' (*Critical Writings*, 145.)

[41] See Senn, *Joyce's Dislocations*, 121–2.

[42] '*A Portrait of the Artist as a Young Man* is in fact the gestation of a soul, and in the metaphor Joyce found his new principle of order. The book begins with Stephen's father and, just before the ending, it depicts the hero's severance from his mother . . . The sense of the soul's development as like that of an embryo not only helped Joyce to the book's imagery, but also encouraged him to work and rework the original elements in the process of gestation. Stephen's growth proceeds in waves, in accretions of flesh, in particularization of needs and desires, around and around but always ultimately forward.' (Ellmann, *James Joyce*, 296–7.)

[43] Gilbert notices only the similarity—i.e. the theme of genetic evolution—when he says: 'The rationale of this sequence of imitations lies in the theme. The technic and the subject of this episode are both 'embryonic development' and the employment of the styles follows an exact historical order.' (Gilbert, *James Joyce's 'Ulysses'*, 255.)

chronological position of a particular phase signifies a value-judgement as well, since the entire sequence is teleologically organized. However, each of these moments is absolutely indispensable to the narrative. The foetus, which is originally sexually indeterminate and devoid of organs of sense-perception, is inevitable as a predecessor for the more perfect phases to emerge. These themes of conception, pre-natal evolution, and childbirth strike a chord in Stephen's and early Joyce's aesthetic. Art is mimesis in so far as it imitates nature in its processes.[44] It also consists in conception, a transfiguring process of gestation and parturition.

The linguistic model, that of the evolution of English prose, presents a counterpoint to this narrative of organic evolution. Here, the chronological sequence does not provide a teleological ordering. Literary style does not develop in the sense in which an embryo does. In embryonic development, what is latent acquires actualization—its history does not bring the realm of the unexpected into play. In the development of language and style, there is no predetermined model to which each given moment is trying to approximate. The style that emerges at the end of the episode is a mixture of cliché and pidgin English, of fragments which do not fall into a coherent order of discourse. However, according to Joyce's letter, the ends of the series, the two opposing forms of 'chaos', do not actually form part of the series.[45] In that case, the evolution concludes with a parody of John Ruskin. It will be naïve to assume that Ruskin occupied, for Joyce, any ideal of stylistic perfection in prose. In fact, the parody of Ruskin comes after that of Newman and Pater, the figures Joyce appreciated most among modern prose writers.[46] Thus the narrative that the model of stylistic evolution unfolds does not follow the continuity of the embryological one.

This model contrasts a series of distinct styles against the series of organic development. What orders the series is the chronological dating of each of these styles. Apart from this, each style is a world of its own, one that does not necessarily retain the characteristics of an earlier stylistic world. Thus we have a series of displacements of one style by another, rather than a progressive growth. I shall illustrate this by the examination of a passage from the 'Oxen of the Sun' (*U*, 14. 228–53).

---

[44] See Chs. 5 and 6, below.    [45] See *Letters*, iii. 16.
[46] Janusko, *James Joyce's 'Oxen'*, 5.

This passage partakes in the embryonic narrative in two ways: by announcing the stage of growth of the embryo and by presenting some features of the embryo which appear for the first time at this stage. An example of the first strategy will be 'how at the end of the second month a human soul was infused'. This is an indication at the verbal level that the passage corresponds to the second month of embryonic growth. This, like many other schematic elements that we examined before, involves a reading that would take the words 'second month' out of their ostensible context in the narrative and relate it directly to a schematic meaning. This passage is peculiar in its thematizing of the embryonic growth at the level of the narrative as well. When Stephen says 'at the second month' he is actually talking about the second month in the embryonic history. However, the third and the seventh months are also announced directly by mentioning the number of the month.

Hereupon Punch Costello dinged with his fist upon the board and would sing a bawdy catch *Staboo Stabella* about a wench that was put in pod of a jolly swashbuckler in Almany which he did straightways now attack:
—*The first three months she was not well, Staboo* . . . (U, 14. 313–16)

The seventh month is announced three times:

and an old whoremaster that kept seven trulls in his house. (U, 14. 620)

Then, though it had poured seven showers, we were neither of us a penny the worse. (U, 14. 773–4)

As I look to be saved I had it from my Kitty who has been wardmaid there any time these seven months. (U, 14. 810–12)

However, in these cases, the number of months seems to be present in two different narratives at the same time. On the one hand, these phrases participate in the ostensible meaning of the sentences in which they occur. On the other hand, they relate to the hidden embryological narrative as well.

The second strategy of presenting the embryological history works in the same way, in its literal relation to the schema. However, its relationship is mediated in the sense that it does not announce the stage in an immediate way—i.e. by naming it. It involves a careful deployment of the embryonic features that have just emerged. A. M. Klein points out a tenuous connection between the feature 'external genitalia appear, but sex cannot be differentiated' and the lines, 'and nature has other ends than we. Then said

Dixon junior to Punch Costello wist he what end.'[47] Janusko is more convincing in his relating 'spleen of lustihead' to the appearance of spleen, a feature that Joyce related to the second month in the notesheets.[48] He points out another connection between Bloom's 'laying hand to jaw' and the appearance of the hand and the jawbone.[49] The interpreters of 'Oxen of the Sun' rely on both authorial evidence and independent assessment of probable correspondences in establishing the embryological elements. A. M. Klein, J. S. Atherton,[50] and Robert Janusko, to mention only a few, have done this with various degrees of critical licence and varying degrees of plausibility.

One reason for the discrepancies in interpretation could arguably be Joyce's own lack of consistency in working out his model. Among Joyce's notes for the episode, one finds an embryological chart, with nine cycles and nine sets of biological features.[51] Several of these elements did not go into the text. In addition, there are new entries in the notesheets, some of which have been worked into the episode and some which have not been. And there is the possibility that Joyce may have used new elements at the time of composition or during revisions, elements which do not have a genetic history at all. This makes it possible to subject any element in the text to an embryological interpretation—or, more precisely, to a critical appropriation into an embryological narrative. The countercheck against this is constituted by the embryological narrative itself, which assigns certain features for each month. But Joyce's assignment of these features vary from many gynaecological texts, and that constitutes another reason for the diversity of versions of the embryological narrative that the critics construct from the text.[52] Thus this narrative provides one ruse of unification in the

---

[47] A. M. Klein, 'Oxen of the Sun', *Here and Now*, 1 (1949), 30.

[48] Janusko, *James Joyce's 'Oxen'*, 48. See Notesheet 12. 78 in James Joyce, *Joyce's 'Ulysses' Notesheets in the British Museum*, ed. Phillip F. Herring (Charlottesville, Va.: University of Virginia Press, 1972). Citations from the notesheets in the following pages will be followed by the notesheet numbers in brackets.    [49] Janusko, *James Joyce's 'Oxen'*, p. 49.

[50] J. S. Atherton, 'Oxen of the Sun', in Hart and Hayman (eds.), *James Joyce's 'Ulysses'*, 313–39.

[51] See Joyce, *Joyce's 'Ulysses' Notesheets*, between pp. 162 and 163. There is a transcript of the chart on pp. 164–5.

[52] E.g. in Klein's version, sexual differentiation occurs in the fourth month. He identifies this in the passage '*Ut novetur sexus omnis corpis mysterium*' (*U*, 393. 1–2). (Klein, 'Oxen of the Sun', 30.) However, sexual differentiation, in Joyce's chart, occurs in the third month.

episode though, by the nature of the facts of composition, it would
be impossible to retrieve one single version of the narrative that
would have critical consensus.

Let us examine how the passage (*U*, 14. 228–53) relates to the
narrative of the evolution of English prose. This passage corresponds, according to Joyce's letter to Budgen, to parodies of
'Malory's *Morte d'Arthur* ("but that Franklin Lenehan was prompt
ever to pour them so that at the least way mirth should not lack"),
then the Elizabethan chronicle style ("about that present time
young Stephen filled all cups")'.[53] Towards the end of this passage,
the words 'all they bachelors' as well as 'jeopard her person' come
from Malory.[54] '[A]ll they bachelors' seems to be a transformation
of 'all they had hoods', a sentence Joyce seems to have copied onto
the notesheets (7. 56). '[J]eopard her person' is literally lifted from
Malory, once again through the notesheets (7. 50). In the passage
that parodies Malory's prose, Janusko finds about twenty-five such
borrowings. Most of them are borrowings of words or phrases. 'Sir
Arthur, king' becomes 'Sir Leopold, king' in the notesheets (7. 47)
and enters the text as 'Sir Leopold' (*U*, 14. 169–70). 'He hath ado
with a knight' enters the notesheets (7. 48) as 'hath ado with' and
becomes 'they had had ado each with other' in the text (*U*, 14.
126–7). Here the purpose and function of the allusions is to evoke a
stylistic world.

Joyce's own main method of evocation in his later fiction,
consisted in the dense deployment of semantemes. For examples,
one need only go through the 'Anna Livia' chapter in *Finnegans
Wake* and the addition of a long list of river-names during the last
stages of revision.[55] Two kinds of semantemes are used here—the
proper names of rivers and the words meaning river in various
languages. Unlike the phonic or the imagistic methods of evocation,
the semantic content of the word is supposed to constitute, along
with other similar words, the requisite ambience. In the 'Oxen of
the Sun', on the other hand, it is the history of these words, their
having been used in Malory's text, that is put to function. Joyce's
parodic technique in this passage is restricted to borrowing. It does

---

[53] *Letters*, i. 139–40.

[54] See, for a discussion of Joyce's borrowings, Janusko, *James Joyce's 'Oxen'*,
55–77, and app. C, pp. 93–155. I follow Janusko's evidence from the Notesheets.

[55] See Fred L. Higginson, *Anna Livia Plurabelle: The Making of a Chapter*
(Minneapolis, Minn.: University of Minnesota Press, 1960).

not involve the borrowing of linguistic forms in the abstract, as in the case of rhetorical figures in 'Aeolus'. The syntactic configurations are invoked only when the lexical elements in relation to which they occurred are also borrowed. The primary strategy, in other words, is that of repetition. Fragments of an earlier text are repeated, literally. This method is distinct from the use of abstract forms, as in 'Aeolus', 'Sirens', and 'Ithaca'. Here the stylistic world is presented by the weaving of these textual elements from Malory into the text. This process of weaving certainly relies on other strategies as well.

For example, the rhythm of the prose changes from passage to passage.

> Before born babe bliss had. Within womb won he worship. Whatever in that one case done commodiously done was. (*U*, 14. 60–1)

The rhythm of this passage is indeed different from the passage we were examining. The textual repetition is here conjoined with an imitation of stylistic rhythms. However, by itself, this imitation produces passages the sources of which are difficult to assign. One example of this is the opening which Joyce originally planned as a Sallustian–Tacitean prelude, but which, Gilbert argues, resembles medieval translations of Latin texts on gynaecology. The specific parodies work through repetition of textual elements and by a narrative mediation which is imitiative of stylistic rhythms.

If this were all that there was to it, the picture that would emerge would be much simpler than it actually is. In the Malory parody, we find a textual repetition of elements from other texts as well. To quote Janusko:

> Between the end of the Mandeville parody ('Thanked be Almighty God') and the beginning of the 'Elizabethan Chronicle' parody there are at least twenty-five phrases that Joyce copied from Malory. But there are also borrowings in these pages from, among others, Wyclif, Fisher, Holinshed, North, Elyot, More, and especially John Bourchier, Lord Berners. It is, in fact, Lord Berners who seems to be a primary source from 'Now let us speak of that fellowship' (*U*, 388. 17), a typical Berners introduction, to the end of the section designated by Joyce as a Malory parody, including the passage in which appear the lines cited by Joyce in his letter as a sample of Malory. Joyce's letter was, of course, written midway during the composition of the chapter, so that it is probable that Joyce either altered

his intention by the time his writing was complete or that he never intended the letter to be a complete and detailed listing.[56]

One consequence of this is that the stylistic world that emerges is also heterogeneous in terms of authorship. There is no single author to whom you can trace back all the elements and, consequently, the narration is actually mediating between elements of disparate origins. One could argue that this can be understood as the representation of an epoch. But again, this would render a certain heterogeneity to the model because, in the later sections, repetitions pertain mostly to a single author. What we have is a series of styles created by the repetition of certain texts and variable narrative mediation.

The sense of history which is implied in this model is less a continuous history than a series of disjunctive moments. The transformations and relations of causality that a unilinear or teleological history rely on are dispensed with. The interaction of this narrative with the narrative of organic development in the same episode point to two antithetical ways of implicating the sign as well. The embryological narrative, as I have tried to show above, endows certain signs with an additional schematic dimension. It is true that this renders the domain of the signs that could have this additional dimension open to critical discrimination. But once a sign is interpreted in relation to the embryological theme, it is inserted into a narrative discourse where some sense of univocity operates. The meaning of the sign is delimited—it could only refer to the features pertaining to the particular month. The linguistic narrative, on the other hand, points to local determinations of the sign. When a sign is implicated in a parodic passage, two things are highlighted. One is, as pointed out earlier, its previous history. The other is the set of discursive regularities which determines it. And both these elements vary from passage to passage. This renders the question of univocity problematic.

One interesting example of this is the occurrence of proper names in this episode. Proper names, which are indicative of character-subjectivities and which recur without variation in most narratives in order to ensure a stabilization of these subjectivities, occur in a variable fashion in this episode. Bloom is referred to as 'traveller Leopold' (*U*, 14. 126), 'childe Leopold' (*U*, 14. 160), 'Sir Leopold'

---

[56] Janusko, *James Joyce's 'Oxen'*, 61–2.

(*U*, 14. 169–70), 'Master Bloom' (*U*, 14. 424), 'Mr Cautious Calmer' (*U*, 14. 469–70), 'Leop. Bloom' (*U*, 14. 504), 'Mr Bloom (*U*, 14. 845), 'Mr Canvasser Bloom' (*U*, 14. 952), 'Leopold' (*U*, 14. 1041), 'Mr L. Bloom (Pubb. Canv.)' (*U*, 14. 1230), and 'Bloom' (*U*, 14. 1393).

These transformations of the name actually point to the discursive regularities in which it is implicated. Do such transformations affect the signified? The answer is both yes and no. From the point of view of the narrative of events, the story carries on and the events are in conformity with what is recounted in the following episodes. But at the same time, since the method of the episode necessitates that Bloom be presented in a certain way in each passage, there is something irreducible about these names too. On the one hand, there is the possibility of a univocal narrative emerging and that of a residual reality attainable, possibly, through translation. On the other hand, there is a closure of each stylistic universe, giving a finality to the signifiers and thus to the possibilities of representation. What is thematized in this opposition is, I think, the implication of representation with discourse. This strategy is taken further in 'Circe' where the transformations are less amenable to recuperation through translation. This is symptomatically present in Bloom's appearance in 'Circe':

*On the farther side under the railway bridge Bloom appears, flushed, panting, cramming bread and chocolate into a sidepocket. From Gillen's hairdresser's window a composite portrait shows him gallant Nelson's image. A concave mirror at the side presents to him lovelorn longlost lugubru Booloohoom. Grave Gladstone sees him level, Bloom for Bloom. He passes, struck by the stare of truculent Wellington, but in the convex mirror grin unstruck the bonham eyes and fatchuck cheekchops of jollypoldy the rixdix doldy.* (*U*, 15. 141–9)

It is interesting to notice the patterns of description that emerge from this passage. Bloom *sees* the first image ('*shows him*'). We are not so sure about his own image in the concave mirror ('*presents to him*'). When it comes to the third image, it is described in terms of the image ('*sees him*'). And the narrator specifies that Bloom does not see the last image, his reflection in the convex mirror. If we can understand the initial descriptions of the images in terms of Bloom's perceptions, it becomes more difficult to understand the later descriptions in the same way. The image is described in its relation to Bloom, had it been viewed by Bloom; but it never actually is seen by him. The perception that is described is freed from a psychological subjectivity here. This is, however, further complicated by another schematic determination. 'Bonham' (i.e. a young pig) performs a Circean transformation on Bloom. These transformations, like that of Bloom's name, cannot be interpreted in terms either of purely objective narration, or of a purely subjective perception. The constitution of these elements is determined by several patterns that operate on the same text. Representation is always implicated in such discursive regularities.

If history is seen as a set of discursive structures which form a chronological series but with no teleological continuity, the search for a pure origin becomes a fruitless task. History, then, would be a history of appropriations of signs, resistant to totalization and open to insertions in an infinite set of future discourses. This is a theme that I have tried to show to be a constant concern of *Ulysses* implicit in the repetition of signs and in allusions. This is highlighted in the 'Oxen of the Sun' in two ways. We have examined, in the previous chapters, the use of verbal elements which connect the 'Oxen of the Sun' to the earlier episodes. This presents the signs as being appropriated by various discourses. The other way of highlighting the lack of a pure origin is by taking as its point of departure medieval translations of Latin texts. Since Latin comes from outside the series and the translated text from far inside the series, a complication sets in. The origin is represented but only in terms of a later discourse.[57] It is an organized disturbance of the series from within rather than a pure full source from which the elements would emerge. Joyce called the beginning and the end 'two opposing forms of chaos'.[58] The welter of pidgin English, jargon, and cliché that constitutes the conclusion, however, retains the representation of moments from within the series. It contains allusions to the Mass, to 'Blessed Damozel', and to Burns's 'Willie brewed a peck o' Maut'. It contains the method of repetition of phrases from Swift, Goldsmith, and Carlyle.[59] It continues the repetition from earlier episodes in phrases such as '*Übermensch*' and 'Elijah is coming'. Thus what is outside the series is presented as contaminated from within.

The linguistic model presents history as a series of discourses

---

[57] For a detailed discussion of this passage, see Ch. 3 above.
[58] *Letters*, iii. 16.        [59] Janusko, *James Joyce's 'Oxen'*, 76–7.

with internal regularities. The conception of historical stages as emerging from and dissolving into forms of chaos and as distinguishable from one another by laws and language is a familiar notion in Vico's *The New Science*.[60] Instead of trying to find Vichean cycles in *Ulysses* and an overschematic tripartite structure in the organization of its episodes, perhaps it is more useful to talk about a possible Vichean inspiration in this concern with language and the consequent notion of history as a series of displacements. One of the methods that inform *The New Science* is the etymological method.[61] Etymology tries to trace the different meanings a sign had at different moments in its history. For Vico, this does not provide an access to the meaning of the sign itself, but it renders intelligible the moments in which it was implicated.[62] In other words, the semantic alliances of the sign are the signs to be interpreted; they are the objects of a historical interpretation. The aim of such an interpretation is to enunciate the rules that characterize each epoch.

*Ulysses* does not insistently use the etymology of words as *Finnegans Wake* does. The plurality of languages and the circulation of signs in them are at least not surface concerns in *Ulysses*. However, this novel is concerned with the plurality of discourses. In *Ulysses*, the history of the sign—whether it be internal to the text or external—is an attempt to thematize the discursive connections in

---

[60] Giambattista Vico, *New Science of Giambattista Vico*, tr. Thomas Goddard Bergin and Max Harold Fish (Ithaca, NY: Cornell University Press, 1968).

[61] Richard Ellmann notes: 'He was particularly drawn to the "roundheaded Neapolitan's" use of etymology and mythology to uncover the significance of events, as if events were the most superficial manifestations of underlying energies.' (Ellmann, *James Joyce*, 554.)

[62] See e.g. Vico's discussion of the etymological relation between 'Jove' and 'law': 'For all these reasons, we begin our treatment of law—the Latin for which is *ius*, contraction of the ancient *Ious* (Jove)—at this most ancient point of all times, at the moment when Jove's idea was born in the minds of the founders of the nations. To the Latin derivation of *ius* from *Ious* there is a striking parallel in Greek: for, as by a happy chance we find Plato observing in the *Cratylus* [412DE], the Greeks called law at first *diaion*. This means pervasive or enduring by a philosophical etymology intruded by Plato himself, whose erudite mythology makes Jove the ether which penetrates and flows through all things [379]. But the historical derivation of *diaion* is from Jove, whom Greeks called *Dios*, whence the Latin expression *sub dio*, which, equally with *sub Iove*, means "under an open sky." For the sake of euphony, *diaion* came later to be pronounced *dikaion*.' These semantic alliances are interpreted in relation to historical stages: 'This then is our point of departure for the discussion of law, which was originally divine, in the proper sense expressed by divination, the science of Jove's auspices, which were the divine institutions by which nations regulated all human institutions.' (Vico, *New Science*, para. 398.)

which the sign is embedded. This is analogous to Vico's use of etymology.[63]

In fact, etymology, in the history of the philosophy of language, has been put to use in two antithetical ways. One is by employing it as a tool in the search for a pure origin of languages, as the 'Ariadne's thread' out of the labyrinth of languages.[64] On the other hand, etymology can be used, as in Vico, to thematize changes in history. The first impulse would search for the pure Adamic word, while the second would rupture the word to reveal the contexts of its use. Joyce's work also seems to have been part of both these impulses. The first is evidenced in his interest in Jousse, in the belief that gesture was the originary language.[65] The second could be found in the non-teleological models of history that come up in *Finnegans Wake* and *Ulysses*. The use of various languages in *Finnegans Wake* and of allusions, repetitions, and various discourses in *Ulysses*, in so far as they resist unification, points in the second direction. The thematization of the history of the sign does not help us to gain mastery over the sign's meaning. It rather reveals the structuredness of all discourse, and the implication of all representation in discourse.

[63] This fits in well with Joyce's remark that he often agreed with Vico that imagination is nothing but the working over of what is remembered and Joyce's remark to Budgen, 'Imagination is memory.' See Frank Budgen, *Myselves when Young* (London: OUP, 1970), 187; Ellmann, *James Joyce*, 661 n.

[64] Leibniz, when he started on his study of etymology, wrote to Ludolf in 1687: 'For nothing is lacking so that learned men, known to you, and in the part also youths, can excell within in a short time, when each of them skilled in particular languages is furnished with the Ariadne thread by you.' (Quoted in Hans Aarsleff, *From Locke to Saussure: Essays on the Study of Language and Intellectual History* (London: Athlone Press, 1982), 100 n.)

[65] For a discussion of Joyce's interest in Jousse's work, see Stephen Heath, 'Joyce in Language' in Colin MacCabe (ed.), *James Joyce: New Perspectives* (Brighton: Harvester Press, 1982), 129–48.

## 5

## Art, Language, and Tradition: Some Remarks On 'Proteus' and Joyce's Aesthetic Theories

JOYCE, in the schema that he prepared for Carlo Linati, specified the sense or meaning of the 'Proteus' episode as 'Prima Materia'.[1] In dramatizing the tension between an everchanging world of primal matter and an artistic consciousness trying to impose order upon it, 'Proteus' thematizes a concern that is central to an understanding of the poetics of *Ulysses*, that of linguistic apprehension and articulation. My purpose in this chapter is to disentangle some of the elements that cluster together in 'Proteus'. I shall try to provide a reading that would throw some light on the concept of language that underlies *Ulysses* and on Joyce's early ideas of poetics and epiphany—as found in the 'Paris' and 'Pola' Notebooks, *Stephen Hero*, and the *Portrait*.

The image of Proteus invokes an opposition between appearance and truth. One learns from the Homeric analogue that Menelaus, to learn the truth concerning his future, both worldly and otherworldly, had to capture Proteus and hold him fast while the old sea-god went through all forms of appearances. The Protean transformations, for Stephen, signify the perennial flux of the objects of perception. They constitute 'the ineluctable modality of the visible'. It is nearing noon-time when the world of vision is most accessible and most displayful in its variety. And it is also at noon-time that the old sea-god comes to laze in the sun. Against this realm of appearance and change, against this realm of sensible intuition, is contrasted the realm of concepts, knowledge, and truth. We know from Stephen's history about his Aristotelianism, about his 'penny worth of Thomist wisdom'. Concepts and theories of form point towards a search for an immutable truth, something permanent and unchanging under the surface of changing appearances. What enigma does the Proteus of primal matter hide from Stephen? And

[1] *Letters*, i. 146.

how does Stephen attempt to cross the frontier between the realms of appearance and truth?

## Languages of the Senses

The metaphor in which these concerns are expressed in 'Proteus' is that of language: 'Signatures of all things I am here to read'. It is worth pausing here to notice that this metaphor was possibly not an alien intrusion on Joyce's part into the Proteus myth. Michael Seidel points out that Victor Bérard, whose *Les Phéniciens et l'Odyssée* Joyce relied on during the composition of *Ulysses*, 'argues that the Proteus legend is very closely connected to the Egyptian myth of the secrets of Thoth passed down to the court of astrologers (magi) and Pharaohs of Egypt, themselves magi.'[2] Thoth is identified in *Ulysses* as the god of writing, 'Thoth, god of libraries, a birdgod, moonycrowned' (*U*, 9. 353). Gilbert mentions, possibly at Joyce's advice, the parallel between the discovery of Thoth's book from under the ocean and Menelaus's attempt to capture Proteus. My purpose in inviting attention to this parallel is to suggest that the acquisition of truth and the mastery of appearances that is involved in the encounter with Proteus get associated with the problematic of language and more specifically writing, through Bérard's connections between Proteus and Thoth. We shall leave this rather esoteric relation which is operative at the level of the schema for the time being and turn to the more immediate ways in which the metaphor of language functions in the text.

We shall return to the initial sentences again: the objects of vision are transformed into a writing and the activity of intellectual apprehension becomes an activity of reading. This visible world of appearances does not provide direct access to the realm of truth. It needs an act of interpretation or reading, a certain deciphering of signs. It is in this transformation of epistemology into semiology that the linguistic metaphor is introduced. This would identify the artistic process as one of recognition in so far as it relates to knowledge, and articulation in so far as it refers to a mastery of signs.

[2] Michael Seidel, *Epic Geography: James Joyce's 'Ulysses'* (Princeton, NJ: Princeton University Press, 1976), 109.

In this change of terrain from questions of knowledge to questions of language, two philosophers come in. One has been announced in the first sentence itself, in the concentration on vision. His presence would be reaffirmed a few lines later:

Limits of the diaphane. But he adds: in bodies. Then he was aware of them bodies before of them coloured. How? By knocking his sconce against them, sure. (*U*, 3. 4–6)

Ostensibly, these lines are about Aristotle and about the reality of matter independent of perception. It can be argued that what is suggested here is a simplistic, materialist representation of Aristotle.[3] But this need not concern us immediately. In the image of knocking one's sconce against the bodies, Stephen is implicitly invoking Dr Johnson's refutation of Bishop Berkeley.[4] Later in the text we come across an explicit reference to Berkeley:

The good bishop of Cloyne took the veil of the temple out of his shovel hat: veil of space with coloured emblems hatched on its field. Hold hard. Coloured on a flat: yes, that's right. (*U*, 3. 416–18)

Berkeley's presence here is affirmed through an allusion to his 'Essay towards a New Theory of Vision'.[5] In a retrospective reading, the entire encounter with the 'ineluctable modality of the visible' in 'Proteus' seems to bear the marks of a constant concern with Berkeley's text.

The ostensible point of departure in the allusion to Berkeley concerns his argument that the experience of distance does not properly belong to the visual sense. The notion of distance arises from the sensation of touch. It is associated with visual perception only through practice and habit. When we speak of seeing an object at a distance, this implies that a judgement is involved which properly belongs to the domain of the sense of touch, but which is here reached through inference based on habit. Berkeley argues that

---

[3] 'Aristotle's definition of substance is in fact complex . . . substance as matter exists potentially and becomes actual only in the form of an individual essence. The principle of actualization, then, is to be found not in matter but in the essence' (Pierre Vitoux, 'Aristotle, Berkeley and Newman in "Proteus" and *Finnegans Wake*', *JJQ* 18: 2 (1981), 164.)

[4] See Weldon Thornton, *Allusions in 'Ulysses': An Annotated List* (Chapel Hill, NC: North Carolina University Press, 1968), 42.

[5] Berkeley, 'Essay towards a New Theory of Vision' (1709), in id., *New Theory of Vision and Other Writings* (London: J. M. Dent, 1910), 1–86.

the ideas of space, outness, and of things placed at a distance are not really proper objects of sight. They are not perceived by the eye any more than they are by the ear. Berkeley suggests the following example to support his argument:

Sitting in my study I hear a coach drive along the street; I look through the casement and see it; I walk out and enter into it; thus, common speech would incline one to think, I heard, saw, and touched one and the same thing, to wit, the coach. It is nevertheless certain, the ideas intromitted by each sense are widely different, and distinct from each other; but having been observed to go together, they are spoken of as one and the same thing. By the variation of the noise I perceive the different distances of the coach, and know that it approaches before I look out. Thus by the ear I perceive distance, just after the same manner as I do by the eye.[6]

Stephen's allusion is mistaken in so far as he attributes the sensation of flatness to vision.[7]

Flat I see, then think distance, near, far, flat I see, east, back. Ah, see now! Falls back suddenly, frozen in stereoscope. Click does the trick.

(U, 3. 418–20)

However, the context in which the allusion to Berkeley is introduced deserves closer attention.

Who watches me here? Who ever anywhere will read these written words? Signs on a white field. Somewhere to someone in your flutiest voice. The good bishop of Cloyne took the veil of the temple out of his shovel hat: veil of space with coloured emblems hatched on its field. (U, 3. 414–18)

The focus in the passage shifts from Stephen's poem to a consideration of Berkeley's theory of vision. This movement re-enacts, in reverse order, the movement in the initial passage from the problematic of visual perception to that of the sign. Berkeley's presence occurs in relation to the transformation of the problem of perception into that of interpretation. The description of the Berkeleyan field of vision as a 'veil of space with coloured emblems hatched on its field' reaffirms this. The object of vision is a sign.

Berkeley treats this question by distinguishing between the objects of vision and touch. He argues that, strictly speaking, we never see and touch one and the same object. The visible figure and

---

[6] Ibid. 33.
[7] 'What we see are not solids, not yet planes variously coloured; they are only diversity of colours.' (Ibid. 85.)

extension are different from the tangible figure and extension. However, one should not conclude that a single thing has two diverse extensions. The true consequence, Berkeley says, is that

the objects of sight and touch are two distinct things. It may perhaps require some thought rightly to conceive this distinction. And the difficulty seems not a little increased, because the combination of visible ideas hath constantly the same name as the combination of tangible ideas wherewith it is connected: which doth of necessity arise from the use and end of language.[8]

Thus language blurs the distinction between the two different objects of sight and touch by conferring the same name on them. The function of language, according to Berkeley, seems similar to the function of habit. It is through habit and custom, Berkeley argues, that we associate the experience of distance with vision or hearing, thus instituting a unification of the experience of different senses. Similarly, language also accomplishes a unification of diverse sense-experiences through names. The objects of various senses are unified under the same name. This unification, according to Berkeley, is philosophically invalid. It is only an equivocation. Berkeley finds the presence of this equivocation in the very mechanism of language. Language equivocates not only between the objects of different senses but between the object and the word as well. In this equivocation, there is a confusion between the referential and the metalinguistic uses of language.

Berkeley explains this confusion in the following passage:

we can no more argue a visible and tangible square to be of the same species, from their being called by the same name, than we can, that a tangible square and the monosyllable consisting of six letters, whereby it is marked, are of the same species because they are both called by the same name: for words not being regarded in their own nature, or otherwise than as they are marks of things, it had been superfluous, and beside the design of language to have given them names distinct from those of the things marked by them . . .[9]

The name equivocates between the object and the word. The name is the name of the object, but it is its own name as well. Language, or custom (inasmuch as it manifests itself in the unreflective use of language), imposes a unity on experience which, in truth, does not exist. But this unity prevails and works because the word and its signification are practically inseparable in the ordinary use of language. They occur together. What is thematized here is the unity of the sign. One could relate Berkeley's idea of the word or the name to the notion of the signifier in modern linguistics. However, the signified is the result of the unification that language has already accomplished. It unites the different objects of the various senses. But is not this unification of experience under the signified and its inseparable relation to the signifier the necessary condition of the possibility of language in general? It seems as if custom, the possibility of equivocation, and the unity of the sign are concurrent at the origin of language.[10]

For Berkeley, this equivocation inherent in the sign is proto-typical of the equivocation between the objects of different senses. Moreover, the model of the sign, the relation of signification, is the relation between the objects of the different senses as well. Berkeley continues:

Visible figures are the marks of tangible figures, and from Sect. LIX. it is plain, that in themselves they are little regarded, or upon any other score than for their connection with tangible figures, which by nature they are ordained to signify. And because this language of nature does not vary in different ages or nations, hence it is, that in all times and places, visible figures are called by the same names as the respective tangible figures suggested by them, and not because they are alike, or of the same sort with them.[11]

Vision is 'by nature . . . ordained' to 'signify' the tangible figure and is 'little regarded' in itself. Here the objects of vision seem to belong to the realm of the signifiers and the objects of touch, to that of the signifieds. The example Berkeley employs several times in the essay to illustrate the disjunction between the senses is that of a congenitally blind person gaining vision for the first time.[12] Such a person, at first, would not find any relation between a chair as an object of vision and the same chair as an object of touch. Later he would learn it through habit, custom, and the use of language. For him, the relationship between the objects of the senses has to be learned, like learning a language or like gaining mastery over a

---

[10] However, we shall find later that for Berkeley, the relation between vision and touch, through which the 'Author of Nature' speaks, is the originary language.

[11] Ibid. 77.

[12] This example occurs several times in the 'Essay'. See e.g. ibid. 56–7.

repertoire of names. Originally he does not possess it because he had no access to the realm of signifiers, or to that of vision. Learning the relationship between vision and touch is thus an apprenticeship in articulation, in gaining mastery over signifiers.

In 'Proteus' too, a recurring metaphor is that of blindness and vision. An elementary opposition is presented in the situation of the short-sighted hero, who keeps replacing perceptions by concepts, speculating on vision at high noon. The possibility of visual experience and an inadequate receptivity are thus pitched against each other.

However, the most insistent use of the image of blindness occurs in Stephen's experiment when he tries to verify whether the world would disappear in the absence of sight.[13]

Stephen closed his eyes to hear his boots crush crackling wrack and shells. You are walking through it howsomever. I am, a stride at a time. A very short space of time through very short times of space. (*U*, 3. 10–12)

Open your eyes now. I will. One moment. Has all vanished since? If I open and am for ever in the black adiaphane. *Basta!* I will see if I can see.
See now. There all the time without you: and ever shall be, world without end. (*U*, 3. 25–8)

If we take the Berkeleyan context seriously, we can read the experiment of blindness as a renunciation of signifiers. If vision acts merely as the sign of the tangible, the signifier is bracketed out in the experiment so that the presence of the signified can be directly ascertained. Stephen satisfies his affirmation of 'Prima Materia' in finding the world there all the time. However, primal matter does not exist apart from its conjunction with an individuating form. And if one looks closer at the experiment, at the moments when the language of vision has been temporarily renounced, one will find that instead of affirming the priority of touch, it is problematizing

[13] Another possible source of this experiment, though less closely related to the context, seems to be Pater's essay 'Pico della Mirandola' in *The Renaissance*. Michael Seidel writes, 'He even closes his eyes just as Pico della Mirandola, to whom he alludes, says all good mystics must do to see real substance.' The passage from Pater reads, 'The word *mystic* has been usually derived from a Greek word which signifies *to shut* as if one shut one's lips brooding on what cannot be uttered; but the Platonists themselves derive it rather from the act of *shutting the eyes*, that one may see the more inwardly.' See Seidel, *Epic Geography*, 117; Walter Pater, *The Renaissance: Studies in Art and Poetry* (London: Macmillan, 1912), 37. See also Berkeley, 'Principles of Human Knowledge', in id., *New Theory of Vision*, 134.

that as well. Immediately as Stephen closes the book of vision, other books are being opened and other modes of reading are commencing. 'Stephen closed his eyes *to hear* his boots crush crackling wrack and shells' (*U*, 3. 10–11, my emphasis). The ineluctable modality of the audible takes over. It is through this contrast that Stephen locates the phenomenological origins of time and space. Touch is present throughout but never thematized directly. Even the solidity of the world, made by the mallet of 'Los *demiurgos*' is communicated through sound: 'Sounds solid' (*U*, 3. 17). For Stephen, the spatial and the temporal relate to two different senses, that of vision and hearing. This is meant less as a strict dichotomy than as an occasion to represent two languages of perception and two modes of articulation. That is why the distinction becomes one between *Nacheinander* and *Nebeneinander*. As words, they signify the mode of perception involved. As terms in an aesthetic vocabulary, through Lessing's *Laocoön*, they signify the spatial and the temporal arts. I have argued in my chapter on time how this tension is constitutive of the narrative mediations in *Ulysses*. I have tried to show here that the focus of Stephen's experiment with vision is not the possibility of ultimate escape from language, but the prevalence of different languages in Berkeley's sense of the word. None the less, even the renunciation of one language is threatened with the anxiety of silence. This theme manifests itself in the possibility of madness and death evoked in the Hamlet image: 'If I fell over a cliff that beetles o'er his base, fell through the *Nebeneinander* ineluctably!' (*U*, 3. 14–15) It comes up again in the possibility of blindness, of being confined in the adiaphane (*U*, 3. 26). However, the concerns that emerge in the experiment are those of the proliferation of languages and of their coherence.

Berkeley also writes about the coherence of the senses. The foundation of this coherence can be discerned in his final elaboration of the visual–tangible relation. Berkeley admits that we are prone to confound the objects of vision with those of touch more easily than linguistic signs with their referents. The reason for this derives from the difference between human languages and the language of the senses. In the case of human languages, the signs vary from one language to another. This makes us realize that they are of human institution. Furthermore, the significance of those signs did not naturally suggest themselves to us. We learn them from experience. The case of the language of the senses, natural to man and universal in its signification, is entirely different. Berkeley argues:

when we find the same signs suggest the same things all over the world; when we know they are not of human institution, and cannot remember that we ever learned their signification, but think that at first sight they would have suggested to us the same things as they do now: all this persuades us they are of the same species as the things respectively represented by them, and that it is by a natural resemblance they suggest them to our minds.[14]

Human languages are variable and founded on convention. The languages of the senses are universal. But that does not exempt the nature of the relation between the objects of the different senses from their linguistic character. Because, 'reluctancy we find, in rejecting any opinion, can be no argument for its truth'.[15]

But there is another sense in which the language of the senses has a privileged position. In contrast to human languages, it is divine in origin.

Upon the whole, I think we may fairly conclude, that the proper objects of vision constitute a universal language of the Author of nature, whereby we are instructed how to regulate our actions, in order to attain those things that are necessary to the preservation and well-being of our bodies, as also to avoid whatever may be hurtful and destructive of them.[16]

A visible square, for instance, suggests to the mind the same tangible square in Europe, that it doth in America. Hence it is that the voice of the Author of nature, which speaks to our eyes, is not liable to that misinterpretation and ambiguity, that languages of human contrivance are unavoidably subject to.[17]

For Berkeley, this freedom from ambiguities makes the language of vision an ideal language. If one argues in Berkeley's terms, it can be said that the perceptions of other senses too would constitute similar linguistic relations. We need only recall Berkeley's idea that sounds can also function as a language. The interesting question that arises here pertains to the foundation of the coherence of all these different languages. If the object of vision is the sign of the object of touch, the tangible sensation has a priority or hierarchical superiority over the visual sense. Berkeley's statements about the significatory status of vision imply such a privileging. But this

---

[14] Berkeley, 'Essay', 79–80.     [15] Ibid. 80.     [16] Ibid. 81.
[17] Ibid. 83.

hierarchy is upset in two ways. Firstly, vision and hearing also have their independent, proper objects, namely colour and sound. These objects can be considered for their own sake rather than as signs of tangible sensations. In other words, these proper objects are their own signifieds. Secondly, Berkeley's whole enterprise is to prove the dependence of the world on our perception. Berkeley concedes the possibility of imagining, without contradiction, a being who has sight, but no sense of touch. Such a person would have the signifiers, but they would not participate in the linguistic relation because the signifieds are absent; in other words they would not be signifiers any more. One cannot make the idea of the real world dependent on any one of the senses, whether it be sight or touch. In the language of the senses, there is not necessarily a clear hierarchy, but inseparability and coherence. And it is this rule of coherence that is divinely given and that functions as the ideal language. The existence of the external world, its endurance apart from human perception, is assured in Berkeley's system by God's eternally perceiving consciousness. And the linguistic relation of coherence between the senses is grounded in God as well. People learn this through habit and custom, but habit and custom are only institutionalizing a relationship that is universal and which in itself is expressive of the voice of the Author of Nature.

## The Original Language and Aesthetic Apprehension

This idea of the language of nature as the primary language takes us to another concern in 'Proteus'. It is a concern with the philosophy of Jacob Boehme signalled in the beginning of the episode: 'Signatures of all things I am here to read'.[18] Boehme too believed that the originary language was the language of nature or *Natursprache*. The Adamic word was natural, pure, and devoid of ambiguity.[19] Both Berkeley and Boehme posit a contrast between the plurality of human languages and the original language of nature. This contrast and an engagement with the questions of

[18] Jacob Boehme, *Signatures of All Things and Other Writings* (Cambridge: James Clarke, 1969).

[19] See George Steiner, *After Babel* (London: OUP, 1975) for the possible Cabbalistic roots of this idea. Cabbalistic tradition is alluded to in 'Proteus' in the reference to 'Adam Kadmon' (*U*, 3. 41).

origin at the levels of apprehension and articulation constitute a major theme in 'Proteus'. The 'art' of the episode is 'philology'. This is reflected both in an affirmation of the difference between various languages and in a process of listening to or reading the *Natursprache*.

One way of determining the thematic relevance of the reflections on Stephen's experience in Paris involves taking into account the linguistic contrasts they make possible in the text. Conversations, the instances of actualization of language in intersubjective contexts, are always either imagined or remembered in this episode. Furthermore, the conversations with uncle Richie can be contrasted with those with Kevin Egan, implicitly contrasting the themes of home and exile. The experience of exile and more generally of social and cultural alienation, is expressed in Joyce primarily as experience of linguistic distance. The themes of otherness, whether in terms of social distance or in terms of geographical frontiers, are communicated in the *Portrait* through metaphors of linguistic difference.

The language in which we are speaking is his before it is mine. How different are the words *home, Christ, ale, master*, on his lips and on mine! His language, so familiar and so foreign, will always be for me an acquired speech. I have not made or accepted its words. My voice holds them at bay. My soul frets in the shadow of his language. (*P*, 194)

Apart from the contexts of home and exile, represented in the contrast between English with Irish rhythms and French, there are contexts of misunderstanding.

She serves me at his beck. *Il est irlandais. Hollandais? Non fromage. Deux irlandais, nous, Irlande, vous savez? Ah, oui!* She thought you wanted a cheese *hollandais*. Your postprandial, do you know that word? Postprandial. There was a fellow I knew once in Barcelona, queer fellow, used to call it his postprandial. Well: *slainte!* (*U*, 3. 219–24)

However, it must be noticed that the plurality of languages is not divisive all the time. It can initiate the possibility of translation. In *Stephen Hero*, we find Stephen exercising his divining agility in translation in trying to predict how *consummatum est* would be translated.

He took no trouble to hear the sermon but every few minutes he heard a new translation of the Word rolling over the congregation. 'It is ended' 'It is accomplished.' This sensation awoke him from his daydream and as the translations followed [each] one another more and more rapidly he found his gambling instinct on the alert. (*SH*, 125)

The possibility of mediating between languages exempts Stephen, in this particular context, from the opposition between the preacher and the congregation: between a preacher who expounds the divine Word and a congregation which cannot understand him.

Here the other woman sighed in her turn and drew her shawl about her:
—On'y, said she, God bless the gintleman, he uses the words that you nor me can't intarprit. (*SH*, 126)

This divisiveness arises from an inability on the preacher's part to translate into the idiom of the congregation. The division is analogous to the distinction Stephen makes in the *Portrait* between the use of words in the literary tradition and that in the market-place, which he illustrates by the example of 'detain' and which the dean does not understand because he is using it in the idiom of the market-place.

The point of unification, in contrast to linguistic and social divisiveness, comes up, as we shall see, in the idea of a literary tradition. In the *Portrait*, Stephen's reflections on the word 'ivy' lead to such a meditation on literary tradition.

Yellow ivy: that was all right. Yellow ivory also. And what about ivory ivy?
The word now shone in his brain, clearer and brighter than any ivory sawn from the mottled tusks of elephants. *Ivory, ivoire, avorio, ebur.* One of the first examples he had learned in Latin had run: *India mittit ebur*; and he recalled the shrewd northern face of the rector who had taught him to construe the Metamorphoses of Ovid in courtly English, made whimsical by the mention of porkers and postherds and chines of bacon ... (*P*, 182–3)

The etymological history of the word through different languages renders it sharp and concrete. This unification, accomplished through an access to the plurality of languages, is founded on ideas of history and culture which are inextricably bound to the notion of literary tradition. I shall return to this point later. At the moment, I shall quote from the subsequent paragraph in the *Portrait* where Stephen's longings for such a culture are expressed.

even for so poor a Latinist as he, the dusky verses were as fragrant as though they had laid all those years in myrtle and lavendar and vervain; but yet it wounded him to think that he would never be but a shy guest at the feast of the world's culture and that the monkish learning, in terms of which he was striving to forge out an esthetic philosophy, was held no higher by the age he lived in than the subtle and curious jargons of heraldry and falconry. (*P*, 183)

Let us turn back briefly from these polyglottal or etymological notions of unity to the idea of a purer unity which is superior to human languages. In the texts of Berkeley and Boehme, such an idea can be found. The purity of the originary language and the inadequacies and the divisiveness of the multiplicity of languages are separated by the moment of Babel. Babel recurs in Boehme's texts as the synonym for confusion and for the misplaced human ingenuity that gives birth to it. What is opposed, here, to the confusion of language in Babel is the notion of 'signature'. This word is used in Boehme's texts in two closely related but distinct senses. On the one hand, it refers to the real essence of things and, on the other, it refers to the presence of divine validation of human perception in the mind of the beholder. Language is dumb without the signature. With it we apprehend the signature of things. It is individual but at the same time revealed in its composition from other fundamental elements. Coleridge, influenced by Boehme, uses a similar idea in his organicist conception of art. In 'Critique of Bertram' in *Biographia Literaria*, he says that '*Forma formans per formam formatum translucens*' (the forming form shining through the formed form) is the definition and perfection of ideal art. For Coleridge, this was 'the specific form [form of the species] shining through individual form . . . the species made individual, or the Individual corresponding in every part to any determined Species, and as if by a kind of translation interpreting it and revealing it.'[20]

This brings us very close to some concerns in Stephen's theory of epiphany and, especially, the controversial interpretation of the Aquinian notion of *claritas* proposed in the *Portrait*. William T. Noon's comments on this issue are very instructive:

The '*claritas* is *quidditas*' remark in the context of the *SH* exposition is quite easily interpreted as a Thomist derivative, whereas the same

[20] S. T. Coleridge, *Biographia Literaria* (1817), ed. James Engell and W. Jackson Bate (Bollingen Series, 75; London: Routledge & Kegan Paul, Ltd., 1983), ii. 215 and n. 3.

statement in the *Portrait* is made to carry the sense of a particularity in determination of essence which aligns it much more closely to the Scotist *haecceitas*. The specific or universal form rather than the individual form is the inner heart of the object as Thomists view the individual thing.[21]

The much more radically individuating idea of *haecceitas*, as proposed in Duns Scotus's writings, is the formal principle of individuation of all created beings. *Claritas* reveals the inalienable particularity of the object in question. Noon argues that this Scotist turn in the *Portrait* is a device of ironical distancing from the hero.

At a time when Joyce was moving towards a Quasi-Thomist interpretation of *quidditas* as the concern for the universally significant and 'essentially' important aspects of reality, he assigned to Stephen in the *Portrait*, possibly to heighten the irony of Stephen's predicament, a solicitude for the uniquely singular and individually ineffable thing.[22]

I think that this need not necessarily be a matter of irony. It could be that in Joyce's own thinking there was a tension or confusion if not a transition from an Aquinian to a Scotist notion of *quidditas*. Noon's argument for irony goes against the correspondence between Joyce's own investigations on questions of aesthetics and Stephen's. It would certainly be possible to produce a reading of the *Portrait* which treats Stephen's Scotism as ironic. However, I believe, it would be difficult to attribute this reading to Joyce. It is not my purpose, at the moment, to trace the full implications of a possible Scotist bias in Joyce's early aesthetic theory. It would involve a closer relation to the post-symbolist theories of art and indeed to Hopkins's theory of the 'inscape'.[23] And if such a reading could be brought to bear upon the structure of *Ulysses*, it could be argued that the schema and the discursive regularities are strategies of inscaping. However, if *quidditas* in the Scotist sense is what Stephen's epiphanies reveal, we could say that the object of art is the revelation of 'ultimate differences', because *haecceitas* is among the ultimate differences. Allan Wolter comments:

The individuating differences are certainly irreducibly simple. They are actual, where the concept of being is potential; they are determining where being is determinable and so on.[24]

---

[21] William T. Noon, *Joyce and Aquinas* (New Haven, Conn., and London: Yale University Press, 1957), 72. [22] Ibid.

[23] Such a particularist reading would bear a closer relation to Walter Pater's ideas of art expressed in the 'Conclusion' to *The Renaissance*.

[24] Allan Bernard Wolter, *Transcendentals and their Use in the Metaphysics of Duns Scotus* (Washington, DC: Catholic University of America Press, 1946), 83–4.

However, these ultimate differences cannot be the objects of knowledge in the present state of existence.

Granting that singularity qua singularity is not intelligible to our intellect in our present state, it is intelligible as such, and will be known one day by our intellect. Even in this life we know singular natures and know that they are singular. We do not perceive the precise formal reason why they are singular.[25]

Aristotle had posited a distinction between the universality of intellectual cognition and the particularity of sense experience. Wolter interprets Scotus's attempt as aimed at qualifying this dichotomy and affirming the possibility of knowing the ultimate differences some day—i.e. in the beatific vision.[26] Joyce's ideas of the three stages of aesthetic apprehension and of *claritas* could be taken to point to a transcendence of intellectual cognition by aesthetic apprehension. In the *Portrait*, Stephen refers to the universalist claims of *claritas* which he had made in *Stephen Hero* and his later rejection of them when he characterizes such claims as 'literary talk'. In the apprehension of the aesthetic image there is an experience of unique singularity which resists abstract universalization. In Joyce's 'Alphabetical Notebook', there is an entry which is illuminating in this context. The entry is, appropriately, under the heading 'Esthetic'.

The instant of inspiration is a spark so brief as to be invisible. The reflection of it on many sides at once from a multitude of cloudy circumstances with no one of which it is united save by the bond of nearest possibility veils its afterglow in an instant in a first confusion of form. This is the instant in which the word is made flesh.[27]

It is in this first confusion of form that the unique singularity of the aesthetic image is expressed. The process of aesthetic apprehension, more schematic, ultimately joins the original moment of inspiration through the apprehension of *quidditas*.

When you have apprehended that basket as one thing and have then analysed it according to its form and apprehended it as a thing you make

---

[25] Ibid. 29.
[26] Ibid.
[27] *James Joyce Archive*, ed. Michael Groden (New York: Garland Press, 1980), vii. 121–2.

the only synthesis which is logically and esthetically permissible. You see that it is that thing which it is and no other thing. The radiance of which he speaks is the scholastic *quidditas*, the *whatness* of a thing. This supreme quality is felt by the artist when the esthetic image is first conceived in his imagination. (*P*, 217)

Thus aesthetic apprehension seems to transcend the limits of ordinary cognition in its apprehension of ultimate differences.

How would this digression on Stephen's aesthetic theory correspond with the ideas of an original universal language? Or with the language of nature? If we take a particularist reading of Boehme's ideas of signature, we could say that the language of nature constitutes the possibility of such an apprehension. Adamic naming was not merely performative, it read the unique particularity of each entity as well. For Boehme, this access to the realm of the pure and original experience of nature was still accessible through mystic experience. Joyce contrasts the mysticism of Boehme with the visionary faculty of Blake.[28] Such a mystical experience would transcend the plurality of human languages by reading the *Natursprache* in a direct access to the pre-Babelian Adamic word.

In the Bible the moment when the Babelian divisiveness is transcended is represented in the image of the Pentecost when the Holy Ghost descends on human beings, enabling them to partake in the gift of tongues. This moment is an inversion of the Babelian moment when lucidity in terms of a particular human language is instituted and lucidity in terms of a universal divine language is lost. For, in the Pentecost, lucidity in terms of ordinary human language is confounded and a participation in the divine allowed.

Joyce seems to equate this post-Babelian annulment of divisiveness with aesthetic apprehension. He notes in the 'Esthetic' entry in the 'Alphabetical Notebook':

art has the gift of tongues.[29]

This idea reappears in *Ulysses*, not in 'Proteus' but in 'Circe'.

STEPHEN

(*looks behind*) So that gesture, not music not odour, would be a universal language, the gift of tongues rendering visible not the lay sense but the first entelechy, the structural rhythm. (*U*, 15. 104–7)

---

28 *Critical Writings*, 83–4.
29 *James Joyce Archive*, ed. Groden, vii. 122.

This refers to the idea of gesture as the original language. Later, Joyce was to get deeply interested in the work of Marcel Jousse who espoused this theory. 'In the beginning was the gest he jousstly says,' recounts *Finnegans Wake* (*FW*, 468. 5). The phrase 'structural rhythm' points to the three requirements of beauty, though in an imprecise way, and 'first entelechy' recalls the 'first confusion of form' in the 'Alphabetical Notebook'. All this points to a similarity in early Joyce and in Stephen between the ideas of a universal language and of art. It might also be possible to give a particularist reading of the 'first entelechy'. Since entelechy is the formal principle in the transformation of the potential to the actual, the phrase could probably be interpreted in the sense of individuating differences.

What needs closer examination is the distance between the language of nature and the post-Babelian vocation of art. For that, we need to return to 'Proteus' to see how those two moments are related.


## Art and Tradition

Such a relation is thematized in Stephen's speculations about the two women on the beach whom he transforms in his imagination into midwives. This establishes the theme of genesis and a speculation on origins.

What has she in the bag? A misbirth with a trailing navelcord, hushed in ruddy wool. The cords of all link back, strandentwining cable of all flesh. That is why mystic monks. Will you be as gods? Gaze in your *omphalos*. Hello! Kinch here. Put me on to Edenville. Aleph, alpha: nought, nought, one. (*U*, 3. 36–40)

It is interesting to notice the mention of mysticism here again. The entry into the Adamic world, for Boehme, was available through a mystic experience of nature. However, there is another interesting cluster of concerns here. It consists in treating history as a series of genetic filiations—a continuity affirmed in the cable of navelcords. This strand relates to ideas of culture and tradition as well. It becomes clearer if we remember that the Martello tower was called *omphalos* in 'Telemachus' and that it was, for Mulligan, a centre for the revival of Greek culture, a new paganism. The origins of

Western culture and its dual ancestry in the Greek and the Hebrew worlds, are an insistent preoccupation in *Ulysses*. Joyce's use of Victor Bérard's theories on the *Odyssey* point to this concern. Having a Jew as the modern Ulysses is indeed one of the indications of this. The relation between the Hellenic and the Hebraic is a complementary opposition that goes back to the origins of Western civilization, and is constitutive of Western culture even up to the present. At least so thinks Matthew Arnold, whose *Culture and Anarchy* Joyce seems to have been familiar with.[30] Thus, reaching back to the origins becomes the search for a certain tradition signalled in the confluence of the Greek and Jewish worlds. This is expressed in the passage cited above, in the code: it contains the first letters of the Hebrew and the Greek alphabet—aleph, alpha. The history of a culture or of a tradition provides a relation between the origins and the present, distinct from the relation proposed by mystic experience. Stephen, in *Ulysses*, does not address himself directly to this relation. However, I think that this is a central concern in Joyce's later work and that any discussion of Joyce's aesthetics would be arguably naïve if it were blind to the concerns of tradition and history. One could even argue that the developments and transformations that the theory of epiphany undergoes in relation to the poetics of later works could be characterized as an increasing preoccupation with these concerns.

Stephen has his own version of the relation to history. However, one encounters problems of equivocity here. Stephen's pronouncement, 'history is a nightmare from which I am trying to awake' (*U*, 2. 377) requires an interpretation in the context, not only of Deasy's subsequent statement (*U*, 2. 380–1), but also of Haines's words in 'Telemachus'.

—I am a servant of two masters, Stephen said, an English and an Italian.
—Italian? Haines said.
  A crazy queen, old and jealous. Kneel down before me.
—And a third, Stephen said, there is who wants me for odd jobs.
—Italian? Haines said again. What do you mean?
—The imperial British state, Stephen answered, his colour rising, and the holy Roman catholic and apostolic church.

[30] Richard Ellmann, *James Joyce* (revd. edn., New York: OUP, 1982), 395. In 'Telemachus', the thoughts on new paganism and *omphalos* are started off by the image of the deaf gardener, 'masked with Matthew Arnold's face'. (*U*, 1. 172–4.)

Haines detached from his underlip some fibres of tobacco before he spoke.

—I can quite understand that, he said calmly. An Irishman must think like that, I daresay. We feel in England that we have treated you rather unfairly. It seems history is to blame. (*U*, 1. 638–49)

The nightmare that Stephen wants to wake from is a history of domination, religious and political. In the dominator's sleep too, ironically, nightmares descend. When the 'panther' image appears again in 'Proteus' as one of the many transformations of the dog, it is no longer a nightmare. But it is still connected with the theme of history.[31]

His hindpaws then scattered the sand: then his forepaws dabbled and delved. Something he buried there, his grandmother. He rooted in the sand, dabbling, delving and stopped to listen to the air, scraped up the sand again with a fury of his claws, soon ceasing, a pard, a panther, got in spousebreach, vulturing the dead. (*U*, 3. 359–64)

The presence of the theme of history here is indicated not only by the images of excavation of the past and of memory, but also in an earlier paragraph where Deasy's description of history is alluded to in describing the dog's encounter with the carcass.

The carcass lay on his path. He stopped, sniffed, stalked round it, brother, nosing closer, went round it, sniffling rapidly like a dog all over the dead dog's bedraggled fell. Dogskull, dogsniff, eyes on the ground, moves to one great goal. Ah, poor dogsbody! Here lies poor dogsbody's body. (*U*, 3. 348–52)

The passage evidently recalls Deasy's statement that all human history moves towards one great goal: the manifestation of God (*U*, 2. 380–1). For Stephen, it is an encounter with death, whether it be in the dreams where his mother comes back to him or in the 'jousts, slush and uproar of battles, the frozen deathspew of the slain, a shout of spearspikes baited with men's bloodied guts' (*U*, 2. 317–18). It is this site of domination, servitude, death, and guilt that Stephen wants to renounce. We know that in the *Portrait* the aesthetic vocation, with its temporary strategies of 'silence, exile and cunning', was meant to be redemptive. Stephen, in *Ulysses*, is certainly not that affirmative, but he still retains the aesthetic

---

[31] See, for some other interpretations of the panther image, Seidel, *Epic Geography*, 119–20.

vocation. The submission to the 'crazy and jealous queen' is in a sense redemptive as well. This vocation involves Stephen in a different engagement with history, in the form of literary tradition.

If we now turn back to the passages I cited earlier on tradition, they appear to fall into place: the literary tradition uses words in a different sense than the market-place, the survival of the human warmth of Horace, the pleasures of translation, the nostalgia for monkish learning. But Stephen, in *Stephen Hero*, does not want to base his theory on tradition.

—No esthetic theory, pursued Stephen relentlessly, is of any value which investigates with the aid of the lantern of tradition. What we symbolise in black the Chinaman may symbolise in yellow: each has his own tradition. Greek beauty laughs at Coptic beauty and the American Indian derides them both. It is almost impossible to reconcile all tradition whereas it is by no means impossible to find the justification of every form of beauty which has been adored on the earth by an examination of the mechanism of esthetic apprehension, whether it be dressed in red, white, yellow or black. We have no reason for thinking that the Chinaman has a different system of digestion from that which we have though our diets are quite dissimilar. (*SH*, 217)

In the *Portrait*, the procedure of Stephen's aesthetic investigation is more explicitly announced as a transcendental inquiry:

The first step in the direction of beauty is to understand the frame and scope of the imagination, to comprehend the act itself of esthetic apprehension. (*P*, 212)

In the determination of aesthetic apprehension the stages are described in purely formal terms. As I have tried to show above, the aesthetic apprehension of singularity is believed to transcend the limits of the ordinary uses of language. Stephen does not thematize the training of the eye of aesthetic apprehension. However, Stephen in the *Portrait*, and much more so in *Ulysses*, is always perceiving the world through eyes trained in the literary tradition. Even the moments of fear when Stephen closes his eyes are couched in literary allusions.

This activation of tradition was not a preoccupation confined to Stephen alone. Throughout *Ulysses*, the organization of different elements is determined by this activation. Whether it be in the overall structures, namely Homer and the medieval *Summa*, or in the individual episodes where a particular art is picked up from the literary tradition as an organizing element, this process is at work. Joyce as arranger is using the literary tradition for the criteria of narrative organization in the novel. This tendency is extended further in *Finnegans Wake*. There, in addition to the use of literary tradition, an encounter with the history of languages becomes an important principle of organization. For the moment, we shall consider the case of *Ulysses* in some detail.

The most striking example of this is given in the 'Oxen of the Sun' episode which I have already examined. The parody of different prose styles provides a clear strategy for evoking the literary tradition. As argued in the preceding chapter, the moments of this narrative show two impulses at variance with each other. The styles parodied are chronologically in a progressive sequence. This is related to the model of embryonic development, a teleologically progressive narrative. But the different styles provide us with widely different universes of discourse, each with its own regularities. To borrow a distinction from text grammar, the texts that underlie the different discourses are different.[32] The coherence of each of these discourses relies on a different set of regularities. And we cannot say that these rules show a progressive evolution towards a stylistic ideal.

Literary tradition, here, is shown as a variety of texts or fields of discourse. The unity of the episode relies on the unity of the action as well as the chronologically precise recollection of all the different styles. In other words, the style of the chapter is the mode of recollection of all these different styles. In *Ulysses*, the primary mode of the encounter with tradition is that of recollection or recapitulation. It is available, all through the novel, in the form of literary allusions, and in the prevalence of leitmotifs from literature which Bloom and Stephen share.

However, if the recapitulation of different moments from the history of the English prose style does not provide an inner logic of unification, what idea of tradition is it that emerges from the unity of the episode? Certainly it is not a monolithic, unitary concept of tradition. It affirms the particularity of each stylistic universe and still produces a unity through the activity of recapitulation. The

---

[32] 'We therefore introduce the concept of TEXT as the basic linguistic unit manifesting itself, as DISCOURSE, in verbal utterances . . . The formal principle of the text must then account for the important empirical notion of COHERENCE.' (T. A. Van Dijk, *Some Aspects of Text Grammars* (The Hague: Mouton, 1972), 3.)

possibility of translation between these universes is hinted at by the continuity of action in the episode. However, there is no style in the episode which would function as the master style or as the most appropriate one. The unity we find in the episode is retrospective and so is the idea of translation that emerges here. The discursive regularities are inalienably specific for each universe. The continuity of reference throughout the episode relies on the recognition of these specific regularities. What all universes do share is the fact of having rules of coherence derived from prior texts. It is in this common element that we can locate an encounter with tradition. Its unity is contradictory. It involves the affirmation of difference in a radical sense.

Now we can return to 'Proteus' and examine how this episode measures the distance from the universal *Natursprache* to a post-Babelian vocation of art. The mediating element, the cable of navel-cords, would be located in the experience of tradition. Stephen does not thematize it directly. But it is present all through the episode, constituting the coherence of his discourse. How does this contradictory idea of tradition relate to the metaphor of linguistic difference that we located at the beginning as a central concern of 'Proteus'? The idea of a multilingual subject is present beneath the coherence of Stephen's discourse. Elements from other languages are presented as they are. The relevance of the word from the foreign language is recognized, but it is subjected to fit into the syntax of the dominant language.

Bald he was and a millionaire, *maestro di color che sanno*. Limit of the diaphane in. Why in? Diaphane, adiaphane. (*U*, 3. 6–8)

The recognition of a plurality of languages and of a unity that results from tradition is presented in this procedure. If we go back to the *Portrait* passage where Stephen's image of ivory is rendered progressively clear through the accumulation of cognates from different languages, moments in the word's etymological history, we can see there the origins of this idea of tradition. It could even be argued that in the distinction between perception and recognition in Joyce's 'Pola Notebook', there was already the possibility of evolving a theory of recognition based on the idea of tradition.[33]

---

[33] 'It has been said that the act of apprehension involves at least two activities—the activity of simple cognition or apprehension and the activity of recognition.' (*Critical Writings*, 148.) Joyce does not develop the idea of recognition in relation to

In the previous chapters I tried to argue that equivocity or the play of identical and different meanings is involved in Joyce's use of repetitions and allusions in *Ulysses*. In the preceding chapter it was argued that there was a tension between the ostensible sense of a sign and the history of its use in *Ulysses*. These tensions point to the plurality of languages and the idea of tradition that makes possible their presentation. This idea of tradition consists in the recapitulation of the history of the use of different languages in a number of texts.

I shall conclude this chapter by commenting on some of Derrida's remarks on *Finnegans Wake* because I think it is the role of tradition that these remarks seek to suppress. Derrida considers *Finnegans Wake* as an act of Babelization. This act has two aspects: one institutes the impossibility of translation, the other makes a gift of the plurality of languages. It repeats the act of the God of Babel:

At the beginning I spoke of resentment. Always possible with respect to Joyce's signature. But it was a way of considering, on a small scale, Joyce's revenge with respect to the God of Babel. But the God of Babel had already tortured his own signature; he was this torment: resentment *a priori* with respect to any possible translator. I order you and forbid you to translate me, to interfere with my name, to give a body of writing to its vocalization. And through this double command he signs. The signature does not come after the law, it is the divided act of the law: revenge, resentment, reprisal, revendication *as* signature. But also as gift and gift of languages. And God lets himself be prayed to, he condescends, he leans over (Loud/low), prayer and laughter absolve perhaps the pain of signature, the act of war with which everything will have begun. This is art, Joyce's art, the space given for his signature made into the work. *He war*, it's a counter-signature, it confirms and contradicts, effaces by subscribing.[34]

The idea of untranslatability implicit in the Babelian moment was elaborated by Derrida in his essay on Walter Benjamin's 'The Task of the Translator'.[35] Derrida posits the logical priority of a

the concept of history. However, it could be argued that this distinction opens up, or constitutes, a temporal dimension to aesthetic acts. Aesthetic recognition seems to rely on memory and repetition as well.

[34] Jacques Derrida, 'Two Words for Joyce', in Derek Attridge and Daniel Ferrer (eds.) *Post-Structuralist Joyce: Essays from the French* (Cambridge: CUP, 1984), 158.

[35] Jacques Derrida, 'Des tours de Babel', tr. Joseph F. Graham, in Joseph F. Graham (ed.), *Difference in Translation* (Ithaca, NY: Cornell University Press, 1985), 165–207. Walter Benjamin's essay appears in id., *Illuminations*, ed. Hannah Arendt, tr. Harry Zohn (London: Jonathan Cape, 1970), 69–82.

language contract among languages over those languages themselves. For him this is implicit in God's command to translate His
name even in the act of forbidding all translation: 'the law does not
command without demanding to be read deciphered, translated. It
demands transference.' Derrida makes this originary language
contract transcendental and anything but knowable.

> The topos of this contract is exceptional, unique and practically impossible
> to think under the ordinary category of contract: in a classical code it
> would have been called transcendental, since in truth it renders possible
> every contract in general, starting with what is called the language contract
> within the limits of a single idiom. Another name, perhaps, for the origin of
> tongues. Not the origin of language but of languages—before language,
> languages.
>   The translation contract, in this transcendental sense, would be the
> contract itself, the absolute contract, the contract form of the contract, that
> which allows a contract to be what it is.[36]

In this unity of the impossibility of translation and the demand to
translate, Derrida discerns the originary form of law. In relation to
Benjamin's essay it is worth pointing out that, for Benjamin, the
importance of translation resides in the possibility of an enhanced
larger language. And this is a symbolic recovery of the original
Adamic language. Translation is not the confirmation of a
transcendental contract, but an asymptotic reconstruction of a lost
intelligibility.

In Joyce too, I believe that plurivocity functions hand in hand
with the idea of a common horizon which emerges through the
holding together and retrospective presentation of all the voices.
Derrida's earlier work did take into account this aspect of Joyce's
work—the recollective repetitive act in relation to tradition.[37]
However in the essays cited above, the Joycean act is described as
Babelian. This is in opposition to the ideas on the vocation of art
that I have tried to develop in this chapter from a reading of Joyce's
ideas on aesthetics, the ideas of language in the 'Proteus' and the
use of tradition in 'Oxen of the Sun'. I think this argument will hold
true in relation to *Finnegans Wake* as well, which is, in many ways,
a meditation on the founding of different laws *in* history.

Just as, for Berkeley, divine language ensures the coherence of the

[36] Derrida, 'Des tours de Babel', 185–6.
[37] Id., *Edmund Husserl's 'Origin of Geometry': An Introduction*, tr. J. P. Leavy
(Brighton: Harvester Press, 1978), 103 ff.

diverse languages of the senses, for Joyce the idea of literary tradition retrospectively ensures a coherence between the different fields of discourses. This coherence is retrospective because it emerges through the presentation of the difference and singularity of these discourses. The vocation of art becomes an arrangement of discourses which reveal their grounding in the common horizon that they have constructed.

# 6

# Conclusion

In the preceding chapters, I attempted to develop an argument about the textual organization of *Ulysses* and about some of the specific effects it generates. I began with an examination of the strategies of repetition used in the text and concluded with a reading of some ideas in Joyce's aesthetic theory in the light of the notion of tradition that emerges in his work. In this chapter, I shall attempt to clarify this notion of tradition and differentiate it from another notion of tradition that one finds in the early modernist moment in English literature.

To facilitate the beginning of this discussion, I shall return to some of the points elaborated in the earlier chapters. While discussing the two modes of repetition in *Ulysses*, we found the pervasive use of disruptive repetition at work in the novel, questioning identities and creating serial connections that cannot be easily totalized. We also found that these events of repetition as well as the large number of organizational patterns deployed by Joyce in *Ulysses* create asymmetries in the text that render a unilinear temporal synthesis impossible and present an experience of differential temporality. I also argued that the specific ways in which memory functions in Joyce further accentuate this problem.

In our discussion of the sign, it was further pointed out that instead of a bipartite relationship, we find a third element, dynamic and temporal, uniting the signifier and the signified. This dynamic element is indeed the temporality of the sign, that determines the signified by the history of the sign's use. Rather than being a totality, the sign opens up its future uses. Here too, we find that this inner temporality of the sign, i.e. the continuous dislocations of the sign, does not constitute a teleological series. It forms a series where elements differ from one another. In Chapter 5 I argued that the notion of epiphany is reliant on a notion of particularity and that the apprehension of particularity takes the form of a performance of literary tradition.

To clarify this last point further, it is important to point out some aspects of Joyce's use of epiphany. In our earlier discussions we found that epiphany contains two distinct meanings in Joyce. Firstly, it is an event in life where the *quidditas* of an object leaps out and reveals itself. Secondly, it is the recording or even the embodiment of this revelation in language. Joyce's earlier notebook of epiphanies needs to be understood in this dual sense. It is the linguistic recording of an apprehension of particulars as well as a linguistic apprehension of particulars. Joyce's oscillation between a cognitivist and an art-critical vocabulary in describing the process of aesthetic apprehension could be understood in this light too. The butcher boy's basket or the ballast office-clock could stand as examples in an aesthetic theory because they have singular essences that can be revealed in life, and this revelation can be recorded and embodied in language so as to become a revelation in the mode of language. Joyce's play on the etymology of aesthetics is in this sense theoretically legitimate—it is a science of perception as well as a science of the apprehension of the beautiful. Epiphany unites both these through its dual sense.

Therefore, the notions of *integritas*, *consonantia*, and *claritas* pertain both to perception and to aesthetic apprehension. They designate the process of differentiation through which the beautiful is apprehended. The work of art itself interiorizes this movement and the three moments in this process become characteristics of the work of art. Jacques Aubert, in his analysis of epiphany and the simulacrum, comments:

The movement has disappeared only in appearance; in sculpture movement corresponding to the truth of bodies has ceased to exist, but rhythm has created an imaginary movement. The artist has put in the work a force that is different from nature but comparable to it.[1]

Aubert argues that this is the sense in which Joyce's comments on *e tekhne mimeitai ten physin* need to be interpreted. Art imitates nature, not in the sense of a similarity between products, but in the sense of a process, a movement. Aubert rightly argues that from the *Portrait* onwards, nature ceases to guarantee or ground the inner movement of the work of art. Art affirms itself in the movement of the work which essentially takes place in a symbolic space.[2] We argued earlier that in the 'Oxen of the Sun', natural evolution and

[1] Jacques Aubert, *Introduction à l'esthétique de James Joyce* (Paris: Didier, 1973), 154 (my tr.).
[2] Ibid. 145.

embryonic growth become represented as series that enter into tension with the model of linguistic evolution. All these series form parts of a movement of differentiation that constitutes the interiorized movement of the work of art.

Thus, epiphany in Joyce's work progressively develops in the direction of a logic of the work of art, the inner differences and movements through which it articulates the singularity of experience. Along with this development, there is a parallel movement on the part of the work of art towards an increased reliance on memory. The difference that marks the *Portrait* from *Stephen Hero* is as much the role of organizing memory in the former as the other factors mentioned. As I argued in the Introduction, the *Portrait* articulates Joyce's solution to the temporal problems of a writing of remembrance as one of style. Memory is embodied as a narrative voice, as a style that characterizes a phase of experience. In other words, memory induces an internal discontinuity to the work of art, in terms of narrative voice or of style.

We have seen some of the ways in which memory functions in *Ulysses*—some of the specific complications that it generates, whether it be in the interior monologue or in the form of allusions and repetitions which rely on a textual memory. The relation between this increasing significance of memory and the development of the notion of the epiphany that I outlined above is not merely external or fortuitous. In a world where stable identities are questioned or dissolved, memory becomes the only source of apprehending the soul as *quidditas*. Stephen's words in *Ulysses* present this:

> But I, entelechy, form of forms, am I by memory because under everchanging forms. (*U*, 9. 208–9).

We know from *Stephen Hero* that epiphany was the revelation of the 'soul' of an object and that soul was equated with 'whatness', *quidditas*, the inalienable singularity. Thus the apprehension of *quidditas* that constitutes epiphany comes to be reliant on memory. This is true not only about the apprehension of one's own self, but also about all singularities that can be objects of artistic embodiment. This chain of associations becomes more complete in Stephen's comments on the universal language in 'Circe', where the first entelechy becomes the 'structural rhythm', the inner temporality of a singularity, whether it be the universe or a work of art.

To summarize, as epiphany moves towards the aesthetic apprehension of a singularity, singularity itself becomes available only
through memory. What is the nature of this memory? Is it the
memory of an unchanging essence lying beneath the everchanging
forms? I think not. Such a hidden identity would be available to the
reflecting consciousness in a direct intuition. Memory would then
be nothing more than a Platonic recollection, or the 'naked'
repetition of a copy, to use Deleuze's vocabulary.[3] Identity can be
founded on memory since it is the 'form of forms' which are
'everchanging'. Memory not only recounts the changing forms but
also notices their difference, a difference that constantly repeats
itself. The only constant here is difference, and the singularity of the
self is the memory of this difference.

Memory induces a series where each element differs from itself,
under everchanging forms. This is the sense in which our findings
about the disuniting function of memory in Joyce's later work need
to be understood. In the *Portrait*, the identity of Stephen is the
memory of the discontinuous worlds he occupies. Memory induces
a discontinuity to the narrative voice precisely because it is this
discontinuity, this rubbing of the differences of style against one
another, that constitutes Stephen's identity. To put this in other
words, the artistic discovery of Stephen is that of a site where the
everchanging forms of his own style could be presented. The
replacement of the narrator by the arranger in *Ulysses* also
designates a site where different stylistic worlds articulate their
differences. If one can speak of homologies in *Finnegans Wake*
between individual and universal memories, or sleep and the
unconscious and death, it is possible only in so far as they are not
coherent worlds that constitute totalities. They rather belong to a
world where voice and identity trace a constantly changing
trajectory. The relations that obtain between characters in
*Finnegans Wake* form clusters of such difference. HCE is Christ
and Parnell and Finnegan, not because there is a superior unity that
subsumes them all, but because they form a series of differences
that constitutes HCE's identity.

This discontinuous memory that functions as a memory of
differences is a symptom of some of Joyce's later textual strategies
that involve a new attitude to tradition. Presumably the roots of

---

[3] See Ch. 1 above.

this attitude can be traced back to the *Portrait* and even to *Stephen Hero*, but it is in *Ulysses* and *Finnegans Wake* that an engagement with the history of representation becomes central to the novel's strategies. Both *Ulysses* and *Finnegans Wake*, which Joyce described as the 'daybook' and the 'nightbook' respectively, deal with a performance of history. In *Ulysses*, Stephen is trying to awake from the 'nightmare of history'. *Finnegans Wake* is the 'ideal book of an ideal insomniac' (*FW*, 120. 13–14), but conveys 'what goes on in a dream during a dream'.[4] Both of them deny the peaceful slumber or the wakeful world an identity.

Some ways in which *Ulysses* proceeds with a performance of tradition were discussed in the last chapter in relation to a close reading of parts of 'Proteus'. Here I shall attempt to articulate a more general discussion of the problem and some of its aspects. We saw that in the meditation on origin, Stephen reaches back to the difference of languages, a difference that is recounted in 'Aleph, Alpha', signalling the Greek and the Judaic which intermingle and animate the representations in several parts of the novel. This is true not only because Joyce uses Victor Bérard's theories about the Semitic origins of the *Odyssey*, nor because he uses a Jew as the image of Ulysses in the novel. It functions to articulate identities as sites of difference, of an inner otherness. Bloom's odyssey brings him back not to a home where his identity can be entirely recuperated, but to a bed where he would see 'the imprint of a human form, male, not his' (*U*, 17. 2124). He brings the otherness of his wanderings back to a home where an inner otherness is found. Stephen Dedalus's name, again, articulates the difference of the two traditions, pointing to the founding of identity on difference. The proposition 'Greekjew is jewgreek. Extremes meet,' only affirms this difference. There is no subsumption of the difference under the rubric of the Greek or the Jew or of a superior third term.

The question of the 'greekjew' is not an abstract philosophical question in *Ulysses*, it is dramatized in the novel as an attitude to otherness which is at the heart of persecution. Anti-Semitism functions in *Ulysses* as a metaphor for this attitude which denies the internal difference that is constitutive of the vision of a live

---

[4] Jacques Mercanton, 'Hours of James Joyce', in Willard Potts (ed.), *Portraits of the Artist in Exile: Recollection of James Joyce by Europeans* (Dublin: Wolfhound Press, 1979), 207.

tradition. It is only appropriate that the anti-Semitic citizen is a Cyclops-figure. He has plucked out the other eye of his vision.

It is also appropriate that the citizen embodies some of the text's ambiguous attitudes towards nationalism. Just as Haines is to Stephen a reminder of his otherness in the context of colonialism, the citizen is to Bloom the reminder of an otherness grounded on racial hostility and on a narrow nationalism. Colonialism, which is the obliteration of other identities and their reduction to a norm, finds its double here—a one-eyed nationalism, equally totalizing and equally excluding. Joyce himself had spoken of a proleptic image of colonialism in his reading of Robinson Crusoe:

> The true symbol of the British conquest is Robinson Crusoe. . . . He is the true prototype of the British Colonist, as Friday (the trusty savage who arrives on an unlucky day) is the symbol of the subject races . . . Saint John the evangelist saw on the island of Patmos the apocalyptic ruin of the universe and the building of the walls of the eternal city sparkling with beryl and emerald, with onyx and jasper, sapphire and ruby. Crusoe saw only one marvel in all the fertile creation around him, the print of a naked foot in virgin sand. And who knows if the latter is not more significant than the former?[5]

The greater empire is indeed the empire of subjection, whether it be religious or political, an appropriation of the human body and soul. Stephen's soul would 'fly by the nets' not only of colonialism, but also of its speculary doubles, the church and narrow nationalism. 'Silence, exile and cunning' outline aspects of this flying by, silence signalling a renunciation of languages that confer an identity, exile the embodiment of an otherness that cannot be erased. Cunning, the Dedalian shrewdness, the devising of the labyrinth of the work of art, is perhaps also the cunning of a memory that will preserve an identity in the memory of ever-changing forms. In Stephen's statement 'Let my country die for me', one can see the subordination of totalizing identities to one's own self, i.e. to a site of difference.

This affirmation of a difference at the heart of identities has serious implications for the notion of tradition. On the one hand, difference animates the origins of a tradition, the irreducible difference between aleph and alpha. On the other hand, tradition itself becomes a site of differences. One of the set of metaphors used

---

[5] James Joyce, 'Daniel Defoe', ed. and tr. Joseph Prescott, *Buffalo Studies*, 1: 1 (1964), 24–5.

in *Ulysses* to explore this is the history of heresy. If the Trinitarian theme provides a Christian counterpart to the theme of paternity in the *Odyssey* and in *Hamlet*, the unity of this counterpart is itself opened up to difference in the recounting of Arian and Sibelian heresies. Heresies are the exclusions on which a dogmatic or monumental tradition founds itself. They speak to us from the wings of a stage occupied by the doctrine. And appropriately, these heresies concern the notion of filiation, a notion that underlies evolutionist notions of tradition. Joyce's activation of heresy, whether it be in the form of the doctrine of consubstantiality or of transubstantiality, shows tradition to be a medley of contradictory voices. Stephen uses these views, often without conceptual resolution, for his own purposes. Often they form elements in a memory series, united contingently or associatively.

Finally, the history of heresy and even of theological literature forms only one strand of allusions in Joyce's work. Even limiting oneself to this specific strand, there is no clear unity in the operation of these allusions in *Ulysses*. On the one hand, Joyce often relies on structures derived from the tradition of Christianity for organizational patterns. He uses Aquinas's ideas on beauty to elaborate his aesthetic theory, and the Aquinian notion of angels to describe the schematism of his episodes. At the same time, often these structures are deployed in relation to an antithetical content, the way Homeric parallels are used in *Ulysses*. The prevalence of parodic and non-parodic attitudes in the use of elements from tradition renders tradition open to antithetical readings within the text. Or, in other words, elements from the same tradition are used for creating antithetical spaces within the text.

Joyce's use of other strands from the tradition of Western representation seems to pose similar problems. Sometimes an image from tradition is doubled or tripled. Aristotle, dominating Stephen's thoughts several times during the day, becomes the author of the Masterpiece in Bloom's monologues and eventually becomes the 'aristocrat' in Molly's. The way Shakespearean texts and the Bible function in *Ulysses* have often been commented on. Similar impulses are at work in the use of theosophy, of Anglo-Irish writing, and of European literature. All of them become part of an immense repertoire from which memory can revive images and combine them with new contexts. Stephen's attempt to 'wake up from the nightmare of history' can be seen as an attempt to

articulate oneself in terms of these phantoms, by recombining them
according to a new and subversive logic.

In our analysis of the opening of 'Proteus' in the last chapter, we
saw how clusters of allusions function in Stephen's interior
monologue. However, these allusions do not necessarily form any
pattern of conceptual rigour. As we saw in the preceding chapter,
they articulate concerns that insistently return to the text, opening
themselves to associational rather logical connections. To contemplate the origins of space and time, Stephen alludes to Aristotle,
Boehme, Shakespeare, Lessing, the Bible. They appear more like
resuscitated phantoms from a past which can be brought alive by a
memory that lets them speak across centuries. The perception of the
sea-shore takes the form of a repetition of elements from tradition.
Jacques Aubert argues that the opening of 'Proteus' is prototypical
of the novel's procedures—the extrication of a potential field, the
discovery of a rhythm, and finally an actualization that corresponds
to the recognition and that results from a play of forces.[6] What I
would like to suggest is that all these various steps are articulated in
terms of a repetition of elements from tradition. The ineluctable
modalities of the visible and the audible, further differentiated into
the signatures of things, reveal their essences as an originary space
and time. The steps of aesthetic apprehension thus accomplished by
Stephen take as their expression the string of allusions and their
associative series.

There are two procedures that are implied in this attitude. On the
one hand, it detaches one specific element, usually a verbal
fragment, from the universe of a text and puts it in communication
with another similar fragment. This *découpage* fragments the
original text in its relation to *Ulysses*. On the other hand, it makes a
plurality of new connections possible so that the allusion can
belong to two texts without being fully determined by either of
them. The original context of 'signatures of all things' does not
entirely determine the use of the phrase in *Ulysses* in a direct way.
Between Boehme's text and the new context of its use, there is
always a fissure, a gap. One needs other elements from the text to
connect them, and many of these other elements could themselves
be allusions or repetitions, thus opening further gaps between
*Ulysses* and its literary past.

[6] Aubert, *Introduction à l'esthétique*, 170.

These two procedures, *découpage* and relocation, constitute an act of performance that goes beyond conventional ideas of citation or allusion. In the latter cases, there is an intelligible voice in the present text that makes it possible for us to locate the scope and limits of the cited piece. In *Ulysses*, on the other hand, the intelligible voices are themselves partially constituted by allusions. The text becomes an act of performance of fragments from the past in constantly changing sites. It is not a single voice that speaks through them, it is a polyphony of voices that do not always form a harmony. This is one of the reasons for the manifest inadequacy of notions such as parody and pastiche in describing Joyce's procedures, even in relation to Homer, let alone to the innumerable other representations that *Ulysses* alludes to. Like the fantasms in 'Circe', they occupy a space where ethical evaluations do not function in a one-to-one way. The fantasms need to enter into relations with other parts of the text or with other fantasms that equally need interpretation. Similarly, allusions do not provide a key to the text, but often provide an opening, an interpretative gap that needs to be filled in with more text. It is said that Joyce sometimes worried whether he possessed the faculty of imagination at all, or whether he was only endowed with that of fancy.[7] This Coleridgean distinction, emanating from an organicist notion of the work of art, defines fancy as a mode of memory emancipated from time and space.[8] Joyce's allusions often function in a way reminiscent of this where the past forms a repertoire rather than a monument. However, it is precisely in using this faculty to present differences in a more radical way than the romanticist synthesis of the imagination, that *Ulysses* realizes its aesthetic vocation. The text presents differences, enacts or performs them, rather than reduces them to a superior identity.

However, to do this, *Ulysses* relies on a number of synthesizing ruses that function only partially. We examined the use of the naturalistic aspirations as well as some of the schematic patterns that function in this way. Allusions too partake in this strategy. This is why one feels that Eliot's formulations on Joyce's 'mythical' method probably do not describe the procedures of *Ulysses* as

---

[7] Mercanton, 'Hours of James Joyce', 224.

[8] S. T. Coleridge, *Biographia Literaria* (1817), ed. James Engell and W. Jackson Bate, (Bollingen Series, 75; London: Routledge & Kegan Paul, Ltd., 1983), i. 305.

much as they describe Eliot's own method.[9] While the Grail myth and literary tradition form two pillars on which the edifice of *The Waste Land* is constructed, Joyce's schematic patterns are scaffolding, exoskeletal, allowing one to make certain connections. Even the interior monologue is seen as a bridge across which he could take his troops.[10] There is a notion of use in Joyce's attitudes to these elements, and this applies no less to the relation of *Ulysses* to tradition.[11] Performance is one form of such use. In our study of the 'Oxen of the Sun', we saw how the notion of discursive regularity, in its differences, forms the only thread of continuity that we can decipher in the model of linguistic evolution. Joyce's use of tradition in general reveals tradition to be a site of discourses, of the presentation of differences. This traces a pattern that is indeed different from Eliot's ideas on tradition in 'Tradition and the Individual Talent'.[12]

For Eliot, tradition is a realm of continuity. It is an organic continuum that extends from the past to the present, an ideal order of monuments where each present poetic act alters this order as a whole.[13] Underlying these characterizations is a notion of tradition as organic totality. This is indeed why the present modifies the past—the present and the past form a totalizing structure together. Joyce's use of tradition, in this respect, is quite different. If tradition is itself disunited, if it is the site of difference itself, the act of artistic creation becomes one of disruptive repetition, of the affirmation of this difference. With each repetitive act, it activates the presence of the text's literary past and multiplies the possible interpretative relations. However, as we saw, this renders tradition itself more fragmented in relation to the text.

It is interesting to identify these rather different notions of tradition in early modernism. The first one is further developed in the *Four Quartets* where a closer symbolic harmony and a more unified notion of tradition assert themselves. Joyce's own method was further developed in *Finnegans Wake* where a contemplation of history and of the evolution and diversity of languages is

[9] T. S. Eliot, 'Ulysses, Order, Myth', *Dial*, 75: 5 (1923), 480–3.

[10] Mercanton, 'Hours of James Joyce', 226.

[11] Joyce remarked to Mercanton: 'I don't know whether Vico's theory is true; it doesn't matter. It's useful to me; that's what counts.' (Ibid. 207.)

[12] T. S. Eliot, 'Tradition and the Individual Talent' (1919), in *Selected Essays* (3rd edn., London: Faber & Faber, Ltd., 1951), 13–22.

[13] Ibid. 15.

accomplished in an even more fluid slippage of identities. The pun epitomizes this impulse, where signification is replaced by the explosion of an internal difference—the two halves of the word do not form a concept. They preserve their difference within the pseudo-identity of the pun.

Once again, to point out these disuniting elements in Joyce is not to make him a simple apologist of difference. It is equally important to emphasize the use of totalizing structures and pseudo-identities in *Ulysses*. I have tried to show how these two impulses work together in Joyce's work. It is not the absence of a schematizing impulse that creates disunities, but an overabundance of such impulses and the diversity of their use. In relation to the question of linguistic evolution, we saw that Joyce used contrary interpretations of etymology and linguistic diversity: on the one hand, the dream of an originary language; on the other, only a retrospective presentation of the differences between languages or discourses.

This coexistence of contrary impulses often makes the attempt to classify Joyce particularly difficult. However, this makes it possible to distinguish Joyce's work from certain strands and labels, including a monumentalist and totalizing strand in early modernism, and what has come to be called the post-modern.

Lyotard, who makes a distinction between modernist and post-modernist sensibilities, classifies Joyce's work as that of 'the sublime, even though a nostalgic one'.

Joyce allows the unrepresentable to become perceptible in his writing itself, in the signifier. The whole range of available narrative and stylistic operators is put to play without concern for the unity of the whole, and new operators are tried. The grammar and vocabulary of literary language are no longer accepted as given; rather they appear as academic forms, as rituals originating in piety (as Nietzsche said) which prevent the unrepresentable from being put forward.[14]

Lyotard goes on to define the post-modern as that which 'in the modern, puts forward the unrepresentable in presentation itself; that which denies itself the solace of good forms, the consensus of a taste which would make it possible to share collectively the

---

[14] Jean-François Lyotard, 'Answering the Question: What is Postmodernism?', tr. Régis Durand, in id., *Postmodern Condition: A Report on Knowledge*, tr. Geoff Bennington and Brian Massumi (Minneapolis: University of Minnesota Press, 1984), 80–1.

nostalgia for the unattainable'.[15] The post-modern would have to be understood in terms of the 'future anterior', since the artist works 'without rules to formulate the rules of what *will have been done*'.[16]

There are two distinct elements in Lyotard's argument. The first concerns the sublime, where nothing can be found in imagination or sensibility to be adequate to a concept. The second concerns attitudes to the past and to principles of organization. I believe that Joyce's work traces a complex trajectory in relation to this second element. Lyotard rightly identifies the Joycean pluralism that puts 'stylistic operators' and 'academic forms' into play without considering the unity of the whole. However, when he argues that these forms, through their 'recognizable consistency offers the viewer solace or pleasure', or further relates this to a 'consensus of taste that would make it possible to share collectively the nostalgia for the unattainable',[17] I think he reduces Joyce's complex attitude to tradition to a rather unitary one. The misrecognition arises from an underestimation of the way repetition functions in Joyce's work and from a reduction of this procedure to 'nostalgia'. The Joycean repetition does not create a recognizable consistency. On the contrary, it creates inconsistencies and asymmetries by putting into play too many operators and patterns in the same zone.

As I argued above, it is the performance of the past as a plurality, as a site of difference, that informs Joyce's attitude to tradition. Memory here does not try out forms that console it, but ruptures the monumental unity of such forms and puts them into circulation. What the text comes to thematize through this strategy is the notion of the rule itself, by presenting differences between rules. However, this works according to a relation that is different from Lyotard's notion of the post-modern as well. Unlike the latter where rules are formulated only retrospectively, in *Ulysses* rules are thematized retrospectively. The novel presents innumerable discursive terrains and rubs their differences against one another without subjecting them to a unifying recollection. The only horizon they form, and only retrospectively, is a horizon where these differences can be thematized. And, as we saw, it is this horizon of differences that constitutes the site of epiphany and of aesthetic vocation in Joyce. The repetition of the past becomes the mode of apprehension of the

[15] Ibid. 81.          [16] Ibid.          [17] Ibid.

particularity of the present. It is this disruptive function of memory that violates the monumentality of the past and differentiates Joyce's work from the nostalgia that Lyotard attributes to his work. And this engagement with a tradition, in the form of a library of fantasms that haunts the text, distinguishes his work from the post-modern.

The four major themes that we considered are related to one another in an integral way. Repetition and its effects, differential temporality, the inner time of the sign, and a performative notion of tradition—they presuppose and illuminate one another. In all these four sites we discovered the coexistence of opposing impulses, of organizing patterns that lead to disunities. Joyce is far more explicit about the role of repetition as an aesthetic vocation and as a historical vision in *Finnegans Wake*. *Ulysses* too joins the repertoire of elements that are repeated and reperformed in *Finnegans Wake*. It slips into the past, only to come alive again and be present at its own wake. However, *Finnegans Wake* remains outside the scope of this book. It has to be the theme for another story.

# Bibliography

## WORKS BY JOYCE

JOYCE, JAMES, *Chamber Music* (London: Elkin Mathews, 1907).
—— *The Critical Writings of James Joyce*, ed. Richard Ellmann and Ellsworth Mason (London: Faber & Faber, Ltd., 1959).
—— 'Daniel Defoe', ed. and tr. Joseph Prescott, *Buffalo Studies*, 1: 1 (1964), 23–5.
—— *Dubliners* (London: Grant Richards, 1914); ed. Robert Scholes (London: Jonathan Cape, 1967).
—— *Epiphanies*, ed. Oscar A. Silverman (Buffalo: Lockwood Memorial Library, 1956).
—— *Exiles: A Play in Three Acts* (London: Grant Richards, 1916; London: Jonathan Cape, 1952).
—— *Finnegans Wake* (1939; London: Faber & Faber, Ltd., 1960).
—— *Giacomo Joyce*, ed. Richard Ellmann (London: Faber & Faber, Ltd., 1968).
—— *The James Joyce Archive*, ed. Michael Groden, 63 vols. (New York: Garland Press, 1977–80).
—— *Joyce's Notes and Early Drafts for 'Ulysses': Selection from the Buffalo Collection*, ed. Phillip F. Herring (Charlottesville, Va.: University of Virginia Press, 1977).
—— *Joyce's 'Ulysses' Notesheets in the British Museum*, ed. Phillip F. Herring (Charlottesville, Va.: University of Virginia Press, 1972).
—— *The Letters of James Joyce*, 3 vols., ed. Stuart Gilbert (vol. i), and Richard Ellmann (vols. ii–iii). (New York: Viking, 1966).
—— *Pomes Pennyeach* (Paris: Shakespeare and Company, 1927).
—— *A Portrait of the Artist as a Young Man* (New York: B. W. Huebsch, 1916; London: Jonathan Cape, 1968).
—— *Stephen Hero*, ed. Theodore Spencer, (1944), revd., J. J. Slocum and H. Cahoon (London: Jonathan Cape, 1956).
—— *Ulysses* (Paris: Shakespeare and Company, 1922); A Critical and Synoptic Edition, ed. Hans Walter Gabler, 3 vols. (New York: Garland Press, 1984).

## OTHER WORKS

AARSLEFF, HANS, *From Locke to Saussure: Essays on the Study of Language and Intellectual History* (London: Athlone Press, 1982).

ADAMS, ROBERT, *After Joyce: Studies in Fiction after 'Ulysses'* (New York: OUP, 1977).

—— *Surface and Symbol: The Consistency of James Joyce's 'Ulysses'* (New York: OUP, 1962).

AQUINAS, THOMAS, *Summa Theologiae*, tr. Timothy McDermott, OP, ii (London: Blackfriars, 1963).

ARISTOTLE, *Complete Works of Aristotle: The Revised Oxford Translation*, ed. Jonathan Barnes, 2 vols. (Princeton, NJ: Princeton University Press, 1984).

*Aristotle's Masterpiece* (London: The Booksellers, n.d.).

ATHERTON, J. S., 'Oxen of the Sun', in Hart and Hayman (eds.), *James Joyce's 'Ulysses': Critical Essays*, 313–39.

—— *Books at the Wake: A Study of Literary Allusions in James Joyce's 'Finnegans Wake'* (London: Faber & Faber, Ltd., 1959).

ATTRIDGE, DEREK, and FERRER, DANIEL (eds.), *Post-Structuralist Joyce: Essays from the French* (Cambridge: CUP, 1984).

AUBERT, JACQUES, *Introduction à l'esthétique de James Joyce* (Paris: Didier, 1973).

AUERBACH, ERICH, *Mimesis*, tr. Willard R. Task (Princeton , NJ: Princeton University Press, 1953).

BAKER, HAROLD D., 'Rite of Passage: "Ithaca", Style and the Structure of *Ulysses*', *JJQ* 23: 3 (1986), 277–97.

BAKHTIN, M. M., *The Dialogic Imagination*, ed. Michael Holquist, tr. Caryl Emerson and Michael Holquist (Austin, Tex.: University of Texas Press, 1981).

—— *Problems of Dostoevsky's Poetics*, ed. and tr. Caryl Emerson (Manchester: Manchester University Press, 1984).

—— *Speech Genres and Other Late Essays*, ed. Caryl Emerson and Michael Holquist, tr. Vernon W. McGee (Austin, Tex.: University of Texas Press, 1986).

BARTHES, ROLAND, 'L'Effet du réel', *Communications*, 11 (1969), 84–9.

BAZARGAN, SUSAN, 'Oxen of the Sun: Maternity, Language and History', *JJQ* 22: 3 (1985), 271–80.

BECKETT, SAMUEL, *The Beckett Trilogy: Molloy, Malone Dies, The Unnamable* (London: Pan Books, 1979).

—— et al., *Our Exagmination round his Factification for Incamination of 'Work in Progress'* (Paris: Shakespeare and Company, 1929).

BEN-ZVI, LINDA, 'Samuel Beckett, Fritz Mauthner, and the Limits of Language', *PMLA* 95: 2 (1980), 183–200.

BENJAMIN, WALTER, *Illuminations*, ed. Hannah Arendt, tr. Harry Zohn (London: Jonathan Cape, 1970).

—— *One Way Street and Other Writings*, tr. Edmund Jephcott and Kingsley Shorter (London: NLB, 1979).

—— *Understanding Brecht*, tr. Anna Bostock (London: NLB, 1973).

BENSTOCK, BERNARD (ed.), *The Seventh of Joyce* (Bloomington, Ind.: Indiana University Press, 1982).

BERGSON, HENRI, *Creative Evolution*, tr. Arthur Mitchell (London: Macmillan, 1960).

—— *Laughter: An Essay on the Meaning of the Comic*, tr. Cloudesley Brereton and Fred Rothwell (London: Macmillan, 1921).

—— *Matter and Memory*, tr. Nancy Margaret Paul and W. Scott Palmer (London: Swan Sonnenschein & Co., Ltd., 1911).

—— *Time and Free Will: An Essay on the Immediate Data of Consciousness*, tr. F. L. Pogson (London: George Allen & Unwin, Ltd., 1910).

BERKELEY, *New Theory of Vision and Other Writings* (London: J. M. Dent, 1910).

BERNSTEIN, JAY, *Philosophy of the Novel: Lukács, Marxism and the Dialectic of Form* (Brighton: Harvester Press, 1984).

BISHOP, JOHN, *Joyce's Book of the Dark: 'Finnegans Wake'* (Madison; Wis.: University of Wisconsin Press, 1986).

BLAMIRES, HARRY, *The Bloomsday Book: A Guide Through Joyce's 'Ulysses'* (London: Methuen, 1966).

BLAVATSKY, H. P., *Isis Unveiled: A Master-Key to the Mysteries of Ancient and Modern Science and Technology*, 2 vols. (London: The Theosophical Publishing Society, 1910).

BLODGET, HARRIET, 'Joyce's Time Mind in *Ulysses*: A New Emphasis', *JJQ* 6: 1 (1967), 22–9.

BOEHME, JACOB, *Signatures of All Things and Other Writings* (Cambridge: James Clarke, 1969).

BOOTH, EDWARD, *Aristotle's Aporetic Ontology in Islamic and Christian Commentators* (Cambridge: CUP, 1984).

BORGES, JORGE LUIS, *Other Inquisitions 1937–1952* (New York: Simon and Schuster, 1965).

—— *Labyrinths*, ed. Donald A. Yates and James E. Irby (Harmondsworth: Penguin, 1981).

BOWEN, ZACK, and CARENS, JAMES F. (eds.), *A Companion to Joyce Studies* (Westport, Conn.: Greenwood Press, 1984).

BROWN, RICHARD, *James Joyce and Sexuality* (Cambridge: CUP, 1985).

BUDGEN, FRANK, *Myselves when Young* (London: OUP, 1970).

—— *James Joyce and the Making of 'Ulysses', and Other Writings*, ed. Clive Hart (London: OUP, 1972).

BURGESS, ANTHONY, *Joysprick: An Introduction to the Language of James Joyce* (London: André Deutsch, 1973).

BUTLER, CHRISTOPHER, *After the Wake: An Essay on the Contemporary Avant-Garde* (Oxford: OUP, 1981).

—— *Interpretation, Deconstruction, and Ideology* (Oxford: OUP, 1984).

CHURCH, MARGARET, *Time and Reality* (Chapel Hill, NC: The University of North Carolina Press, 1963).

CIXOUS, HÉLÈNE, *The Exile of James Joyce*, tr. Sally A. J. Purcell (London: John Calder, 1976).
—— 'Joyce: the (r)use of writing', in Attridge and Ferrer (eds.), *Post-Structuralist Joyce*, 15–30.
COLERIDGE, S. T., *Biographia Literaria* (1817), ed. James Engell and W. Jackson Bate, 2 vols. (Bollingen Series, 75; London: Routledge & Kegan Paul, Ltd., 1983).
CONNOR, STEVEN, *Samuel Beckett: Repetition, Theory and the Text* (Oxford: Basil Blackwell, 1988).
COPE, JACKSON I., *Joyce's Cities: Archaeologies of the Soul* (Baltimore: Johns Hopkins University Press, 1981).
CROCE, BENEDETTO, *The Philosophy of Giambattista Vico*, tr. R. G. Collingwood (New York: Russell and Russell, Inc., 1964).
CROSS, RICHARD K., *Flaubert and Joyce: The Rite of Fiction* (Princeton, NJ: Princeton University Press, 1971).
DAHL, LISA, *Linguistic Features of the Stream-of-Consciousness Techniques of James Joyce, Virginia Woolf and Eugene O'Neill* (Turku: Turun Yliopisto, 1970).
DELEUZE, GILLES, *Bergsonism*, tr. Hugh Tomlinson (New York: Zone Books, 1988).
—— *Différence et répétition* (Paris: Presses Universitaires de France, 1968).
—— *Kant's Critical Philosophy*, tr. Hugh Tomlinson and Barbara Habberjam (London: Athlone Press, 1984).
—— *Proust and Signs*, tr. Richard Howard (London: Allen Lane, 1973).
—— *Sacher-Masoch: An Interpretation, together with the Entire Text of 'Venus in Furs' from a French Rendering by Aude Willm*, tr. Jean McNeil (London: Faber & Faber, Ltd., 1971).
DEMING, ROBERT (ed.), *James Joyce: The Critical Heritage*, 2 vols. (London: Routledge & Kegan Paul, Ltd., 1970).
DERRIDA, JACQUES, 'Des tours de Babel', tr. Joseph F. Graham in Joseph F. Graham (ed.), *Difference in Translation* (Ithaca, NY: Cornell University Press, 1985), 165–207.
—— *Dissemination*, tr. B. Johnson (Chicago: University of Chicago Press, 1981).
—— *Edmund Husserl's 'Origin of Geometry': An Introduction*, tr. J. P. Leavy (Brighton: Harvester Press, 1978).
—— *Margins of Philosophy*, tr. Alan Bass (Chicago: University of Chicago Press, 1983).
—— *Of Grammatology*, tr. G. C. Spivak (Baltimore: Johns Hopkins University Press, 1976).
—— *Positions*, tr. A. Bass (Chicago: University of Chicago Press, 1971).
—— *Speech and Phenomena and Other Essays on Husserl's Theory of*

*Signs*, tr. David B. Allison (Evanston, Ill.: Northwestern University Press, 1973).

—— 'Two Words for Joyce', in Attridge and Ferrer (eds.), *Post-Structuralist Joyce*, 145–59.

—— *Writing and Difference*, tr. Alan Bass (Chicago: University of Chicago Press, 1978).

DOCHERTY, THOMAS, *Reading (Absent) Character* (Oxford: OUP, 1984).

DUNCAN, JOSEPH E., 'Modality of the Audible in Joyce's *Ulysses*', *PMLA* 72 (1957), 286–95.

DUNS SCOTUS, JOHN, *Philosophical Writings: A Selection*, tr. Allan Wolter, OFM (Indianapolis: Hackett Publishing Co., 1987).

ECO, UMBERTO, *Aesthetics of Chaosmos: The Middle Ages of James Joyce*, tr. Ellen Esrock (Tulsa: University of Tulsa Press, 1982).

EISENSTEIN, SERGEI, *Film Form: Essays in Film Theory*, ed. and tr. Jay Leyda (London: Dennis Dobson, Ltd., 1951).

—— *The Film Sense*, tr. Jay Leyda (London: Faber & Faber, Ltd., 1986).

—— 'Notes for a Film of *Capital*', *October*, 2 (1976), 3–26.

ELIOT, T. S., *Selected Essays*, (3rd edn., London: Faber & Faber, Ltd., 1951).

—— 'Ulysses, Order, Myth', *Dial*, 75: 5 (1923), 480–3.

ELLMANN, RICHARD, *Ulysses on the Liffey* (London: Faber & Faber, Ltd., 1972).

—— *The Consciousness of Joyce* (London: Faber & Faber, Ltd., 1977).

—— *James Joyce* (revd. edn., New York: OUP, 1982).

FLAUBERT, GUSTAVE, *La Tentation de saint Antoine* (1874), tr. Kitty Mrosovsky as *The Temptation of Saint Antony* (Harmondsworth: Penguin, 1983).

—— *Bouvard and Pécuchet*, tr. A. J. Krailsheimer (Harmondsworth: Penguin, 1976).

FOUCAULT, MICHEL, *The Archaeology of Knowledge*, tr. A. M. Sheridan Smith (London: Tavistock, 1972).

—— *Death and the Labyrinth: The World of Raymond Roussel*, tr. Charles Ruas (London: Athlone Press, 1987).

—— *Language, Counter-Memory, Practice*, ed. D. F. Bouchard, tr. D. F. Bouchard and Sherry Simon (Oxford: Basil Blackwell, 1977).

—— 'The Order of Discourse', tr. Ian McLeod in Robert Young (ed.), *Untying the Text* (London: Routledge & Kegan Paul, Ltd., 1981), 48–78.

FRANK, JOSEPH, *The Widening Gyre: Crisis and Mastery in Modern Literature* (New Brunswick, NJ: Rutgers University Press, 1963).

FRENCH, MERYLIN, *The Book as World: James Joyce's 'Ulysses'* (Cambridge, Mass.: Harvard University Press, 1976).

FRIEDMAN, M., *Stream of Consciousness: A Study of Literary Method* (New Haven, Conn.: Yale University Press, 1955).

FRYE, NORTHROP, *Anatomy of Criticism* (Princeton, NJ: Princeton University Press, 1957).

GADAMER, HANS-GEORG, *Relevance of the Beautiful and Other Essays*, ed. Robert Bernasconi, tr. Nicholas Walker (Cambridge: CUP, 1986).

—— *Truth and Method*, tr. William Glen-Deopel (London: Sheed and Ward, 1975).

GENETTE, GÉRARD, *Narrative Discourse*, tr. Jane E. Lewin (Oxford: Basil Blackwell, 1980).

GIFFORD, DON, and SEIDMAN, ROBERT J., *Notes for Joyce: An Annotation of James Joyce's 'Ulysses'* (New York: E. P. Dutton, 1974).

GILBERT, STUART, *James Joyce's 'Ulysses': A Study* (Harmondsworth: Penguin, 1963).

—— 'Why a Revolution of the Word?', *Modern Quarterly*, 5 (1929), 284–5.

GILSON, ETIENNE, *History of Christian Philosophy in the Middle Ages* (London: Sheed and Ward, 1955).

GIVENS, SEON (ed.), *James Joyce: Two Decades of Criticism* (New York: Vanguard, 1963).

GOLDBERG, S. L., *The Classical Temper: A Study of James Joyce's 'Ulysses'* (London: Chatto & Windus, Ltd., 1961).

GOLDMAN, ARNOLD, *The Joyce Paradox: Form and Freedom in his Fiction* (Evanston, Ill.: Northwestern University Press, 1966).

GOSE, ELLIOT, Jun., *The Transformation Process in Joyce's 'Ulysses'* (Toronto: University of Toronto Press, 1980).

GOTTFRIED, ROY K., *The Art of Joyce's Syntax in 'Ulysses'* (London: Macmillan, 1980).

GRODEN, MICHAEL, *'Ulysses' in Progress* (Princeton, NJ: Princeton University Press, 1977).

HAMBURGER, KATE, *The Logic of Literature* (Bloomington, Ind.: Indiana University Press, 1973).

HANLEY, MILES L., *Word Index to James Joyce's 'Ulysses'* (Madison, Wis.: University of Wisconsin Press, 1962).

HANNA, THOMAS (ed.), *The Bergsonian Heritage* (New York: Columbia University Press, 1962).

HART, CLIVE, *Structure and Motif in 'Finnegans Wake'* (London: Faber, & Faber, Ltd., 1962).

—— and HAYMAN, DAVID (eds.), *James Joyce's 'Ulysses': Critical Essays* (Berkeley, Calif.: University of California Press, 1974).

—— and KNUTH, LEO, *A Topographical Guide to 'Ulysses'*, 2 vols. (Colchester: A Wake Newslitter Press, 1975).

HAY, LOUIS (ed.), *Genèse de Babel: Joyce et la création* (Paris: Éditions du CNRS, 1985).

HAYMAN, DAVID, *'Ulysses': The Mechanics of Meaning* (Englewood Cliffs, NJ: Prentice Hall, Inc., 1970).

—— 'Language of/as Gesture in Joyce', in Louis Bonnerot (ed.), *Ulysses cinquante ans après: témoignages franco-anglais sur le chef-d'œuvre de James Joyce* (Paris: Didier, 1974), 209–21.

—— 'Joyce → Beckett/Joyce', *Journal of Beckett Studies*, 7 (1982), 101–7.

HEATH, STEPHEN, 'Ambiviolences', in Attridge and Ferrer, *Post-Structuralist Joyce*, 31–68.

—— 'Joyce in Language', in MacCabe (ed.), *James Joyce: New Perspectives*, 129–48.

HEGEL, GEORG WILHELM FRIEDRICH, *Phenomenology of Spirit*, tr. A. V. Miller (Oxford: OUP, 1977).

HEIDEGGER, MARTIN, *Being and Time*, tr. John Macquarrie and Edward Robinson (Oxford: Basil Blackwell, 1962).

—— *Poetry, Language, Thought*, tr. Albert Hofstadter (New York: Harper and Row, 1971).

HIGGINSON, FRED L., *Anna Livia Plurabelle: The Making of a Chapter* (Minneapolis: University of Minnesota Press, 1960).

HOLLINGTON, MICHAEL, 'Svevo, Joyce and Modernist Time,' in Malcolm Bradbury and James McFarlane (eds.), *Modernism* (Harmondsworth: Penguin, 1976).

HOMER, *The Odyssey*, tr. S. H. Butcher and A. Lang (London: Macmillan, 1906); tr. Walter Shewring (Oxford: OUP, 1980).

HUMPHREY, ROBERT, *Stream of Consciousness in the Modern Novel* (Berkeley, Calif.: University of California Press, 1954).

HUSSERL, EDMUND, *The Phenomenology of Internal Time Consciousness*, tr. James S. Churchill (Bloomington, Ind.: Indiana University Press, 1964).

JAMESON, FREDRIC, '*Ulysses* in History', in W. J. McCormack and Alistair Stead (eds.), *James Joyce and Modern Literature* (London: Routledge & Kegan Paul, Ltd., 1982).

JANUSKO, ROBERT, *The Sources and Structures of James Joyce's 'Oxen'* (Essex: Bowker Publishing Co., 1983).

JEFFERSON, ANN, *The Nouveau Roman and the Poetics of Fiction* (Cambridge: CUP, 1980).

KAFKA, FRANZ, *The Penguin Complete Short Stories of Franz Kafka*, ed. Nahum N. Glatzer (Harmondsworth: Penguin in association with Secker & Warburg, Ltd., 1983).

—— *The Penguin Complete Novels of Franz Kafka*, tr. Willa and Edwin Muir (Harmondsworth: Penguin, 1983).

KAIN, RICHARD M., *Fabulous Voyager: James Joyce's 'Ulysses'* (Chicago: University of Chicago Press, 1947).

KANT, IMMANUEL, *The Critique of Pure Reason*, tr. Norman Kemp-Smith (London: Macmillan, 1933).

—— *The Critique of Judgement*, tr. James Creed Meredith (Oxford: Clarendon Press, 1952).

KENNER, HUGH, *Dublin's Joyce* (London: Chatto & Windus, Ltd., 1955).
—— *Joyce's Voices* (London: Faber & Faber, Ltd., 1978).
—— *Ulysses* (London: George Allen & Unwin, Ltd., 1980).
KERMODE, FRANK, *The Sense of an Ending: Studies in the Theory of Fiction* (New York: OUP, 1967).
KESTNER, JOSEPH A., *The Spatiality of the Novel* (Detroit: Wayne State University Press, 1978).
KIERKEGAARD, SØREN, *Fear and Trembling and Repetition*, ed. and tr. Howard V. Hong and Edna H. Hong (Princeton, NJ: Princeton University Press, 1983).
KLAWITTER, ROBERT, 'Henry Bergson and Joyce's Fictional World', *Comparative Literature Studies*, 3 (1966), 429–37.
KLEIN, A. M., 'Oxen of the Sun', *Here and Now*, 1 (1949), 28–48.
KRISTEVA, JULIA, *Revolution in Poetic Language* (New York: Columbia University Press, 1984).
KUMAR, SHIV K., *Bergson and the Stream of Consciousness Novel* (London: Blackie & Son, Ltd., 1962).
LARBAUD, VALERY, preface to Édouard Dujardin, *Les Lauriers sont coupés* (Paris: Bibliothèque 10/18, 1968).
LAWRENCE, KAREN, *The Odyssey of Style in 'Ulysses'* (Princeton, NJ: Princeton University Press, 1981).
LESSING, GOTTHOLD EPHRAIM, *Laocoön: An Essay on the Limits of Paintings and Poetry* (1766), tr. Edward Allen McCormick (Indianapolis: Bobbs-Merrill, 1962).
LEVIN, HARRY, *James Joyce: A Critical Introduction* (London: Faber & Faber, Ltd., 1944).
LEVINE, JENNIFER SCHIFFER, 'Originality and Repetition in *Finnegans Wake* and *Ulysses*', *PMLA* 94: 1 (1979), 106–20.
LEWIS, WYNDHAM, *Time and Western Man* (London: Chatto & Windus, Ltd., 1927).
LITZ, WALTON, *The Art of James Joyce: Method and Design in 'Ulysses' and 'Finnegans Wake'* (London: OUP, 1961).
—— 'Ithaca', in Hart and Hayman (eds.), *James Joyce's 'Ulysses': Critical Essays*, 385–405.
LOSS, ARCHIE K., *Joyce's Visible Art: The Work of Joyce and the Visual Arts 1904–1922* (Ann Arbor, Mich.: UMI Research Press, 1984).
LUKÁCS, GEORG, *Writer and Critic and Other Essays*, ed. and tr. Arthur Kahn (London: Merlin, 1970).
—— *Studies in European Realism*, tr. Edith Bone (London: Merlin, 1978).
—— *Theory of the Novel: A Historico-Philosophical Essay on the Forms of Great Epic Literature*, tr. Anna Bostock (London: Merlin, 1971).
—— *The Meaning of Contemporary Realism*, tr. John and Neckie Mander (London: Merlin, 1962).
LYONS, F. S. L., *Ireland Since the Famine* (London: Fontana, 1973).

LYOTARD, JEAN-FRANÇOIS, *The Postmodern Condition: A Report on Knowledge*, tr. Geoff Bennington and Brian Massumi (Minneapolis: University of Minnesota Press, 1984).

MACCABE, COLIN, *James Joyce and the Revolution of the Word* (London: Macmillan, 1979).

—— (ed.), *James Joyce: New Perspectives* (Brighton: Harvester Press, 1982).

McARTHUR, MURRAY, 'Rose of Castile/Rows of Cast Steel: Figural Parallelism in *Ulysses*' *JJQ* 24: 4 (1987), 411–22.

McGRATH, F. C., 'Laughing in his Sleeve: The Sources of Stephen's Aesthetic', *JJQ* 23: 3 (1986), 259–75.

McHUGH, ROLAND, *The Sigla of 'Finnegans Wake'* (London: Edward Arnold, 1976).

McLUHAN, MARSHALL, 'James Joyce: Trivial and Quadrivial', *Thought*, 28 (1953), 75–98.

—— 'Joyce, Aquinas and the Poetic Process', *Renascence*, 4 (1951), 3–11.

MANGANIELLO, DOMINIC, *Joyce's Politics* (London: Routledge & Kegan Paul, Ltd., 1980).

MENDILOW, A. A., *Time and the Novel* (New York: Humanities Press, 1972).

MERCANTON, JACQUES, 'Hours of James Joyce', in Potts (ed.), *Portraits of the Artist in Exile*, 205–52.

MEYERHOFF, HANS, *Time in Literature* (Berkeley, Calif.: University of California Press, 1960).

MILLER, J. HILLIS, *Fiction and Repetition* (Oxford: Basil Blackwell, 1982).

MOSES, MICHAEL VALDES, 'The Sadly Rejoycing Slave: Beckett, Joyce and the Art of Destructive Parody', *Modern Fiction Studies*, 31: 4 (1985), 659–74.

MOSELEY, VIRGINIA, *Joyce and the Bible* (DeKalb, Ill.: Northern Illinois University Press, 1967).

MURILLO, L. A., *The Cyclical Night: Irony in James Joyce and Jorge Luis Borges* (Cambridge, Mass.: Harvard University Press, 1968).

NIETZSCHE, FRIEDRICH, *The Basic Writings of Nietzsche*, ed. and tr. Walter Kaufmann (New York: Random House, 1968).

NOON, WILLIAM T., *Joyce and Aquinas* (New Haven, Conn.: Yale University Press, 1957).

NORRIS, MARGOT, *The Decentered Universe of 'Finnegans Wake': A Structuralist Analysis* (Baltimore: Johns Hopkins University Press, 1974).

*Obscenity in Books: The Decision of the United States District Court of Appeals in the case of 'Ulysses' by James Joyce 1933–1934* (London: John Lane and Bodley Head, 1954).

PATER, WALTER, *The Renaissance: Studies in Art and Poetry* (London: Macmillan, 1912).

PLATO, *The Republic*, tr. Paul Shorey (Cambridge, Mass.: Harvard University Press, 1953).

POTTS, WILLARD (ed.), *Portraits of the Artist in Exile: Recollection of James Joyce by Europeans* (Dublin: Wolfhound Press, 1979).

POULET, GEORGES, *Studies in Human Time*, tr. Elliott Coleman (New York: Harper Torch Books, 1959).

—— *Proustian Space*, tr. Elliott Coleman (Baltimore: Johns Hopkins University Press, 1977).

POWER, ARTHUR, *Conversations with James Joyce*, ed. Clive Hart (London: Millington, Ltd., 1974).

PROUST, MARCEL, *À la recherche du temps perdu* (1913–27), tr. C. K. Scott Moncrieff and Terence Kilmartin as *Remembrance of Things Past*, 3 vols. (London: Chatto & Windus, Ltd., 1981–2).

—— *A Selection from his Miscellaneous Writings*, ed. and tr. Gerard Hopkins (London: Allan Wingate, 1948).

RABATÉ, JEAN-MICHEL, 'Portrait of the Artist as a Boggyman', *Oxford Literary Review*, 7: 1–2 (1986), 62–90.

RICARDOU, JEAN, 'Time of the Narration, Time of the Fiction', tr. Joseph Kestner, *JJQ* 16: 1–2, (1978–9), 7–15.

RICŒUR, PAUL, *Time and Narrative*, tr. Katherine McLaughlin and David Pellauer, 3 vols. (Chicago: University of Chicago Press, 1984–8).

—— 'Narrative Time', in W. J. T. Mitchell (ed.), *On Narrative* (Chicago: University of Chicago Press, 1981), 165–86.

RIQUELME, JOHN PAUL, *Teller and Tale in Joyce's Fiction: Oscillating Perspectives* (Baltimore: Johns Hopkins University Press, 1983).

ROPPEN, GEORG, and SOMMER, RICHARD, *Strangers and Pilgrims: An Essay on the Metaphor of Journey* (Oslo: Norwegian Universities Press, 1964).

ROSE, GILLIAN, *Dialectic of Nihilism* (Oxford: Basil Blackwell, 1984).

SAID, EDWARD, *Beginnings: Intention and Method* (Baltimore: Johns Hopkins University Press, 1975).

—— *The World, The Text and the Critic* (London: Faber & Faber, Ltd., 1983).

SALDIVAR, RAMÓN, *Figural Language in the Novel: The Flowers of Speech from Cervantes to Joyce* (Princeton, NJ: Princeton University Press, 1984).

SCHECHNER, MARK, *Joyce in Nighttown: A Psychoanalytic Inquiry into 'Ulysses'* (Berkeley, Calif.: University of California Press, 1974).

SCHLOSSMAN, BERYL, *Joyce's Catholic Comedy of Language* (Madison, Wis.: University of Wisconsin Press, 1985).

SCHOLES, ROBERT, and KAIN, RICHARD M. (eds.), *The Workshop of Dedalus: James Joyce and the Raw Materials of 'A Portrait of the Artist as a Young Man'* (Evanston, Ill.: Northwestern University Press, 1965).

SCHUTTE, WILLIAM M., *Index of Recurrent Elements in James Joyce's 'Ulysses'* (Carbondale, Ill.: Southern Illinois University Press, 1982).

—— *Joyce and Shakespeare: A Study in the Meaning of 'Ulysses'* (New Haven, Conn.: Yale University Press, 1957).

SCOTT, BONNIE KIME, *Joyce and Feminism* (Brighton: Harvester Press, 1984).

SEIDEL, MICHAEL, *Epic Geography: James Joyce's 'Ulysses'* (Princeton, NJ: Princeton University Press, 1976).

—— *Exile and the Narrative Imagination* (New Haven, Conn.: Yale University Press, 1986).

SENN, FRITZ, 'Esthetic Theories', *JJQ* 2: 2 (1965), 134–6.

—— *Joyce's Dislocutions: Essays on Reading as Translation*, ed. J. P. Riquelme (Baltimore: Johns Hopkins University Press, 1984).

SERRES, MICHEL, *Hermes: Literature and Philosophy* (Baltimore: Johns Hopkins University Press, 1982).

SHAKESPEARE, WILLIAM, *Shakespeare: The Complete Works*, ed. G. B. Harrison (New York: Harcourt, Brace and Co., 1948).

SHATTUCK, ROGER, *Proust's Binoculars: A Study of Memory, Time and Recognition in 'À la recherche du temps perdu'* (London: Chatto & Windus, Ltd., 1964).

SPERBER, DAN, and WILSON, DEIRDRE, *Relevance: Communication and Cognition* (Oxford: Basil Blackwell, 1986).

STEINBERG, ERWIN R., *The Stream of Consciousness and Beyond in 'Ulysses'* (Pittsburgh: University of Pittsburgh Press, 1973).

STEINER, GEORGE, *After Babel* (London: OUP, 1975).

THORNTON, WELDON, *Allusions in 'Ulysses': An Annotated List* (Chapel Hill, NC: North Carolina University Press, 1968).

TINDALL, WILLIAM YORK, *James Joyce: His Way of Interpreting the Modern World* (New York: Scribner's, 1950).

—— *A Reader's Guide to James Joyce* (New York: Noonday, 1959).

TODOROV, TZVETAN, *The Poetics of Prose*, tr. Richard Howard (Oxford: Basil Blackwell, 1977).

—— *Theories of the Symbol*, tr. Catherine Porter (Oxford: Basil Blackwell, 1982).

VAN DIJK, TEUN A., *Discourse and Literature: New Approaches to the Analysis of Literary Genres* (Amsterdam: John Benjamins Publishing Co., 1985).

—— *Some Aspects of Text Grammars* (The Hague: Mouton, 1972).

—— *Text and Context: Explorations in the Semantics and Pragmatics of Discourse* (London: Longman, 1977).

VICO, GIAMBATTISTA, *The New Science of Giambattista Vico*, tr. Thomas Goddard Bergin and Max Harold Fish (Ithaca, NY: Cornell University Press, 1968).

VITOUX, PIERRE, 'Aristotle, Berkeley and Newman in "Proteus" and *Finnegans Wake*', *JJQ* 18: 2 (1981), 161–75.

WEILER, GERSHON, *Mauthner's Critique of Language* (Cambridge: CUP, 1970).

WHITE, HAYDEN, *Metahistory: The Historical Imagination in Nineteenth Century Europe* (Baltimore: Johns Hopkins University Press, 1975).

WHITTACKER, STEPHEN, 'Joyce and Skeat', *JJQ* 24: 2 (1987), 177–92.

WILSON, EDMUND, *Axel's Castle: A Study of the Imaginative Literature of 1870–1930* (New York: Scribner's, 1931).

WOLTER, ALLAN BERNARD, *Transcendentals and their Use in the Metaphysics of Duns Scotus* (Washington, DC: Catholic University of America Press, 1946).

# Index